BE CIVIL!

BE CIVIL!

A guide to learning civil
litigation and evidence

VIRGINIA DUNN

Worth Publishing

First published 2011 by Worth Publishing Ltd
www.worthpublishing.com

© Worth Publishing Ltd 2011

Second Edition published 2014 by Worth Publishing Ltd
www.worthpublishing.com

© Worth Publishing Ltd 2014

Printed and bound in Great Britain by TJ International Ltd., Padstow, Cornwall.

British Library Cataloguing in Publication Data
A catalogue record for this book is available from the British Library

ISBN 9781903269336

Cover and text design by Anna Murphy, Layout by Stephen Hall

Preface to the first edition

If you are reading this, my guess is you are getting ready to sit a professional examination. Whether you are at the beginning or end of your course or, having already qualified, are embarking on a change of direction in early practice, this book is intended to help. Its purpose is to make civil litigation easier and more fun to understand, so that when the time comes, you really know what you are talking about.

My experience of teaching has shown me that most students look upon civil procedure, not so much as a Cinderella subject, but as one of the ugly step-sisters. It often seems to them like an avalanche of apparently disjointed rules and regulations, so that what is covered in class one week is forgotten the next. And anyway (they think) crime is *so* much more fun. This attitude makes it hard to get to grips with the subject. My approach is intended as an antidote.

The key to learning civil litigation is to see the big picture. If, for example, you are putting together a jigsaw puzzle, it is much more difficult if you do not know what it should look like when it is completed. That is what I hope to provide. You have been (or are about) to look at all the individual pieces of the civil litigation puzzle in some detail on your course. This book is the picture on the box.

It is intended to augment, not replace, your own learning. It can assist with classroom preparation, by allowing you to focus intelligently on the subject matter, research more knowledgeably and contribute intelligently to discussions, rather than merely writing down everything you see and hear. It should be especially helpful as you prepare for examinations by reinforcing the bigger picture while reviewing the essential individual concepts. I also offer many revision tips. This book should also remind you of the value of common sense (an under-rated commodity) in learning how to think about and understand any aspect of the law, including civil procedure and evidence.

This book is the product of many years of helping students to learn and enjoy its subject. In particular it is an elaboration of the revision notes they had access to when I taught full-time at the Inns of Court School of Law/City Law School. I am grateful to all of my students – past and present – for teaching me to teach them better. Many colleagues at City Law School were also very supportive of this enterprise, in particular: Lisa Laurenti (who keeps me teaching and learning), Catherine Hill (who keeps me in touch with my roots), Ros Carne (who tried, with limited success, to curb my enthusiasm for exclamation marks), Robert McPeake (whose library extended to *Hart's Rules*) and especially Stuart Sime, who spent time he did not have to make some very useful editorial suggestions. My most grateful thanks, however, go to Ronnie Lachkovic (who runs the BPTC Civil Litigation course at City Law School) and Sir Peter Coulson, who kindly wrote the Foreword. Ronnie (who doubles as Lady Coulson) not only took a personal interest in the book (and its author), but also the time to read virtually all of the manuscript, which is very much improved as a result. Neither she, nor anyone else of course, should be held accountable for any of its content, and any errors which remain are mine alone.

I should also thank my supportive daughters, Eden, Kate and Rachael Sanders, who have become adept at making their own or ready-meals (which they sometimes like better than mine, if the truth be told) while I was chained to my desk. Finally, I should like to pay tribute to Martin Wood and Andrea Perry at Worth Publishing for their help in producing this book. It took patience, professionalism and good humour, which they have in abundance.

The dedication is to two people very close to my heart, always: my husband Ray Sanders, a social security appeal judge, who died in 2002, and Rosie Samwell-Smith, former BVC course director at the ICSL, who died in 2010. How I wish they were here to see this.

VVD
London
March 2011

For Ray and Rosie

About the author

Virginia V Dunn, BA, MA, Barrister began practice in civil and family law and spent most of the last 30 years teaching students training for the Bar at the Inns of Court School of Law, now the City Law School. She has taught a range of subjects there, including litigation and evidence. For much of the time, she co-ordinated the civil litigation course, and has first-hand knowledge of how the subject is taught and assessed. She is currently a Visiting Lecturer there. She contributes to the City Law School's Bar Manuals supporting training for the Bar, and has written for the Institute of Legal Executives. This book is the culmination of many years helping students to enjoy learning the subject with her popular revision notes. In 2013 she published a companion guide for criminal procedure entitled *It's Criminal!: Guide to learning criminal litigation, evidence and sentencing*.

Preface

Since *Be Civil! A guide to learning civil litigation and evidence* was published in 2011, two important changes have occurred affecting the teaching and assessing of Civil Litigation, Evidence and Remedies on the Bar Vocation Training Course (BPTC).

The first is that the examinations are now centrally set by the Bar Standards Board (BSB). Centrally set assessments pose special challenges (for practically everyone, not just students!) and for this reason I have added and emphasised more of the procedural detail which two years of assessing these examinations has taught me students need to know. I have also completely rewritten Chapter 20 on examination preparation and technique. It is important not only to 'know your stuff' when you walk into the exam hall, but also to be well aware of the sorts of questions you will have to answer. As all barristers come to learn - good preparation is critical.

Secondly, the Civil Procedure Rules are an ever-evolving creature, but there have been radical changes since 2011, impinging especially on the funding, costs and case management of civil litigation. This second edition includes the changes introduced on 1 April 2013, which implemented most of the recommendations made by Sir Rupert Jackson's Review of Civil Litigation Costs (December 2009, Ministry of Justice), as well as some important case law generated by them in the last year. The Jackson reforms impact on various aspects of the rules and are discussed in detail throughout the relevant chapters of this book; they have brought about the most significant changes to civil procedure since the Woolf reforms of 1998.

As this book was going to print, another raft of amendments to the CPR came into being (in April 2014), and so reference is made to these when, where, and to the extent this was possible. These principally affect the jurisdiction of the (now unitary) County Court and modernise aspects of enforcement of judgments. It is important to note, however, that these changes will not find their way onto the BPTC syllabus until the academic year 2014-15, so anyone sitting the exams in summer 2014 need not worry about them for this purpose.

Do not forget, however, that whatever your motivation for reading this book, it is important to keep yourself up to date thereafter. Big rule changes and procedural innovations almost always generate interpretation and fine-tuning. I have to stop somewhere, which is where you have to start!

And remember always to check your assessment syllabus so that you are clear, year on year, about what will be examined and to what extent.   The setting and assessing of these examinations centrally has been an education in itself for the BSB - there has been a recent review of the syllabus (to keep it focused on matters most relevant to early civil practice) and advice from BPTC providers about what level of detail should be expected on the various topics which are assessed. For example, in future, subjects like Judicial Review could come off the syllabus altogether and a code of sorts may eventually be adopted which gives some indication about which topics will by tested by Multiple Choice Question only (MCQ) (the 'outline' or 'overview' subjects), leaving the rest of the syllabus as fair game for both the Multiple Choice and the more detailed and challenging Short Answer Question (SAQ). At the time of writing, however, these remain proposals and possibilities only; it does not look as if there will be any significant change to the BPTC syllabus until 2015-16 at the earliest. So if taking examinations, always consult your current syllabus and follow the lead of your tutors and course directors.

Finally, I remain grateful to family and friends, and Worth Publishing, for their help and support in producing this second edition, in particular my colleague Lisa Laurenti, who never got back her contributor's copy of the 2014 edition of Blackstone's Civil Practice! As always, special mention must go to my editor Andrea Perry and to City Law School's Ronnie Lachkovic, both of whom remain committed to this series of Law Guides, despite having many other demands on their time and energy. They have all helped to improve this edition - as usual, any errors of content are mine alone. Finally, my thanks for the constructive and positive comments from the many students and young practitioners who say they have benefitted from this book - which, after all, is the point of it.

VVD
London
May 2014

Foreword

One of the principal aims of the Woolf reforms and the Civil Procedure Rules was to streamline civil litigation, and make it simpler and more straightforward. It might be said that, with the White Book running to two fat volumes, we have yet to fully achieve that ambition. And although there can be little doubt that the situation has improved considerably since my early days in practice, it is also undeniable that a student confronting the CPR for the first time needs a sensible place to start the process of assimilation.

That is where this useful book comes in. 'Be Civil!' presents a convenient, short guide to the basic rules of civil practice and procedure, expressed in clear and direct language. It will be an admirable companion for those wrestling with the subject for the first time. And it even manages the difficult feat of making its subject matter both interesting and fun. I have no doubt that it will be very popular with students and new practitioners.

The Hon Sir Peter Coulson
Member of the Civil Procedure Rules Committee

Glossary of terms

Affidavit
This is a written, sworn statement containing evidence. It was at one time commonly used to support interim applications, so will still be referred to in older cases. Affidavits are still used for freezing and search orders, but most interim applications nowadays present their supporting evidence by means of witness statements.

Alternative Dispute Resolution (ADR)
This is a collective description for methods of resolving disputes otherwise than through the normal litigation process.

Civil Procedure Rules (CPR)
One of the primary sources of procedural law in England and Wales. It was brought in as a new procedural code in 1999.

Cross-examination *(compare with examination-in-chief)*
Questioning of a witness by a party other than the party who called the witness.

Damages
A sum of money awarded by the court as compensation to the claimant. 'Additional' damages punish a defendant's objectionable behaviour and 'exemplary' damages compensate a claimant for it.

Disbursements
In a legal context, money paid by solicitors on behalf of their client.

Evidence-in-Chief
The evidence given by a witness for the party who called him.

Examination-in-Chief
The questioning process by which a party's evidence-in-chief is elicited orally.

Joint liability *(see also several liability)*
Parties who are jointly liable share a single liability and each party can be held liable for the whole of it.

Overriding Objective
The principal aspiration of the CPR, which is to deal with cases justly and at proportionate cost.

Obiter
Judicial observation in a case which is not strictly binding, as it is not the point to be decided in the case.

Plaintiff	Pre-CPR description for a Claimant.
Pleadings	This is an old-fashioned way of referring to statements of case.
Practice Form	Form to be used for a particular purpose, as specified by a practice direction.
Quia timet	Literally, 'because he fears'. Used to describe an injunction restraining a threatened wrong.
Set aside	Cancelling a judgment or order or step taken by a party in the proceedings.
Several liability *(see also joint liability)*	A person who is severally liable with others may remain liable for the whole claim even where judgment has been obtained against others.
Stay	A stay imposes a halt on proceedings, apart from taking any steps allowed by the rules or the terms of the stay. Proceedings can continue if, but only if the stay is lifted.
Tort	A civil wrong, other than breach of contract, which is compensated by damages.
Tortfeasor	A person who has committed a tort.
Westlaw	An online legal resource.

Abbreviations and references

ADR	Alternative Dispute Resolution
BCP	Blackstone's Civil Practice
BPTC	Bar Professional Training Course
BSB	Bar Standards Board
BVC	Bar Vocation Course (before re-named BPTC)
CFA	Conditional Fee Agreement
CH	Chancery Division (of the High Court)
CJEU	Court of Justice of the European Union (formerly European Court of Justice/ECJ)
CPR	Civil Procedure Rules
CRU	Compensation Recovery Unit
DBA	Damages Based Agreement
ECHR	European Court of Human Rights
GLO	Group Litigation Order
LAA	Legal Aid Agency (replacing Legal Services Commission)
LEI	Legal Expenses Insurance
MIB	Motor Insurance Bureau
MR	Master of the Roles
para/s.	paragraph/s in CPR and BCP and WB etc
PD	Practice Direction
PI	Personal Injuries
PSLA	Pain, suffering, loss of amenity element of personal injuries damages
r/rr.	rule/s
RSC	Rules of Supreme Court (predecessor to CPR)
RTA	Road traffic accident
SATs	Standard Achievement Tests (school assessments)
SI	Statutory Instrument
s/ss.	section/s
TCC	Technology and Construction Court
WB	The White Book (Civil Procedure)
WFO	Worldwide freezing order

Case References

AC	Appeal Court
All ER	All England Law Reports
BCC	British Company Cases
BLR	Business Law Reports
CostsLR	Costs Law Reports
CPLR	Civil Procedure Law Reports (Westlaw)
EWCA	Neutral case citation for Court of Appeal case
EWHC	Neutral case citation for High Court case
FSR	Fleet Street Reports
KB	Kings Bench (Older Law Report Citation)
LS Med	Medical Law Reports
LSG	Law Society Gazette
NLJ	New Law Journal
PIQR	Personal Injuries Quantum Reports
QB	Queen's Bench Division of the High Court
RPC	Reports of Patent, Design and Trade Mark cases
RTR	Road Traffic Reports
UKHL	Neutral case citation for House of Lords case
UKPC	Neutral case citation for Privy Council case
WLR	Weekly Law Reports
[ ]	Indicates para/section of judgment

Statute References

AJA 1999	Access to Justice Act 1999
CA 2013	Courts Act 2013
CCA 1984	County Courts Act 1984
CEA 1972	Civil Evidence Act 1972
CEA 1995	Civil Evidence Act 1995
CJJA 1982	Civil Judgments and Jurisdiction Act 1982
FAA 1976	Fatal Accidents Act 1976
HRA 1998	Human Rights Act 1998
LA 1980	Limitation Act 1980
LASPO 2012	Legal Aid, Sentencing and Punishment of Offenders Act 2012
LDA 1986	Latent Damage Act 1986
MCA 2005	Mental Capacity Act 2005
SCA 1981	Senior Courts (formerly Supreme Court) Act 1981
SoGA 1979	Sale of Goods Act 1979

County Court Remedies Regulations 2014
County Court Jurisdiction Order 2014

Contents

BE CIVIL!

Introduction

This book sets out the nuts and bolts of the way in which disputes are resolved in the civil courts of England and Wales. It is written primarily for students on the Bar Professional Training Course ('BPTC'), but will also be of use to solicitors and other practitioners. It can be used both as an overview, as your course progresses, and as a revision guide, as you prepare for your professional examinations or experience early practice. What it is not is a substitute for your own learning. This book can do a lot for you, but it cannot do everything.

So there are some ground rules. *The first is that you must learn your way around the accepted practitioner texts.* If you are on the BPTC, you will have been given what is known in the trade (for obvious reasons if you are looking at a copy) as the 'White Book'.[1] This is still the favoured reference book of many judges, so you must familiarise yourself with it, and know how to use it. But tak e it gradually - you do not need to go all the way on the first date!

The White Book comes in two volumes. The first contains the relevant rules and other primary source material, accompanied by explanatory notes as appropriate. This commentary is, of course, a secondary source of information, although it will lead you to relevant case law. One of the advantages of this lay-out is that the primary and secondary source materials appear side-by-side, and

1   There is also a 'Green Book' (yes, it is green). There was a time when this was used only for procedure in the County Court, and the White Book, only for that in the High Court, but because the rules are now essentially the same for both jurisdictions, this division of labour no longer exists (although solicitors and County Court practitioners may be a little more apt to use the Green Book). Both books are set out in similar ways, so if you can use the one, you can use the other.

are easily distinguished one from the other,[2] so it is easy to move from one to the other, although at times the volume of the commentary seems to swamp the (often much) shorter recital of the actual rules. Volume II contains procedural legislation (more primary source material), specialist information, and some very useful general guidance in Sections 11 to 15. Have a look inside the cover to each volume for a guide to its contents. When I refer to the White Book in my footnotes, I will use the abbreviation 'WB'.

You may also have been given (or have access to) Blackstone's Civil Practice ('BCP'). This is the newer kid on the block. It performs a similar function to the White Book in that it contains the same sort of primary and secondary source material, but the presentation is different. BCP is rather more of a cross between a textbook and a practitioner reference work, and for this reason tends to be more helpful to students. It is certainly a bit easier on the eye. It comes in one volume, the first half of which is complete commentary. All of the primary source material is in the second half. This allows you to read both the secondary and primary source material in coherent sections, but it does mean you can find yourself having to flip back and forth between the explanatory text and the actual rules, which can be a little frustrating at times. Even so, BCP also covers some areas of interest which the White Book does not (for example, guidance on drafting statements of case), includes useful tables and examples, and you may find its procedural checklists easier to follow and more user-friendly than the White Book's. Again, look at the contents summary for a quick guide to what is inside.

In short, both works have strengths and drawbacks. I will thus make what I hope is even-handed reference to both throughout this book[3], bearing in mind the needs of the novice and the requirements for the BPTC. Both works are published

---

2   For example, the rules are all in bold, and the font size is different when you move to the commentary.

3   References will be to the most up-to-date editions available at the time of writing, namely WB 2013 and BCP 2014.

annually and produce supplements when between editions.[4] Both contain print which is getting so vanishingly small (although I think the White Book wins the prize here) that at times you will wish you had a magnifying glass (I am sure I have seen 'terms and conditions' in a bigger font!). Similarly, both are printed on paper which you may fear will dissolve in your hands, but it won't. It is surprisingly resilient! You just need to be patient and in the right frame of mind when you use these books. Take it slowly and do not rush.

To the extent that you are not provided with copies by your course, they will be in any decent law library. Consult them there - do not feel you must purchase them! You may, at times, find **BCP** more accessible, certainly in terms of learning the subject, but even so you *must also* become *confident at navigating the White Book*, which the Bar Standards Board (**BSB**) currently favours. But let's be honest - no-one reads these books for pleasure. They are reference works for practitioners who understand the subject and need to keep up-to-date. Their primary purpose is to inform, not teach. So, you do not have to love them, but you do need to know *how to use* them. The more you understand the subject, the easier it will become. But when your pupil supervisor turns to you in court and asks you to look up something for her quickly in the White Book, she needs a fast result, not a blank stare.

You may also have been provided with other textbooks and materials for your course, which you should use as required or needed. Stuart Sime's *A Practical Approach to Civil Procedure* ('Sime')[5] is a comprehensive and knowledgeable work, regularly updated and with lots of useful examples of various documents and court forms. He rather charmingly manages to marry up many of his chapter numbers with the Parts of the CPR they are discussing. His is an excellent and popular textbook, to which I will refer from time to time, but remember that it is not a practitioner text, as such - do not confuse the two.[6]

---

4   If using the 2013 edition of the WB, it is very important to use the latest supplement, because this is where some very important changes to the rules are set out. These are included in the 2014 edition of BCP (published in 2013) and will be incorporated into the 2014 edition of the WB.

5   Oxford University Press, at the time of writing in its sixteenth edition (2013)

6   Although Stuart Sime is one of the editors of BCP, so he can, and does, do both! At times the two sound very similar on that account.

The second ground rule is that you yourself must engage with the primary source material. It is nothing to be afraid of. The Civil Procedure Rules (CPR) are written in clear, straightforward language (the same might not always be said of the practitioner commentary). There aren't so many statutory provisions to deal with (unlike criminal procedure), and what there is you will know intimately by the end of your course (for example, Limitation Act 1980). At the end of the day, you must not simply rely on what someone else tells you the law is - go that one step further and have a look yourself.

In particular, I want you to *read some cases.* By that I do not mean the headnotes or summaries or a précis or a case analysis (although read those too if you wish) - I mean *actual judgments given by actual judges!* This, of course, is another primary source of the law. For some reason students tend to come to their professional training courses, if not with an aversion to reading cases, then with a very strong desire to find a way to avoid doing so. I do not know whether this is because they were made to read *Re Diplock*[7] when they were five years old or what, but such an attitude is short-sighted and utterly counter-productive. *There is no better way to learn* about the law than to see it in operation, and that is just what the cases do. A well-written judgment, which sets out the facts and relevant law clearly, and explains why the case has been decided the way that it has, will teach you a whole lot more about the rules and principles involved than any secondary source - and it is usually much more interesting to read.[8]

To encourage you in this endeavour, at the end of most chapters I have suggested you read a judgment[9] in one or two cases. They are all accessible on-line.[10] It will not necessarily be the leading case in the subject, nor the most recent, nor the most talked-about[11] - I have tried to choose cases which are particularly well written, or fun to read, or even a bit bizarre, so that you can see how useful they are. All of

7   A very old, and very long case!

8   Practitioner secondary sources are often updated in such a piecemeal way as to make them less rather than more readable over time (at least until they are completely re-written).

9   And I mean the judgment - you can skip all the preliminaries and go straight there. Some reports set out the legal argument as well, which can be interesting too, but I want you to focus on what the judge says.

10   Through Westlaw or other online legal resource service, provided by most teaching institutions for their law students.

11   These will be referred to in the relevant chapters themselves, so feel free to read them too.

them will tell you a lot about civil litigation and should show you that, contrary to the popular belief of many students, *cases are your friends.*

Finally, remember that even when major change is not being implemented, the civil procedure rules continue to evolve and it is important to know how to keep up to date (for example by keeping your eyes and ears open and always checking the most recent supplement to the practitioner texts). Your course tutors will give crucial guidance and any exam syllabus will test you on the state of play up to a given date. But don't forget that life, and the law, do not end there.

So if you do your part, I will do mine. This book will boost your understanding of civil litigation and evidence, principally by showing you how the various pieces of the 'procedural puzzle' fit together. This is the key to understanding the subject. If you can see the big picture clearly, the smaller detail will more easily fall (and fit) into place.

You must never try to learn rules in an intellectual vacuum. Think of all the games you know. Football. Monopoly. Even Snakes and Ladders has rules. As a general proposition, such rules will always be based on consistency, predictability, fairness and the purpose of the game. Those governing civil litigation are not really very different. To help you understand these rules, I use a thematic approach, which might be a little different from the way in which you have been taught. I hope this will help reinforce what you have been learning and give you further insight into the subject. Similarly, this book may well cover areas which are not on your particular examination syllabus: but naturally, the focus throughout is litigation.[12] There are some study tips at the end of most chapters, and I close the book with a brief guide to approaching revision and the different sorts of examination questions which you may encounter.

---

12 Remedies, as such, are
   not covered in detail.

The main rules of the civil litigation game are, of course, the Civil Procedure Rules ('CPR'), which originally came into being in 1999 - additional detail about implementation is set out in Practice Directions ('PD'), which immediately follow the rules to which they relate. These embody what became known as the Woolf reforms, named for the judge whose task it was to devise what was then a completely new and modern system. The principal impetus behind the CPR was a desire to take the pace and direction of litigation out of the hands of the parties (for which read 'the lawyers') and place them firmly in the hands of the court. This was a radical departure at the time.[13] The idea was that litigation (where this is, as a last resort, necessary) should become:

- more efficient, both in terms of costs and time, because it proceeds more quickly and only real contests get to trial;
- more accessible, to the extent it is less legalistic and easier to understand;
- more proportionate, so that cases proceed in a manner and at a pace commensurate with their complexity;

and so ...

- more *just* overall than was the case before the CPR.

The CPR transformed the procedural landscape (from which other areas of litigation, notably family and criminal law, have borrowed). But the costs of litigation still proved difficult to control (and at times eye-watering in amount) and so Lord Justice Jackson was asked to 'review' this aspect of the process and suggest changes which would better promote access to justice, but at proportionate cost. This he did, and the upshot is what are now known as the 'Jackson reforms', which have made significant

---

13 The vocabulary of litigation was also updated. For example, 'plaintiffs' became 'claimants', 'claim forms' replaced the 'writs' which started proceedings in the High Court and so on. So be prepared when reading older cases. For the sake of consistency, I shall use the modern vocabulary in this book, even when referring to events which occurred before the CPR.

changes to several aspects of the rules - most of which were brought into effect in April 2013. In a nutshell, what these amendments did was to boost the importance of proportionality in the rules (both in spirit and in practice), especially where case *and* costs management is concerned, and place more emphasis on encouraging parties to solve their difference without recourse to a courtroom. Lord Justice Jackson's preface to the supplement to the 2013 White Book (to be updated for the 2014 edition) is a neat overview of the changes and is well worth reading.

But to start at the beginning: the aspirations of both the Woolf and Jackson reforms are manifested and expressed in the *'overriding objective'* of the CPR, which is to enable the court 'to deal with cases justly *and at proportionate cost'*.[14] What this means in practical terms is explained in CPR, r 1.1(2). It is worth setting this out in full.

'Dealing with a case justly **and at proportionate cost** includes,[15] so far as is practicable -

(a) ensuring the parties are on an equal footing;

(b) saving expense;

(c) dealing with the case in ways which are proportionate -

(i) to the amount of money involved;

(ii) to the importance of the case;

(iii) to the complexity of the issues; *and*

(iv) to the financial position of each party;

(d) ensuring that the case is dealt with expeditiously and fairly;

(e) allotting to it an appropriate share of the court's resources, while taking into account the need to allot resources to other cases; *and*

(f) enforcing compliance with rules, practice directions and orders.

---

14 I have indicated in bold the amendments to the overriding objective recently added as part of the Jackson reforms.

15 Note the use in this rule of the word 'includes'. The list is not exhaustive.

Tape a copy of CPR, r 1.1 (2) (as it now reads) to your fridge or bathroom mirror, because the overriding objective and its constituents are of primary importance to understanding civil litigation. *They give the rules purpose and also dominate their content. It is essential to always bear them in mind.* Everyone, the parties as well as the court actively managing cases, is under a duty to comply with the overriding objective.[16] So CPR can also stand for -

Court Control and compliance with rules and court orders ...

Proportionality ...

Resolution by efficient and cost effective means.

If you begin by eating, sleeping and dreaming about the overriding objective (within reason), then you will have made a good start.

Civil jurisdiction is exercised mainly[17] by the High Court, which has some regional outposts, but is based at the Royal Courts of Justice in London, and by the County Court (which from April 2014 will be a single court sitting at various locations all the country).[18] The High Court, along with the Crown Court (a criminal court) and the Court of Appeal used to be known together as the Supreme Court of England and Wales, but when the House of Lords (the highest appellate court in the land) was re-branded 'The Supreme Court', this meant that suddenly there were too many chiefs. So the High Court, Crown Court and the Court of Appeal became the Senior Courts.[19]

The High Court, which deals with the more important and complex civil cases, is itself divided into three divisions:

---

16 CPR, r 1.2 and 1.3
17 Some civil jurisdiction is exercised by magistrates' courts (for example, on regulatory matters) and some by specialist tribunals (for example, employment tribunals).
18 The Courts Act 2013, s 17 replaces what were local County Courts with a single jurisdiction to be exercised at various local outposts (like the High Court when it sits out of London). The enforcement date is 22 April 2014. As a result, it looks as if individual County Courts will be redesignated as 'hearing centres. Titles on statements of case will change accordingly. Watch this space.
19 And the Supreme Court Act 1981, which is the primary source of their procedural powers, became the Senior Courts Act 1981

(i)   The Chancery Division ('ChD'), which specialises in land, trust, probate and such cases;

(ii) Family Division, where matrimonial and related cases are assigned;

(iii) The Queen's Bench Division ('QBD'), where most tort and contract cases appropriate for the High Court are started. The Administrative Court, which hears judicial review cases, is part of the QBD.

There are other specialist courts in the High Court, including the Commercial Court (part of the QBD), the Companies Court (part of the ChD) and the Technology and Construction Court ('TCC'),[20] but this book concentrates on mainstream litigation, which will tend to proceed either in the County Court (for the more straightforward and lower value cases) or the Queen's Bench (or Chancery Division) of the High Court.

So off we go. But before we start, there is one *final ground rule*, and that is: *you should have fun* reading this book. And if, by the end of it, you have *understood* what you have read, both in principle and in application (as opposed to merely memorising or 'learning' it), and if you have also abided by my ground rules, then you should be well able to meet the challenge that awaits you.

---

20 These tend to have their own special ways of doing things. For further information on these specialist courts see BCP, para 2.15ff.

PART ONE
getting started

CHAPTER 2

Litigation lite:
pre-action conduct

Courtroom drama may make good television, but by and large it is a costly, time-consuming and forbidding way to resolve disputes. Parties who can settle their differences on sensible and agreed terms will retain ownership of, and faith in, the outcome. For that reason, it has always been a matter of common sense as well as good practice that litigation should be seen as a last and not a first resort.

An important innovation of the CPR was the introduction of a formalised system for the early exchange of information about legal disputes, which is intended to increase the opportunities for a fair settlement without proceedings ever having to be issued. This manifests itself in the various pre-action protocols, which exist for, and are tailored to the needs of certain specific types of disputes,[1] including personal injuries claims.[2] In addition, there is an overarching Practice Direction which gives guidance about pre-action conduct generally, and in particular for those cases not covered by a specific protocol.[3] I shall refer to these last two as the 'PI protocol' and the 'Pre-action conduct PD', respectively.

Pre-action conduct tends to be the expertise of solicitors, who are there on the front line from the beginning. After all, the idea is to avoid, not incur legal costs! Nevertheless, it is important for barristers to have a clear grasp of the fundamentals because compliance (or lack of compliance) with proper pre-action behaviour can

1 For example, building disputes, clinical negligence cases, mortgage possession claims, defamation cases. See the full list in WB, Section C

2 The Pre-Action Protocol for Personal Injury Claims is primarily intended for claims up to £25,000 (the usual fast track limit), but those worth more should follow the spirit of the protocol, if not necessarily the exact letter (para 2.4). As to track allocation see Ch 8.

3 Practice Direction - Pre-action Conduct

have serious consequences down the line, especially where case management[4] and costs orders[5] are concerned.

You can find the various Protocols set out in all practitioner texts.[6] Although you should be aware of the existence of the other published protocols, for examination purposes the BPTC[7] like this chapter, focuses on the generic Pre-action conduct PD and the PI protocol referred to above.[8] BCP also includes a helpful one-page procedural checklist for both of these.[9]

It is important to grasp the essential framework and function of the protocols. The necessary detail will fall into place so long as you understand the two main objectives of appropriate pre-action conduct:

(1) to empower the parties to resolve their dispute fairly without having to litigate if possible;

and

(2) in cases where going to court cannot be avoided, to ensure that the case proceeds as quickly and efficiently as possible when it gets there.[10]

The PI protocol was a trailblazer. It was one of the first to be published and provided a prototype for those which followed.[11] It contains four essential elements.

A. STANDARD 'LETTER BEFORE CLAIM' DETAILING THE NATURE OF THE CLAIM

This used to be called a letter *of* claim, but this sounded too much like the real deal and so the name was changed to make the pre-action context clearer: letter *before* claim. Previous communications between the parties may well have made clear the prospective claimant's concerns and expectations, but it is this specific letter

---

4 See Ch. 13
5 See Ch. 18
6 WB, Vol 1, Sec C or BCP, Appendix 2, which begin by listing them all. Check your exam syllabus for the exact knowledge required.
7 For 2013/2014. This may change in future).
8 But be aware that the new RTA protocol now applies to a sub-group of personal injuries actions, that is to say RTA claims worth no more than £10,000 where liability is not disputed. See below.
9 Procedural checklists 1 and 2
10 See pre-action conduct PD, para 1.1
11 The newest protocols, however, mark a significant procedural departure from the others. See below.

which starts off the formal pre-action process. Two copies should be sent to the defendant[12] (or one to the defendant and one to the relevant insurers, if known). The letter before claim should be concise but include sufficient detail (for example, what went wrong, why the claimant holds the defendant responsible and so forth) so that the defendant can understand and investigate the issues raised without having to ask for more information. It should contain, and seek from the defendant, any relevant documents.[13] The letter should be professional, not spiteful in tone and must inform defendants of any funding arrangement which can impact directly on them (for example, if the claimant is publicly funded).[14] A fill-in-the-blanks example is appended to the PI protocol.[15] Most solicitors would have something similar on their template data base.

Where no specific protocol applies, the Pre-action Conduct PD makes clear that where the defendant is unrepresented, the letter before claim must refer explicitly to that practice direction, draw attention to the risks of non-compliance and warn the defendant that ignoring the letter may result in proceedings being issued and increasing the defendant's liability to costs.[16]

B. PROMPT IDENTIFICATION OF ISSUES

The PI protocol requires that defendants should acknowledge receipt of a 'letter before claim' within 21 days, naming any relevant insurer (if not already known). Having done that they then have up to *three months to investigate* the claim (not surprisingly, the generic Pre-action conduct PD is more flexible - it requires that the defendant be given a 'reasonable period' to make a full response, which will vary depending on the complexity of the allegations. It could be 14 days in a simple debt case, in which case the defendant need not acknowledge receipt, but could just respond in that short period[17]).

---

12 Although strictly speaking no-one is being sued yet, it is now common to refer to the parties as 'claimant' and 'defendant' once the pre-action protocol process has got underway.

13 See the list of documents suitable in various types of personal injuries action at PI Protocol, Annex B.

14 Or other funding agreement which *impacts* on a defendant. Precise details need not be disclosed. From April 2013, CFA funding no longer poses costs risks to defendants, so it is not required that they be told about it. See further Ch. 18

15 At PI Protocol, Annex A. There is also an example in Sime, fig 5.1.

16 Pre-action conduct PD, annex A, para 2.3

17 *Ibid*, para 3.1

A defendant should provide the claimant with the documentary evidence and/or other clear explanation for any denial of liability. An allegation of, say, contributory negligence should be clearly set out and met with an equally detailed response by the claimant.[18] The idea is that there is *early* identification of the *real* issue in dispute. As soon as possible the PI protocol requires that the claimant should provide the defendant with a schedule of past and future loss and expense and *both* sides should consider whether the claimant has needs which could be met by *rehabilitation* treatment or other measures.[19] The earlier rehabilitation is factored into the equation (and indeed begun), the better for everyone.

C. EARLY EXCHANGE OF RELEVANT EVIDENCE, INCLUDING EXPERT EVIDENCE

Relevant documents are exchanged almost from the outset. Different types of personal injuries cases call for the disclosure of different kinds of documentary evidence.[20] For example, a current MOT certificate might be relevant to a road traffic accident claim,[21] but not in a workplace accident case, where health and safety compliance documents would be more to the point.

The hope is that very early on, both sides should be in a position to assess the strength (or weakness) of their respective cases - and negotiate accordingly. Expert evidence[22] can be a crucial component of this picture. In personal injuries cases, this usually takes the form of medical reports, but other expertise (for example, from an engineer, or car mechanic) may also be relevant.

There are several ways in which expert evidence can be exchanged and/or presented, both before and after proceedings are issued in civil cases. The various protocols differ in their requirements, depending on what the nature of such cases usually requires. The generic Pre-action conduct PD merely requires the parties to

---

18 A counterclaim would require the defendant, in effect, to send his own letter before claim. As to counterclaims generally, see Ch. 5

19 Para 4.1 and PI Protocol, Annex D.
20 See PI Protocol, Annex B.
21 Bear in mind that for the most minor road traffic accidents, occurring after 30 April 2010 and where liability is *admitted*, the new RTA Protocol will apply. See below.

22 See below Ch. 17 on the nature of expert evidence generally in civil litigation.

'consider how best to minimise the expense'[23] and sets out various ways this might be done in its Annex C. One important way expense is saved is by the use of a *single* expert on an issue (rather than one for each party), which can come about in a number of ways. Put generally, a single expert can be:

- jointly selected or agreed (where both sides participate in the selection of, and can put questions to the expert, but only one side pays for and gives instructions to the expert, calls the evidence and retains legal professional privilege in the evidence, unless and until it is disclosed to the other side[24]);

or

- jointly instructed (where both parties participate in the selection of *and* also instruct the expert who will send each side a copy of the report. Generally the costs of such reports are shared. This is the norm in fast track cases which *litigate*[25]);

or

- one party could get expert evidence independently and hope its use can be agreed and sanctioned by the court.

The PI protocol shows a distinct preference for the first of these. The notes of guidance say that the protocol encourages 'joint selection of, and access to, experts'[26] and the body of the protocol sets out a process resulting in joint selection, but not joint instruction of an agreed single expert in the pre-action period.[27]

However, so far as *medical* evidence in particular is concerned, however, the guidance notes to the PI protocol also recognises that a patient may well seek, or have already obtained, a medical opinion from his or her own doctor in the process

---

23 para 9.4.
24 *Carlson v Townsend* [2001] CPLR 405, and see generally below in Ch. 17
25 See generally Ch. 17. The terminology distinguishing joint selection from joint instruction can be confusing. 'Single joint expert' is not particularly

descriptive but in the context of litigation refers to the expert whom both sides select *and* instruct: CPR, r 35.1(2). The pre-action protocols are a little less precise in their vocabulary. The important thing is to be clear what you mean in your own mind (and writing).

26 Para 2.14
27 Joint selection works like this: the claimant sends a list of possible experts to the defendant, who then indicates whether he objects to any of them. The claimant is free to choose and instruct any remaining on the list. If

of formulating a cause of action. It therefore anticipates, indeed 'promotes'[28] the practice of a claimant, having obtained an informal medical report, disclosing this to the defendant, who can then query the report and/or agree it without the need for obtaining his own or selecting another expert. Such an expert would, again, remain the claimant's expert. This is the cheapest option, but is probably only viable when the medical evidence is relatively uncontroversial. Even at this stage, a defendant may not find the claimant's own doctor to be completely free of bias.

A claimant wanting to use his own (that is, the treating) doctor as the single expert *at trial*, however, may well find that the defendant and/or the court would consider this expert insufficiently objective for those purposes, resulting in the evidence being excluded. Care should thus be taken from the outset, since, even if the claimant wins, the costs for such (unusable) reports may not ultimately be recoverable.

D.   REALITY CHECKS, FURTHER NEGOTIATIONS AND THE IMPORTANCE OF ADR

The protocols and Pre-action conduct PD all reinforce the message that litigation should be a last resort, and stress the importance of 'reality checks' and serious thought being given to whether there might be some other, alternative, way to resolve the dispute (known colloquially as 'ADR'). In most cases 'the court will want to know what steps' the parties have taken to settle their differences[29] and it would certainly be frowned upon if proceedings were started while meaningful negotiations were on-going, unless (for example) the limitation period was about to expire.[30] As Sir Rupert Jackson put it: 'The aim is that, in general, no case should come to trial without the parties having undertaken some form of ADR to seek to settle the case'.[31]

It is important to note, however, that the duty is to *consider* ADR, not necessarily

---

the defendant objects to them all, the claimant is still free to instruct one from the list, but both he and the defendant may have to explain their list, choice and objections to the court who can, if necessary, decide who has and who has not

acted unreasonably. Similarly, explanations would be necessary if both decided to instruct separate experts. See para 3.15- 3.21

28 Para 2.14
29 See wording of Part 1 of the directions questionnaire.

30 See generally, Ch. 10
31 To assist in this process, an ADR handbook was published in April 2013 (*The Jackson ADR Handbook*, OUP). See the introduction to the WB supplement, at p xii.

to engage in it. This is made emphatically clear in the PI protocol.[32] Not all cases are suitable for ADR.[33]

To an extent, the pre-action protocols and the Pre-action conduct PD create a system of pre-litigation litigation, but without the wigs and gowns, expense and bad tempers that flare when the bureaucracy bears down and parties begin to lose control over the outcome. You might think of it as 'litigation-lite'. Certainly if, despite everything, proceedings are issued, the groundwork will have been laid for the expeditious conduct and progress of proceedings. Many of the steps of the litigation process, especially where disclosure, choice of expert and exchange of evidence is concerned, will already have taken place.

The low value protocols

Recent additions to the protocol library are those dealing with low value (now up to £25,000 [34]) road traffic accidents (RTA) and employers/public liability (EL/PL) personal injury claims (but not those destined for the small claims track), arising from accidents occurring after 30 April 2010 and where liability is *not* contested. Such cases are straightforward cases where defendants are (or should be insured) and where the only real issue is quantifying loss and damage. The purpose of the protocols is to provide a streamlined, highly regulated system (mostly on-line communication with strict time and costs limits) which is designed to produce a just result to the parties, rather than profits to businesses (like those who advertise on TV) who began 'feeding off' such cases in the interests of their bottom line.[35] The detail of these protocols is not on the BPTC exam syllabus for 2013/2014[36], but you should know of their existence and purpose. They are procedurally different from all the others. They basically involve three stages:

---

32 At para 2.19
33 For a good example,see *Halsey v Milton Keynes General NHS* [2004] 1 WLR 3002.
34 Increased from £10,000 from July 2013

35 This 'commoditisation' of resolving such disputes was identified as a problem in the Jackson Review (2009). These protocols are part of the solution. See discussion in Sime, 9.01ff.

36 But check subsequent years

(i) Claimant sends defendant's insurer a Claim Notification Form (CNF). Defendant given a short time to decide whether to admit liability. If liability is denied, or the defendant raises contributory negligence, the claim leaves the protocol. Claimant's costs fixed for this stage (currently £200).

(ii) Quantification of damages. Time limited negotiation should follow the obtaining and disclosure of medical evidence. Claimant's costs again fixed (currently £300).

(iii) If quantum cannot be agreed (or the claimant is a child, for example), the claimant can get the matter before the court using the Part 8 claim form.[37] Costs continue to be fixed (for solicitors and advocates).[38]

Finally, remember that compliance with proper pre-action conduct is a cornerstone of the CPR and is viewed very seriously. The fact that the parties have complied must be pleaded in relevant statements of case. The court will not look kindly on someone who approaches the protocol in the wrong spirit,[39] and it has an armory of effective penalties for willful non-compliance.[40] In particular, it will not be pre-disposed to assist a party seeking a helpful direction or extension of time who has failed, in some fundamental and inexcusable way, to engage with the ethos of the protocols. Adverse costs orders are another important sanction. Having said that, the court will not concern itself with minor or technical infractions. Sometimes, circumstances will justify a departure from the protocol, especially if mediation is in progress or being attempted.[41] Any punishment for non-compliance should, of course, be in keeping with the (new look) overriding objective, but should also fit the crime.

---

37 See Ch. 3

38 See generally Ch. 18

39 See e.g. *King v Telegraph Group Ltd*, [2004] EWCA Civ 613, [2005] 1 WLR 2282 where the court penalised the claimant by putting a cap on the costs which the defendant might have to pay because the letter before claim was written 'in a vituperative tone calculated to raise the temperature and inflate the parties' costs'.

40 And see generally case management at Ch. 13

41 As in *Roundstone Nurseries Ltd v Stephenson Holdings Ltd* [2009] EWHC 1431 (TCC)

revision tips

- Be aware of the existence and applicability of the pre-action protocols not tested in detail. But focus on the pre-action conduct PD and the PI protocol. The latter is specific to personal injuries actions; the former has to be more flexible to accommodate a range of cases not covered by an existing protocol. Know them both, but do not confuse them – appreciate their similarities as well as their differences.

- The BCP checklist for both the PI protocol and the pre-action conduct PD will help.

- Always double check your examination syllabus to ensure you have the required level of understanding of the relevant protocols. Solicitors' exam syllabus, for example, may well test a wider knowledge of the pre-action protocols than the BTPC's, which itself can change from year to year.

- The court cannot ultimately force a party to *engage* in ADR, because everyone is entitled to fair access to the courts (Art 6 ECHR), but it can penalise a party for not giving it serious *consideration*. Not every case is suitable for ADR (e.g. where the merits are obviously all on one side), but litigation should always be viewed as a last (and not very pleasant) resort.

It is worth reading …

Lightman J's judgment in *Hurst v Leeming* [2002] EWHC 1051 (Ch). This is something of a cautionary tale, I suppose, given that the claimant is a solicitor and the defendant, a barrister, but don't let that put you off. It is short and to the point and a precursor of sorts to the (more important) *Halsey* case. Too bad we could not have been there for the 'frank exchange of views' between the judge and the defendant on the merits of the latter's utterly hopeless case. Counselling might have been more appropriate than mediation!

CHAPTER 3

Proceedings and parties

If a dispute does not settle in the pre-action phase, then it will become necessary, if the case is to be pursued, to commence proceedings.[1] This raises questions of where and how to start an action, and against whom. This is also a convenient chapter for discussing special rules about joining parties to proceedings.

1.   WHERE TO START?

An important effect of the CPR was to end, generally speaking, the distinction between High Court and County Court procedure. The latter had been created in the image of the former, and so, despite some significant differences, there were always many similarities.[2] The CPR instituted a unitary code of practice, which applies to all civil courts, although some specialist areas, such as family law (which has its own CPR-like procedure), are specifically excluded. Recent changes in April, 2014 have continued this process by converting a localised County Court system into one national court (like the High Court) and making various adjustments in order to streamline the organisation, save costs and make what is now *the* County Court more of an equal, if still junior partner in dispensing civil justice. Where a party brings

---

1   The focus here, as on the BPTC, is on mainstream County and High Court actions.

2   County Court jurisdiction is entirely the creature of statute; the County Courts Act 1984, as amended ('CCA 1984'). The High Court has a longer pedigree and an inherent jurisdiction, but its procedures are governed primarily by what is now called the Senior Courts Act 1981('SCA 1981').

a civil action will depend both on rules about *jurisdiction* (which court is capable of dealing with the claim) and rules about *commencement* (where to start off a claim). It is important not to confuse the two concepts.

There are certain types of cases where only the High Court has jurisdiction. These include libel, judicial review, certain specialist and human rights claims, and equity cases exceeding £350,000 (recently raised from £30,000).[3] There are even a very few cases where only the County Court has jurisdiction, for example certain unlawful discrimination and lower value consumer credit claims.[4] But in the *general run* of contract and tort cases[5], the High Court and County Court have *concurrent* jurisdiction, which is to say that either has the power to deal with such cases.

Although jurisdiction is concurrent in such cases, there are, nevertheless, important rules about commencement which dictate where certain actions must be started. In particular:

(i) Cases seeking damages for personal injuries and fatal accident cases: claims for less than £50,000 must be commenced in the County Court.[6] There are two points to note here:

   (a) The amount sought must be one which a claimant can 'resonably expect' to recover. Most personal injury claims are, realistically, worth less than £50,000.

   (b) When calculating a claim for these purposes, certain aspects of a case (for example costs, interest, contributory negligence) are to be disregarded.[7]

(ii) Generally, as regards all other types of money claims: those which do not exceed £100,000 must be commenced in the County Court.[8]

---

3   County Court Jurisdiction Order 2014 (S1 2014/503). This threshold had not been changed since 1981 which explains why the increase is such a big one. It means a lot more Chancery work can now be dealt with in the County Court.

4   Certain housing applications may only be brought in the County Court if the costs of doing so are to be recovered. See Sime, paras 3.19-21

5   CCA 1984, s 15

6   CPR, PD 7A, para 2.2. The actual wording is 'proceedings which include a claim for damages for personal injuries', so the latter need not be the only claim being made for the rule to be applicable.

Bear in mind that these are fundamentally rules about *commencement, not jurisdiction*. Their purpose is to force litigants to begin 'smaller' claims in the County Court, where they will most likely be tried (if the case gets that far). Note, too, the possible sanctions for non-compliance with these commencement rules. Deliberate or tactical flouting can result in the claim being struck out. More usually, there will be a penalty in costs, either at the end of the trial, assuming the case litigated all the way in the High Court when it should have been brought in the County Court[9] - or when the case is transferred from the High Court to the County Court where it belongs.[10]

Further, it is important to understand that it does *not* follow from these rules that claims crossing the relevant thresholds must be started in the High Court. Such actions *may* also be commenced in the County Court, although where the claimant believes that the High Court could better deal with the claim because of its complexity or its public importance, then the case should be started there. Such considerations would also dictate where claims for remedies other than money (for example, an injunction) should most appropriately be commenced.[11]

Equally, the court, for the same sorts of reasons, can transfer cases from the High Court to the County Court (and vice versa!) as part of its extensive case management powers, either on its own initiative or on application by any party. Thus, where appropriate, a high value claim may be transferred to the County Court even if properly started off in the High Court although this may not happen so often now that the threshold for being allowed to commence non-personal injury money claims in the High Court has been raised to £100,000. Moreover, where a case may ultimately be tried is another factor which will influence where a claimant, with a choice, decides to start off his action.

---

7   Ibid and Art 9 High Court and County Courts Jurisdiction Order, 1991 (SI 1991/1724 as amended).
8   CPR, PD 7A para 2.1 This threshold for non-PI claims was raised from £25,000 as of 22 April 2014: High Court and County Court Jurisdiction (Amendment) Order 2014 (SI 2014/821).
9   A winner's costs could be reduced by up to 25% to reflect the fact that the case could have litigated more cheaply in the County Court. See SCA1981, s 51(8),(9)
10 *Ibid*, s 51. This is the most typical outcome. See also *Restick v Crickmore* [1994] 1 WLR 420, CA.
11 CPR, PD 7A para 2.4

2. HOW TO START?

Civil proceedings involving run of the mill factual disputes (for example, negligence, breach of contract, breach of trust) are started by means of the issue of a Part 7 claim form, which comes in one standard form (to be adapted as necessary).[12] The claim form is issued by the court at the request of the claimant, whether personally or, more usually, acting through his or her solicitor. The claim form is the lead document in what are known generically as statements of case.[13] It kicks off the proceedings, although it need not set out all the specifics of the case against the defendant. This is done in the particulars of claim, which should set out in detail the cause of action, the facts relied upon by the claimant and the remedy sought.[14] In personal injuries actions, a medical report and schedule of past and future loss and expense ought to accompany the particulars of claim.[15]

The particulars of clam itself can either be (a) contained on the claim form itself, (b) come as a separate document *with* (or 'attached' to) the claim form, or (c) follow within *14 days* of service of the claim form (and in any event while the claim form is still valid for service).[16]

Where practicable the particulars of claim should be set out on the claim form[17] (typically where it is short) or accompany the claim form. However, where neither is possible (for example because the draft is long or complicated or time is a factor), the claim form itself must give concise details of the nature of the claim, remedy sought and (where money is at stake) contain a statement of value (that is, less than £10,000; £10,000-£25,000; more than £25,000; or don't know). These values, as you can probably tell, are for track allocation purposes.[18] If commenced in the High Court, the claim form must state that the relevant threshold has been crossed, or that it is a specialist High Court case.

---

12 Some specialist courts like the Commercial Court use their own special forms.

13 See generally CPR, Part 16, para 4. As to validity of the claims form, see Ch. 12

14 CPR, r 16.4

15 CPR, PD 16

16 CPR r 7.4(1)(a) and (b)

17 See example in Sime, figure 6.1

18 CPR, r 16.3 and see generally Ch. 8

If the particulars of claim are not actually contained on the claim form, the latter should state whether they are 'attached' to (that is, included with) the claim form or will follow later. It must also contain a statement of truth. If served separately, a copy and certificate of service of the particulars of claim must be filed with the court.[19]Not all disputes, of course, are fact-based. Those which are essentially about legal questions or issues are initiated by using a Part 8 claim form. Typically such actions ask the court to construe a document such as a Will or a deed. In such cases, the so-called 'weapons of litigation',[20] which are pertinent to contentious disputes of fact, are not generally deployed. Written evidence is served with the Part 8 claim form (as opposed to particulars of claim) and any trial will essentially involve legal submissions on the basis of that evidence rather than cross-examination of witnesses of fact.

So, for example, *compare*:

- claim for breach of contract (Part 7) versus asking the court to answer the legal question, 'What does this contractual term mean?' (Part 8)
- claim for breach of trust (Part 7) versus asking the court to construe a Will so the trustees know to whom to give the estate's assets (Part 8)

Certain procedural applications also use Part 8 claim forms as required by relevant rules, statutes and practice directions.[21] Broadly speaking, where no claim has been brought, but an issue requires a judge's determination, then Part 8 is the usual mechanism to bring the matter to the court's attention. Part 8 is also used for specialist proceedings. In the main, these will only be of interest if you practise in these areas,[22] but you should be aware of the existence of this alternative procedure. Part 8 claims may be started off at any County Court hearing centre, unless a rule, practice direction or enactment provides otherwise.

The vast majority of claims, of course, are factually based claims (in other

19 CPR, r 7.4(3)
20 Especially orders for disclosure of documents, and testing of oral evidence at trial.

21 For example, the approval of children's settlements per CPR, r 21.10(2). See CPR, PD 8A, para 3.1-3.3

22 Although it is worth noting that the new RTA protocol makes use of a 'modified' Part 8 procedure.

words, Part 7) and are for money - and most of these are started in the County Court. Money only claims in the County Court (whether for a specific sum or not[23]) should be issued from the main Business Centre at Northampton[24] and will be sent to the Money Claims Centre at Salford)[25]. Claimants should indicate on the form which hearing centre they would prefer to deal with their case ('preferred hearing centre'), and this is where *undefended* cases will often be sent for matters (such as the amount or rate of payment) to be finalised. *Defended* cases tend to go to the *defendant's* preferred or local hearing centre, but will usually not end up there until after directions questionnaires have been filed (or any stay pending attempts to settle have expired), when it will be clearer what steps next need to be taken in the case.

Not surprisingly, claimants can even make money claims online these days, so long as certain basic conditions are met - for example, neither party must be a child or protected party[26] and the amount claimed must not exceed £100,000. The claim form is issued and the fees paid on-line using the court service portal at www.moneyclaim.gov.uk. The particulars of claim can be contained on the form if short enough (no more than 1080 characters) - otherwise they may be filed and served separately. Service is effected by the court and defendants can respond electronically, or by traditional (hard copy) methods if they prefer.[27]

3.   WHOM TO SUE: PARTIES AND JOINDER

A.   PARTIES

When starting proceedings, one needs to make clear who is suing whom[28] - and for what. This is often fairly obvious, but thought must be given to the rules regarding special types of parties, as well as to what happens when there is more than one party on each side.

---

23 Some of these were known, temporarily, as 'designated money claims'. This term has now been abandoned.

24 Formerly Northampton County Court. Individual County Courts will be re-branded hearing centres once the unified system

comes into being in April 2014. Part 8 claims can be started off at any hearing centre, unless a rule, PD or statute provides otherwise.

25 CPR, PD 7A, para 4A.1
26 See discussion below
27 See generally CPR, PD 7E, summarised in Sime,6.12.

28 This needs to be made clear on the statements of case. The full name of each party must be given, including an individual's full and proper title. See PD 16, para 2.6. See also helpful summary of how various types of parties are named in proceedings

As regards the first of these, the following merit special mention, if only because they commonly feature in litigation and regularly crop up in examinations.

(i) Children

An individual attains full age at 18. Until then, a person is, legally speaking, considered to be 'acting under a disability'.[29] In the past (and in older cases) such people have been referred to variously as minors or infants, but the CPR now uses the more modern description 'child' or 'children'.

Children must sue and defend by their '*litigation friend*', although the court may order that a child is able to conduct proceedings on his or her own behalf.[30] Remember that the child is the party (for example, claimant or defendant), but he or she must litigate by means of a litigation friend. The title of the proceedings would reflect this in the following way:

Miss WENDY DARLING   Claimant
(a child by MR GEORGE DARLING, her litigation friend)

A person assuming the role of a child's litigation friend usually does so voluntarily and so *without* the need for a court order. Typically such a person would be the child's parent or guardian, but in any case it must be someone with no conflicting interests, who is capable of acting fairly and competently and who, if the child is a claimant, will undertake to pay any costs ordered against the child.[31] The litigation friend must file a certificate of suitability with the court.[32] In the rare instances where no appropriate person steps forward to be a child's litigation friend, the court can make an order that one is appointed.[33]

It is important to note that settlements of monetary claims made by a child

---

in BCP at table 14.1 and Sime at table 19.2.

29 As are persons lacking mental capacity to conduct proceedings, who are now called 'protected parties' in accordance with the Mental Capacity Act 2005 ('MCA 2005'). See below.

30 CPR, r 21.2 (2) and (3). This is uncommon, but might be appropriate for an older child in certain circumstances.

31 CPR, r 21.4(3), and see e.g., *Nottingham County Council v Botomley* [2010] MedLR 407

32 CPR, r 21.5. see example in Sime, Fig 19.1

33 CPR, r 21.6

require *special* attention. There are two principal reasons for this: children need protection from exploitative or disadvantageous settlements, and defendants need to be confident that a settlement made in good faith is effectively final.[34] The court should be asked to approve the proposed settlement as being in the child's best interests (in view of the strengths and weaknesses of the case, the risks of and expected delays in litigation and so forth[35]). If it does so, the court will also give relevant directions to ensure the money is used and applied properly.

The procedure for seeking court approval varies depending on whether the offer of settlement is made before or after proceedings have started. Thus -

(a) *If no action has yet been commenced* in respect of a child's claim, a Part 8 claim form is the mechanism used for seeking the court's approval for the settlement.[36] It should set out the details of the claim and the terms of the proposed compromise. Seeking court approval for a pre-action compromise is always advisable, if not actually required by the rules, because without it the settlement could unravel.

(b) *Once proceedings have been commenced*, the rules specifically state that any settlement, to be valid, *must* be approved by the court.[37] In such cases, a Part 7 claim form will already have been issued and so the application for approval of the child settlement is, like all interim applications, made under CPR part 23.[38]

It is easier, of course, to make things compulsory once the court has been seized of the case. If no action has been started, the rules can do little else but provide a mechanism for seeking court approval. The critical point is that in either case, until a proposed children's settlement is approved by the court, there is no binding agreement, and either party can resile from it.[39]

---

34 At common law a child will not be bound by an out-of-court settlement unless made for his benefit. Court approval of the settlement gives the defendant a valid discharge from liability.

35 The court will need a lot of information before it to make such a determination, especially if the claim is for personal injuries. This includes an opinion on the merits of the case. See, e.g., PD 21, para 5.1

36 CPR, r 21.10(2)
37 CPR, r 21.10(1)
38 See generally Ch. 4
39 *Drinkall v Whitwood* [2004] 1 WLR 462

(ii) Persons suffering mental incapacity

Persons lacking the mental capacity[40] to conduct litigation are known as 'protected parties' and, like children, they are treated as persons 'acting under a disability'. Thus the rules discussed in (a) above also apply to such litigants[41], with appropriate adaptations - for example, the protected person would not be described in the court documents as a child (unless he or she was also a child) and it will be clearer when a child, by virtue of his having reached 18, ceases to be acting under the disability of childhood. But otherwise, like children, protected persons require a litigation friend to sue and be sued, and court approval should be sought for any settlement of monetary claims made by such litigants.

(iii) Partnerships and sole traders

A partnership is the association of two or more persons who co-own a business for profit. A partnership typically trades under a firm name.[42] Generally speaking, it is 'one for all and all for one' in partnerships; in most situations each partner, who was a partner at the relevant time, will be bound by acts done on behalf of the firm and liable in respect of them.[43]

Unless it is inappropriate to do so, claims by or against a partnership must use the *firm name* under which the partnership carried on business *at the time* the cause of action arose.[44] There was a time when this was merely an alternative to suing in the name of all of the individual partners (which could be very tiresome if there were a lot of them), but it was so routinely preferred that it seemed sensible to make it the rule, rather than a matter of choice. As to when it might be 'inappropriate' to sue or be sued in the name of a firm, your guess is as good as mine - like the proverbial elephant, such a situation may be difficult to describe, but you will probably know it when you see it.

---

40 There is a presumption of mental capacity, which is displaced when it is shown that an individual has an impairment which prevents them from making the necessary decisions. See formula set out in MCA 2005, s 3, at WB at 21.0.3

41 CPR, Part 21 is entitled 'Children and Protected Parties'

42 Note that just because a business calls itself 'Jones and Co' does not make it a registered company.

43 See generally Partnership Act 1890

44 Assuming it has a name. See PD 7A, para 5A.3

In the title to proceedings, the fact that a partnership is named is signified by putting the words 'a firm' in brackets after the name, as in *Warner v Penningtons (a firm).*[45]

Compare the rules about naming partnerships in proceedings (whether as claimant or defendant) with the rule about suing a sole trader. The latter is merely an individual carrying on business whether in his own or another name. Such individuals, if not trading in their own name,[46] may be sued in their 'business name as if it were the name of a partnership'.[47] This option helps the claimant who might not know the name of the person behind the business name. A sole trader bringing a claim presumably knows his own name, so it is unnecessary to give him this option! Whether the individual's name is known or not, the title should reflect the status of sole trader. For example, therefore, a defendant might be described as 'BITS 'N' BOBS (a trading name)' or (if both names are known) 'MR ROBERT SMITH t/a BITS 'N' BOBS'.

(iv) Companies

Limited companies registered under the Companies Act 2006 (or a predecessor) must sue and be sued using the full, registered company name.[48] If the company does not end its name with the traditional 'Ltd', 'plc', or 'LLP' (the hybrid 'limited liability partnership', which in the UK is more a corporate body than a partnership), then its name should be followed by an accurate description of how its liability is limited. Different companies can have similar sounding names, and it is important to be accurate.

The essential difference between a partnership and a limited company, technically speaking, is that the latter is a legal artifice, created so as to limit the liability of its owners.[49] It is capable of suing and being sued.[50] A partnership is, in a sense, the sum of its human parts, whereas a registered company has its own legal

---

45 [2010] EWHC 1753 (Admin). See suggested reading in Ch. 17
46 PD 7A, para 5C.1
47 PD 7A, para 5C.2
48 If the company is in liquidation, then the words '(in liquidation)' should indicate this.

49 This is why 'limited' is part of the description!
50 Compare this with the status of unincorporated associations which have no separate legal personality, some of which may nevertheless sue or be sued in their names (e.g. trades unions can,

but most social and sports clubs cannot). Where a charity is unincorporated proceedings may be brought against it by suing an officer of the charity 'on behalf of' the (named) charity. Alternatively, the trustees of the charity may be named as parties. See

personality, which is distinct from the human individuals through which it must act. One sues in the name of a firm because it is convenient (and the rules say so); one sues in the name of a limited company because there is no alternative.

(v) Bankrupts, trusts and deceased persons

When a person becomes bankrupt, generally speaking, all causes of action (other than for personal injuries and defamation) vest in the 'trustee in bankruptcy', whose official name appears, for example, as 'the trustee of the estate of MR JUSTIN PENNY, a Bankrupt'.[51] If a claimant becomes bankrupt in the course of proceedings, the trustee in bankruptcy may carry on with it, if the court agrees to substitute the name of the trustee for the bankrupt's name.[52] If, on the other hand, it is the defendant who goes bankrupt, this is obviously very bad news for the claimant. Whether the case proceeds really depends on the circumstances,[53] but if there is no money to be had from the defendant, a claimant would have to be very wary of throwing good money after bad.

Claims involving trust property generally may be brought by or against the trustees without joining the beneficiaries, and any judgment will bind the latter unless the court orders otherwise.[54]

A claim will only cease upon the death of a claimant if the cause of action is personal to him or her, such as a libel action. Otherwise the executors or administrators of the estate can take over the claim. Again, this would necessitate an order to substitute the one party for the other[55]. Similarly, on the death of a defendant, a claimant may apply for an order to continue the action against his personal representatives.[56] If an action is commenced against someone who was in fact dead when the claim was issued, it will be treated as if it were brought against the estate of that deceased.[57]

---

generally Sime, 19.33-45/ BCP para 14.35-14.41

51 The trustees in bankruptcy do not have to disclose their own names: Insolvency Act 1986, s 305 (4)

52 This is a good example of the use of the court's powers under CPR, r 19.2. See below at Ch. 11

53 It could be 'stayed' or could continue on conditions. See Insolvency Act 1986, s 285

54 CPR, r 19.7A

55 Substitution of personal representatives in proceedings started before expiry of the relevant limitation period does not infringe the limitation rules, whether the death occurred before or after limitation expired: *Roberts v Gill and Co* [2011] 1 AC 240, at [103]. See generally Ch. 10.

56 CPR, r 19.2/8

57 CPR, r 19.8(3).

B.   JOINDER OF PARTIES AND CAUSES OF ACTION

If you, as a claimant, want to sue one person or one firm or one company in respect of one cause of action, that is straightforward enough.   But what if you have more than one person you want to sue … or there is more than one of you who wants to sue … or you have more than one cause of action in respect of which you want to sue? The CPR give claimants very wide latitude to combine - or ' join', as it is called - causes of action or parties into one claim form without seeking permission, although the court will always have the last case management word on which claims will be heard together and which will not.

Common sense will very much dictate decisions on this, taking account of the overriding objective, especially the need to save expense and deal with cases expeditiously and fairly.

It is useful to distinguish between joining causes of action and joining parties to proceedings, particularly as these two things may be happening simultaneously! It also helps to differentiate between what claimants and defendants can do in this context.

(i)   Joining causes of action

(a) By claimant

A claimant may use a single claim form to start *all* claims which can be 'conveniently disposed of' in the same proceedings.[58] No permission of the court is necessary. This is a nice, simple rule, ostensibly giving the claimant wide scope for making common sense decisions about combining causes of action in one claim form.[59]Although there need not be any special connection between the actions, the wording of the rule suggests some link between them: even if it might seem 'convenient' to a claimant to use only one form to bring various, possibly disparate, claims against a single defendant, the wording of the rule refers to how convenient it would be to 'dispose'

---

58 CPR, r 7.3

59 A typical example might be where the claimant's case against the defendant can be formulated in alternative ways, for example negligence and occupier's liability.

of the actions together. The court will focus on this too - ultimately it will be the one to decide whether to hear cases together or separately.[60]

(b) By defendant

A defendant with a claim against the claimant can raise it by way of a *counterclaim*. This is one type of 'additional claim' referred to in CPR Part 20.[61] Thus, a defendant can join a cause of action to the one(s) brought against him by 'countering' with his own claim against the claimant, no matter what the cause of action or remedy sought. No permission is required if the counterclaim is against the claimant *alone* and is filed at the *same time as the defence*, at the end of which document it typically appears.[62] No connection between the claim and counterclaim is required, although if they are completely unrelated, the court may well separate the two in due course.

(ii) Joining parties

(a) By claimant

CPR, r 19.1 says that 'any number of claimants or defendants may be joined as parties to a claim'. In conjunction with CPR, r 7.3, referred to above, this gives a claimant the freedom,[63] when starting all claims which can be 'conveniently disposed of' on the one claim form, to join as many parties to those claims as are relevant so to dispose of them. Again, as a matter of common sense, it follows that 'convenience' will require, when deciding whether to join various claimants or defendants to one or more causes of action, a degree of interrelationship between the parties and the claim(s).[64] Suppose, for example, a claimant had building work done which went badly wrong, both because of poor workmanship on the part of the builders, but also because of the lack of supervision of those builders by the architects overseeing the work. It would make sense to sue both the builders and the architects in the one claim

---

60 See below
61 Part 20 is discussed further below.
62 CPR, r 20.4(2), 20.5(1). Where permission is needed, a Part 20 claim form will be required: CPR, r 20.7

63 This freedom is limited where claimants are jointly entitled to a remedy, when the rules make joining them all as co-claimants obligatory. See CPR, r 19.3

64 The current rules do not require this as the old rules did, but it seems logical as a matter of common sense when adding defendants to a claim

because, even though there are two separate contracts or causes of action, the allegation is that both parties, in their own ways, were responsible for the loss and damage.

CPR, r 7.3 and 19.1 are very open-ended and together give the claimant a great deal of latitude as regards joinder at this initial stage.[65]

(b) By defendant

Defendants can bring parties into proceedings in two ways. First, if a defendant is counterclaiming, he can join co-defendants to that counterclaim *with the permission of the court.*[66] Secondly, defendants can bring in parties by way of Third Party proceedings, another form of 'additional claim', which is discussed in detail below.

It is always important to remember that what the parties have joined together, perfectly appropriately under the rules, the court can always put asunder. The court, as part of its case management mandate, will be the ultimate arbiter of what is and is not 'convenient' to be disposed of together and will *sever* causes of action and order separate trials whenever it believes that this will further the overriding objective. To a great extent, of course, both solicitors and barristers should anticipate when this might happen - and act accordingly.

Equally, where two actions have been started separately, the court has the power to order that they be *consolidated* into one action, if this would further the overriding objective.[67] In one sense consolidation is the mirror image of severance. But do not confuse consolidation with Representative Actions[68] or Group Litigation.[69]

Finally, once *litigation has started*, the court has equally wide powers to put right situations where, say, a potential party was not joined at the outset or one party needs to be replaced by another.[70] Thus the court has a wide discretion to remove, add or substitute parties after the action has started. Again, common sense considerations

---

65 We are discussing the rules about deciding whose names to put on the claim form, and in respect of which claims, when *commencing* proceedings. Usually no permission of the court is needed. Adding parties or causes of action at a *later* stage almost always requires the permission of the court. See generally at Ch. 11.

66 CPR, r 20.5. For example, suppose a claimant brings an action against a defendant for payment for (lawful) services rendered. This defendant is in fact owed money by the claimant and his brother (which may explain the lack of payment). The defendant will no doubt want to counterclaim in respect of the debt, but if he wants to claim from both debtors, he

apply, so that the court may order that a new party be added to proceedings, or indeed removed, if doing so helps the court 'resolve' all matters in dispute.[71] The court can do this on its own initiative or on application, but remember that the permission of the court is *always* required to add or substitute parties once the claim form has been served. Note too that this area of litigation also impinges on matters of limitation and amendment, discussed below.[72]

4.   THIRD PARTY PROCEDURE AND OTHER ADDITIONAL CLAIMS

A.   THIRD PARTY CLAIMS

A defendant in an action can make certain linked claims against a person *not yet* a party to the action brought against him. Such have historically been called third party claims and the party brought into the action, a 'third party'. The CPR lumps these sorts of claims in with counterclaims and claims between existing defendants, referring to them globally as 'Additional Claims'.[73] The expression 'third party', however, continues to be used in advocacy and in the title of proceedings to distinguish third party claims from the other types of additional claims (so that the various parties are described as Claimant v Defendant v Third Party[74]) and I will use it here.

Let's start with a given set of facts:

C is injured in an accident while a passenger in D's car. C sues D. Let's call the driver of the other car involved in the accident T.

Before the introduction of the CPR, there were only four types of claim which a defendant could initiate against a third party, namely:

will need permission to 'join' the brother to the counterclaim against the existing claimant. It might be quite straightforward, but still requires permission (and some consequential directions) because so far the brother has apparently had nothing to do with the litigation.

67 CPR, r 3.1(2)(g)

68 These are relatively rare these days, but may be a convenient way of litigating a dispute where otherwise a large number of persons would need to be named as parties (either as claimants or defendants), which would be inefficient both in terms of time and expense. If all the people to be represented have the same interest in the outcome, then one or more persons can bring (or be allowed to continue

(i)   A 'contribution' claim

This is a claim that the third party is wholly or partly to blame for the claimant's loss.[75] Thus, in our example, D could bring in T as a third party claiming that T (who, like D, owed C a duty of care) was wholly or partly to blame for the accident through his poor driving, and seek a 'contribution' from T (commensurate with his actual contribution to the accident) to anything that D may have to pay C in the main action.

(ii)   An 'indemnity' claim.

This is a claim that the third party is under an *obligation* to the defendant, usually arising in contract, to reimburse the defendant for some or all of what the defendant may be ordered to pay to the claimant. Note that this is *not* an allegation that the third party shares responsibility for the claimant's loss. It is a different animal from a contribution claim and the two should not be confused. A simple example of an indemnity claim involves insurance. Insurance companies rarely pay out on the whole of a claim, since there is usually an 'excess' to be paid by the policy holder or not all losses may be covered by the policy; so it is a little dangerous to think of an indemnity as always equivalent to a 100% contribution! But so-called indemnity clauses are common in building contracts, where a total indemnity will be more usual. It all depends on the extent of the obligation!

In our example, if the defendant's motor insurance company denied their obligations to him under his policy, he could join the company as a third party and claim an indemnity from them. In effect, the defendant would be saying to the third party: *"Under our contract of insurance, you promised you would pay if I was found liable in these circumstances, so if I have to pay anything in damages to the claimant in respect of this accident, I want you to meet your obligation to indemnify me under my insurance policy".*

---

to pursue or defend the action) as representatives of all the others. See CPR, r 19.6(1). 'Same interest' is a strict requirement which is interpreted with some flexibility. See, for example, *Smith v Cardiff Corporation* [1954] QB 210 and WB, 19.6.3

69   This is rather like the class action in the USA and is a relatively recent addition to our system. Group Litigation Orders (and an order of the court is required) are intended to assist in multi-party claims where there are common questions of law

or fact, and other existing procedures are incapable of providing a cost effective and expeditious way of dealing with the action. They are typically used in cases where a large number of people have been affected (albeit in different ways) by a

It may be useful to think of these two third party claims as *defensive* in nature because they are dependent on the claimant succeeding against the defendant. If the main action settles, with the defendant agreeing to pay something to the claimant, there will still be a question of what, if anything, the third party should pay to the defendant.[76] *But if the defendant is not liable to pay anything to the claimant in the action, there is nothing to contribute to or in respect of which to indemnify.*

(iii) A claim for the defendant's own remedy

A defendant can also claim his own remedy or relief against a third party so long as it is the same or similar to that claimed by the claimant and it arises out of the same or similar facts. So, in our example, D, having sought a contribution from T, might also go on to say, in effect: "*... and by the way, T, while you were injuring C, you also injured me in that accident, and I want damages from you for my own injuries and losses caused by your negligent driving.*"

This type of claim might usefully be thought of as *offensive* in nature because it is *not* dependent on the claimant's claim succeeding against the defendant. Although it commonly goes hand-in-hand with a contribution claim, regardless of what happens to the main action, this claim for the defendant's own remedy can continue in its own right, just as if it had been brought separately. *This is an important distinction, which is often tested in assessments.*

(iv) A connected question of law or fact

Finally, there has traditionally been a 'safety net' category of third party claims, which caters for situations where there are questions or issues needing adjudication which are common to both the main claim (C v D) and the third party claim (D v T). Such may not fall neatly into categories (i) to (iii) above, but the original and third party claims are so inter-related that it would be silly not to deal with them together.

disaster of some kind, e.g. industrial accident, investment mis-selling, damaging side-effects of drugs). Funding of such cases can be very problematic. See Sime, para 19.74 and CPR, PD 19B

70 CPR, r 19.2
71 See CPR, r 19.2(2)-(4)

72 See Chs. 10 & 11
73 See generally CPR, Part 20 and WB editorial introduction at 20.0.2
74 If a defendant needs to bring in more than one new party against whom he has *separate* claims (or if a third party wants to make an additional

claim against a new party) these will be called 'Fourth Party', 'Fifth Party', and so on. If an *identical* claim were to be made by a defendant against two new parties they would be referred to as the 'First Named Third Party' and the 'Second Named Third

Suppose, for example, I was sued by someone who claims ownership of the White Book which I use and think is mine. The cause of action against me would be the tort of conversion or trespass to property (the civil law's answer to the theft, in effect). As the defendant, I could bring in the person who sold me the disputed White Book as a third party because if the claimant were to succeed against me, it would mean that I paid money for something that belongs to someone else. My cause of action against the third party would be breach of contract. The issue or question common to both claims is "*Who has good title?*" It obviously makes sense to deal with the two cases together, because the answer to that question will determine the outcome of both cases. Otherwise I might be running up and down the hallway giving evidence in two cases in different rooms with two different judges, but telling both courts the same thing. And what would happen if one judge decided the book was mine, but the other decided it wasn't?!

Indeed, the whole point of third party proceedings has always been to avoid this sort of multiplicity of action and the risk of different results where the logical connection between the main action and third party claim dictates that the two matters be heard together. This is still the purpose of Part 20 procedure under the CPR, which is stated as being to enable additional claims 'to be managed in the most convenient and effective manner'. But because Part 20 is not simply about third party claims, one gets to essentially the same destination as under the old rules, but by a slightly different route.

The old rules had mandated that only claims (a)-(d) mentioned above were capable of getting off the ground as third party claims. The CPR specifically refers only to types (i) and (ii) (contribution and indemnity claims) as viable third party claims, but not to types (iii) and (iv) as such. Instead it gives a defendant free rein to claim any 'other remedy' from the third party.[77] It then leaves it to the court, in the exercise of its discretion and case management powers, to *detach*, as it were, such of those claims as

---

Party': PD 20 para 7

75 A right to a contribution arises where liability is joint or several, i.e. where two or more persons are liable to the same claimant for the 'same damage'. See Sime at 20.07. If a third party is not capable of being liable to the same

claimant, for the 'same damage' there can be no claim for a contribution. *Cooperative Retail Services Ltd v Taylor Young Partnership Ltd* [2002] 1 WLR 1419 (HL)

76 See *Stott v West Yorkshire Road Car Ltd* [1972] 2 QB 651. There might even be

an issue as to whether the settlement is legitimate. This is why, when people are insured against claims, the insurance company (who *will be picking up most of the tab*) wants to be in charge of how the case is handled, and in particular whether to settle

it decides should not be heard together with the main action. CPR, r 20.9 specifically uses the language of the old rules in describing the 'matters to which the court should have regard' in deciding whether a third party claim should be 'dealt with separately' from the main claim, including (but not limited to) references to whether the defendant is seeking from the third party 'substantially the same remedy' as the claimant (as in type (iii) above) or whether there is a 'question connected with the subject matter' of the main action to be determined (as in type (iv) above).[78]

In effect, as regards third party claims type (iii) and (iv) as described above, these are now simply factors which the court will look at when deciding whether or not to let the claim continue as a third party claim. Practitioners, of course, ought to be able to predict when a claim by a defendant would appropriately be tried with the main action as a third party claim, but ultimately it is for the court to decide this.[79] In the normal course of events, both common sense and the overriding objective would dictate that claims falling within categories (iii) and (iv) mentioned above ought to be heard together with the main action as third party claims.

When bringing in a third party, a Part 20 claim form must be issued and served on the other parties (including the ones to be added!).[80] If the third party claim is issued *before* or at the same time as the defence is filed, no permission of the court is needed.[81] Otherwise, permission is required and in such cases, the matters set out at CPR, r 20.9, referred to above, will be relevant. It is because the defence and the third party claim interact with one another [82] that the filing of the defence is the procedural point around which the question of permission turns. If, for example, a defence has already been filed and served, and the defendant later seeks to add a third party to the proceedings, the defence document which is in the hands of any existing party/ies will, in effect, need to be 'recalled' to be amended and re-served to incorporate the name and relevant act or omission of the third party.

---

or not (and for how much).

77 CPR, r 20.2(1)(b). No permission is required if made early enough. See below.

78 CPR, r 20.9(2). In addition it adds a more generic consideration, i.e. the degree of 'connection' between the main and third party claim, thus opening up possibilities and giving the court a bit more discretion than it had under the old rules.

79 We have noted that under CPR, r 19.2 the court may add, substitute etc a party to ongoing litigation if this would help determine all of the issues in dispute or there is some other relevant connection between the claim against the party to be added and the ongoing litigation. *Do not confuse this* with a defendant's ability to make (or seek permission to make) third party claims under Part 20.

B.   ADDITIONAL CLAIMS AGAINST CO-DEFENDANTS

So far, two types of 'additional claim' under Part 20 have been discussed: counterclaims and third party claims. There is one more that needs mentioning. Where two or more defendants have been sued by a claimant, so that they are *already parties* to the action, they can make the same sorts of claims against one another that a defendant can make when bringing in a third party (who until then is *not* a party to the action).

At this point the jargon can get confusing because practitioners still persist in using the old-fashioned term 'contribution notice' to describe the mechanism by which such a claim is made (even when the claim is not for a contribution!).[83] Moreover, if a co-defendant, who is not otherwise in a hostile relationship with the other defendants, merely wants to ask the judge to use his existing powers to apportion liability in a particular way, even though this is a contribution claim of sorts, no formal notice need be issued, thereby saving unnecessary expense.[84]

If, however, there is some other issue or claim being made between co-defendants (an order for disclosure of documents, perhaps, or a claim for an indemnity or damages for some other remedy or relief), a Part 20 claim form must be issued and served. These kinds of additional claims might be (and sometimes are) more accurately described as 'party and party claims' to distinguish them from third party claims.

---

80 CPR, r 20.7(2)
81 CPR, r 20.7(3)
82 For example, the name of the third party will need to be added to the title of the proceedings.
83 The rules do not use this expression, but some commentators and practitioners still do.

84 Where there is joint and several liability, a judge has power to apportion liability amongst defendants whether they ask him to or not: Civil Liability (Contribution) Act 1978. If all a co-defendant wants to do is argue for a

30:70 split in his favour (as opposed to, say, 50:50) then only unofficial notice to the other defendant(s) is required. A defendant serving formal notice when not necessary to do so may not recover the costs.

revision tips

- If the main action folds or is otherwise unsuccessful, whether the third party proceedings can continue independently essentially depends on whether the third party claim is 'defensive' or not. If it is 'defensive', it will die a death with the main claim. To the extent that it is 'offensive' in nature, or there is otherwise a live issue to be determined between the parties, then the third party claim can carry on independently. With claims involving 'connected questions' of law or fact, you will need in each case to look at the relationship between the main action and third party claim - they often stand or fall together.

- Remember that, subject to the court's case management powers, *only claimants* decide who the defendants will be. And *only defendants* bring in third parties

- *Note too that a claimant cannot obtain judgment against a third party.* If a claimant suspects that the third party might conceivably be the entire villain, then that claimant should turn the third party into a defendant!! He can do that by amendment (see Ch. 11).

It is worth reading ...

The judgment of Lord Denning MR in *Stott v West Yorkshire Road Car Ltd* [1972] 2 QB 651. It is short and explains the factual background. The relevant legislation has changed, and so too some of the descriptions used (claimants were called plaintiffs and District Judges were called registrars back then). But it is a good example of a typical third party scenario. Anyway, if you have never read a Denning judgment, then you are in for a treat. They are models of clarity.

It may also be worth dipping into PD 16 to remind yourself of matters which should be included (in various circumstances) on statements of case, some (but not all) of which I cover at various points in this book and much of which BPTC students will have come across in drafting classes.

CHAPTER 4

Interim applications and service

1.   MAKING INTERIM APPLICATIONS

The issuing of the claim form begins the *interim* (sometimes called interlocutory) phase of the proceedings which, despite sounding rather temporary, in effect covers all the preparatory stage(s) through which a case passes until trial or settlement is reached.[1] In most defended cases, directions will be given at the track allocation stage, which is usually some weeks after proceedings have been served. These deal with requirements common to almost every case as it litigates (such as disclosure of documents and the exchange of evidence). Somewhere along the line, however, a party may still need or want to ask the court to make some other (or different) order prior to the substantive trial of the action. These are known as interim applications.

It has always been true that most cases are concluded pre-trial, which is why the focus of any civil litigation course (and indeed this book) is on what does (or does not) go on in this interim period between the initiation of a claim and (if the case does not settle) the trial of the substantive action. The CPR rules are designed to control this aspect of litigation to such an extent that even fewer cases reach trial than did before, and those which do, get there much more quickly.

CPR Part 23 sets out the general rules about interim applications, to which

1   If you think of litigation as a linear continuum, with commencement of proceedings at one end, and trial at the other, everything in between (and sometimes even pre-action) is the interim phase.

2   'Master' is a curiously archaic judicial title which survived the modernising ethos of the CPR. Masters sit in London at the Royal Courts of Justice in London. Their out-of-London equivalent is the more prosaically titled High Court District Judge.

3   See below Ch. 6

4   Out of London, it is not uncommon for one person to act as both a High Court and County Court District Judge, as the cases arise.

reference is often made in other parts of the rules.

In High Court cases, *most* interim applications are made to a '*master*', who is essentially a procedural judge, with no significant trial jurisdiction.[2] There are some interim applications, however, which must be made to a High Court *judge*, most notably most *injunctions*.[3]

In the County Court, the equivalent of a master is a *District Judge*.[4] It is thus to a District Judge that most interim applications requiring a hearing in the County Court are made. Those applications with which a District Judge cannot deal are made to the Circuit Judge. *Unlike masters*, County Court District Judges have a certain amount of trial jurisdiction; they can try cases where the claim does *not exceed* £25,000[5] and so also grant injunctions in such cases. Otherwise, it is the Circuit Judge who tries cases in the County Court, and who has the general power to grant injunctions there.

Most interim applications are made by giving the other side notice ('inter partes' in the old jargon).[6] The reason for this is obvious - where the matter is of any importance, all interested parties are entitled to be alerted and have their say on the matter. Similarly, most applications are to be made in writing by using the official standard form notice *of application*.[7]

Exceptionally[8] interim applications are made without giving the other side notice ('ex parte' in the old jargon). Sometimes this happens out of necessity, for example when there is no defendant on record or the matter does not essentially concern the defendant at that time.[9] Otherwise, applications are only made without notice either because the matter is so *urgent* that there is *no time* to give formal notice[10] or where *secrecy* is vital.[11] It is very important to note that where applications are made without giving the other side notice, the applicant comes under a *duty* to make what is known as 'full and frank disclosure' of all material facts, including those adverse

---

5 In other words, small claims or fast track cases. They can also hear certain possession actions and hearings to assess damages in the County Court.

6 CPR, r 23.4

7 CPR, r 23.3 and R *(Simmons) v Bolton* *Metropolitan Borough Council* [2011] EWHC 2729. See example at Sime, Fig 23.1. Do not get confused, as well you might, between an application made by notice of application (referring to the document used) and an application made *on* or with notice (letting the other side know about the application by serving on them the application notice).

8 Only if permitted by a rule, practice direction or court order may an application be made without notice: CPR, r 23.4(2).

9 For example, an application

to the application. This is exactly what it sounds like, and amounts to an obligation, in effect, to *compensate* for the other side's absence, *not to exploit it*. It is a crucial and continuing duty in any application made without notice, and sanctions for a failure to comply can be severe.[12]

Most interim applications must be supported by *written evidence*.[13] The rules allow such to be provided in several ways. It can either be:

(i)   included on the notice of application itself, if it contains a statement of truth;

(ii) found in any statement of case served in the proceedings, which should already contain a statement of truth;

(iii) contained in a witness statement (that is, statement of evidence of a relevant person), including a statement of truth, to be served with the notice of application;

or

(iv) contained in an affidavit (that is, a sworn statement) to be served with the notice of application.

Because affidavits cost rather more than witness statements (due to the costs of being 'sworn'), a litigant will not generally recover the costs of making an affidavit. The 'statement of truth' now performs much the same function as swearing to the truth of an affidavit, but more cheaply. Thus, most interim applications are supported by witness statements, except where affidavits are specifically required by the rules.[14]

Unless the application is a very simple one, a draft of the order sought should also be included. If long and/or complex, the draft should be included on disk as well as hard copy (which makes it easier for the court to adapt it to its own liking!).[15]

---

to extend the validity of the claim form (see Ch. 12). These are made by means of an application notice, but without sending a copy to the other side.

10 In which case, informal notice should be given: CPR, PD 23A, para 4.2.

11 Typical examples are applications for freezing and search orders. See generally Ch. 7

12 See generally Sime, 23.23-23.28.

13 Complex cases in the High Court can require additional documents, including chronologies and skeleton arguments.

14 For example when applying for freezing and search orders – see Ch. 7. But watch out when reading older cases. At one time all interim applications were supported by affidavit evidence.

15 CPR, PD 23A, para 12.1

In most cases the written notice and supporting documentation must be filed at court and served by the applicant on all other parties at least three clear days before the date on which the application is to be heard (known as the 'return date' since that is when everyone returns to court to deal with the application). Any evidence in reply should be filed and served as soon as practicable thereafter. Some applications, which are thought to be more complex, involve longer notice periods (for example, summary judgment, interim payments). These are discussed in more detail in later chapters.

In this context it is worth noting that the expression 'service' refers to the act of providing the document to the other side; 'filing' refers to providing the document to the court. Often these two things go hand-in-hand, but not inevitably. A without notice application is an obvious example - the application will have to be filed, but the other side will not be served with a copy.

The rules seek to encourage dealing with interim applications 'on the papers', that is to say without the need for parties to attend a (costly) hearing. This furthers the overriding objective by saving time and money. Thus, the court may determine an interim application without a hearing either if the parties agree or the court considers that a hearing would be unnecessary.[16] A party who is not happy about the latter may apply to have that decision set aside, varied or stayed.[17]

The court's case management powers are extensive.[18] They include keeping the scope of what goes on during the interim hearing within proportionate bounds[19], conducting hearings by telephone[20], and making orders when no-one has even asked for one.[21] Again, in the latter case, an unhappy party can trigger a hearing by applying to set aside the order, but may have to pay for the costs of doing so.

The person making the application is called the 'applicant' and the person responding is called the 'respondent'. These terms might be used interchangeably

16 CPR, r 23.8
17 CPR, r 3.3(5)(a)
18 CPR, r 3.1(2) sets out some of the typical orders the court might make on interim applications. And see Ch. 13
19 See, e.g., *VTB Capital plc v Nutrick International Corpn* [2013] 2 WLR 398

20 CPR, r 3.1(2)(d). And see Sime at 23.50
21 This is known as the court 'acting on its own initiative', and is an important part of the court's ability to control proceedings before it. See CPR, r 3.3
22 Skeleton arguments are usually required for

applications before County Court or High Court judges, unless the matter is very simple or time is short. These provide a concise summary of the party's submissions and give the opportunity for pre-reading. They are, in their own way, a piece of written advocacy, with claimant and defendant, where the claimant is also the applicant. But sometimes the defendant in the main action is the one applying for the interim order, so you must be careful with your terminology - both in your own mind and for the benefit of the judge. Applications should always be made as soon and expeditiously as the circumstances allow.

There are the obvious exceptions, but generally speaking hearings on interim applications are heard in public. Most are pretty mundane, however, and would not be apt to draw in the crowds. The more complicated the matter, the more apt one would be to instruct counsel, file and exchange skeleton arguments[22] and so forth. Disputes of *fact* on interim applications [23] raise the question of how the court should deal with these, given the lack of oral testimony and opportunity to test the evidence, which after all is just set out on pieces of paper.[24] It is generally thought that such questions are decided by asking whether the applicant has established a 'good arguable case' on the matter - a middling sort of standard, which in essence amounts to saying that the court should be as satisfied as it can be in the circumstances, given the limitations inherent in hearings based on written evidence but at the same time wanting to avoid mini-trials of matters raised on interim applications.[25]

Where interim applications are dealt with in less than a day (as most are), the court will normally make a summary assessment of costs immediately after making its order.[26]

2. SERVICE IN THE JURISDICTION

A. SERVICE OF THE CLAIM FORM

Service of the claim form is the next procedural step after issuing proceedings. A

---

but they are not a substitute for oral argument. See WB, Vol 2 and guidance in Chancery Guide (at Section 1 paras 7.18 – 7.38)

23 Do not confuse a factual dispute in this context with the merits of the substantive action. As we shall see, how strong the

latter must be shown to be at the interim stage varies depending on the nature of the interim application.

24 It is always worth remembering that it is not the advocate's role to give evidence. His or her job is to get the court to view the available evidence in a

particular way.

25 See, e.g., *WWP Holdings Italy SRL v Bennett* [2007] 1 WLR 2316

26 CPR PD 44, para 9.2 and see generally Ch. 18

claim form issued for service inside the jurisdiction remains valid for four months.[27] It must be served during this time, unless an extension is granted.[28]

The service rules include considerations of *how, where and by whom* service is to be effected. The first thing to remember is that generally, any document prepared or issued *by the court*, which includes the claim form, will be served by the court.[29] This is the most stress-free form of service. But there are times when this does not happen.[30] One is the rare occasion when the rules or the court require personal service by the claimant.[31] Another, much more commonly invoked insofar as service of the claim form is concerned, is where a claimant notifies the court of a desire to serve the claim form himself.[32] In such circumstances, CPR, r 6.3 provides a variety of permissible methods.

Personal service

This is effected by leaving the claim form with the relevant person.

First class post, DX or other 'next business day' delivery service

The claim form may be sent to an appropriate address by first class post or other method of mail transmission (it need not be the Royal Mail), which provides for delivery on the *next business day* (the claimant having taken reasonable steps to ascertain the correct, current address). This includes using the document exchange (DX) system, which is commonly used to transport documents between business offices, and also normally arrives the *next business day*. DX is permissible only if the defendant has provided a DX number for service or the relevant information otherwise appears on correspondence and no unwillingness to be served in this way has been stated.

---

27 The claim form is valid for service *outside* the jurisdiction for *6 months*: CPR, r 7.5(1)

28 See generally Ch. 12

29 Usually by first class post, although it is for the court to choose. CPR, r 6.4(2) and PD 6A,8. Where documents are prepared

by the parties themselves, they are responsible for service unless the court orders otherwise. See CPR, r 6.21

30 CPR, r 6.4(1)

31 CPR, r 6.5(1). An example is a claim form relating to committal proceedings.

32 CPR, r 6.4(1)(b). In such cases, a certificate of service must be filed within 21 days, unless all defendants have acknowledged service by that time: CPR, r 6.17(2)

Leaving the claim form at an address

The claim form may be left at an address given for service or the usual or last known residence/place of business (the claimant again having taken reasonable steps to ascertain the correct current address.

Fax or email

Before service is permitted by fax or other electronic means, the party who is to be served, or his legal representative, must have expressly indicated *in writing* a willingness to be served in this way and provided a fax-number, email address or other electronic identification as appropriate. This willingness must be *explicitly* given by an unrepresented party (a fax number on the litigant's notepaper is not enough). But where service is to be made on the party's *solicitors*, the willingness to be served by *fax* is sufficiently indicated by including the relevant fax number on the solicitor's writing paper (it is sort of assumed that solicitors' offices are geared up for and expected to look at their incoming faxes). However, a litigant's solicitor's willingness to be served by *e-mail* must, *in addition*, actually state that the e-mail address provided on the writing paper may be used for this purpose (this is because e-mail is rather more personal than the office fax machine). A party seeking to serve by electronic means should in any case first ask whether the recipient has any limitations on such transmission (for example, on the size of an attachment to an e-mail).

All of these service options require the claimant to take a certain step ('the required step'), as set out in CPR, r 7.5(1).[33] Having chosen a method, it is important that service is made *to the right person or place*. One important rule is that where the defendant's *solicitor* is *authorised* to accept service on the defendant's behalf and the claimant has been given written notice both of this fact and the relevant address,

---

33 See also PD 6A for more detail on each step.   34 CPR, r 6.7(1)   35 CPR, r 6.8

then the claim form *must* be served at that address.[34] Otherwise, service should be effected at the address given for service[35] (which, again, could be the address of the defendant's solicitors). Failing that, the appropriate address for service will be the defendant's 'usual or last known address.' The defendant's last *known* address can be used, even if the claimant knows the defendant no longer lives there, so long as the claimant took reasonable steps to discover a current address, and was unable to do so (or to serve in some other way).[36]

When did service occur?

Once service has been effected on the right person/place and in an appropriate way, the next question is *when* service will have occurred. Previously this was calculated on a rather piecemeal basis, depending on the service option selected. Now it is dealt with by a strict, but generic and uniform rule, which says that service of the claim form takes effect on the second business day after completion of the required step.[37] This even applies to personal service, which in real time is instantaneously! So regardless of what step is required/taken, and regardless of when or indeed whether the claim form might actually have been received, service of the claim form is *deemed* to have taken place on the second *business* day after the relevant step was taken. Watch out for holidays and weekends - they are not business days![38]

The effect of deeming provisions

It is important to understand the effect of such deeming provisions. Where they apply, service takes effect on the deemed date *and no other*. They create, in effect, an irrebuttable presumption of law[39] and no evidence is admissible to prove that the claim form arrived on some other date, or even not at all. This may sound severe, but the deeming provisions inject some predictability into this aspect of litigation,

---

36 CPR, r 6.9 and *Mersey Property Holdings v Kilgour* [2004] EWHC 1638 (TCC). As to alternative service, read on.

37 CPR, r 6.14
38 CPR, r 6.2(b). So, if the relevant step is taken on a Friday, service is deemed to occur on the following Tuesday (assuming Monday is not a Bank Holiday).

39 See generally below at Ch. 17

and only very rarely does the outcome of a case turn on service of the claim form.[40]

The advantage of letting the court serve the claim form is obvious - the claimant does not need to provide a certificate of service or otherwise prove, or worry about being responsible for service, as is the case when a DIY option is chosen.[41] The latter, however, can give the litigant some control over when and how service is effected and for that reason some claimants prefer to do it themselves.

B.   SERVICE OF DOCUMENTS OTHER THAN THE CLAIM FORM

You will notice that CPR, Part 6 is divided into distinct sections, so that there is, in effect, one set of rules for service of the claim form (Part II) and a second set for service of documents *other than* the claim form (Part III). There are many similarities between the two, and often the same or similar wording is used.[42] For example, when any party is acting through solicitors, and their business address has been provided, *all* documents in a case should be served on that address.[43] But there are also some discrepancies. For example, notice the somewhat subtle difference in the deeming provisions as regards service by post of documents other than the claim form ('second day after posting if that day is a business day; or if not, the next business day after that day'). And insofar as electric service of such documents, where a fax number or e-mail address has been included on a statement of case or response to a claim filed with the court, then this itself is sufficient indication of a willingness to be served in this fashion. Remember too that there is no generic overarching deeming provision for service of documents other than the claim form (like there is for service of the claim form) and so as the method of serving such other documents becomes more instantaneous in nature, then service is equally deemed to occur more quickly (for example, service by email or indeed personal service).[44]

---

40 But where limitation is at issue, the date of service can suddenly become very important. See generally, Ch. 10.

41 CPR, r 6.17(2)

42 This is partly because only the rules about serving the claim form were overhauled in 2008, and not the rules about service of other documents.

43 CPR, r 6.23(2)

44 CPR, r 6.26

Normally, service of other documents is even less controversial than service of the claim form in the general run of the case, but you still want to be aware of the fact (and basic detail) of the differences. It can crop up in exams.

C. SPECIAL CASES

Finally, be aware of special rules about serving claim forms (and other documents) on particular types of parties[45] and what to do if none of the sanctioned methods of serving the claim form seem to work. Pay attention, in particular, to the following.

Serving children

Where the *defendant is a child* (but not also a protected party), the claim form must be served on one the child's parents or guardians (or, if no such person exists), on an adult with whom the child resides or in whose care the child is.[46] These are the sorts of persons who would typically assume the role of 'litigation friend' once proceedings are brought. Once the litigation friend is identified, then service of all subsequent documents would be on that person.[47]

Serving partnerships

As discussed in Chapter 3, partnerships should generally be sued in the name of the firm. Special refinements to the service rules thus become necessary, because a firm is not a legal entity and so poses some service quandaries. A firm is not a person, so how, for example, would you serve a firm 'personally'?

If the court effects service on a partnership, it will normally do so by first class post to the firm's address (or other address given for service). For a claimant wishing to serve the claim form himself the possibilities are as follows:

---

45 As discussed in Ch. 3

46 CPR, r 6.13(1). Analogous provisions apply to protected parties: CPR, r 6.13(2)

47 CPR, r 6.25(2)

(a) If the claimant has been notified of *solicitors who are authorised* to accept service on the firm's behalf, the claimant must serve the defendant firm at this address. This can be effected by post, leaving the claim form, DX or other electronic means as appropriate.

(b) The partnership can be served *'personally'* by leaving the claim form with any of the partners or leaving it with a person having, at the time of service, the control or management of the partnership business at the principal place of business of the partnership.[48]

(c) Service can also be effected by post, leaving, faxing and so on the claim form at the *principal or last known place of business* of the firm or other address provided by the defendant.

Note that a proprietor of a business, even if a sole trader (and not a firm) can be served either at his own usual or last known residence or the address of his principal or last know place of business.[49]

Serving claim forms on companies

Companies dance to a slightly different drummer. They can be served either under the CPR rules, or they can be served at their registered offices under the Companies Act 2006. The former allow service at the 'principal office' or any place of business of the company which has a real connection with the claim, or personal service on a senior person in the company. This provides rather more latitude for place of service, than simply the registered office. Having said that, if serving the claim form by post on the registered office under the Companies Act 2006, it will be deemed to be delivered 'in the ordinary course of posting', unless proved to the contrary. So a rebuttable presumption in that case![50]

---

48 CPR, r 6.5(3)(c) 49 CPR, r 6.9(2) 50 Presumptions are discussed in Ch. 17

Contractually agreed service

The rules also allow for a contractually agreed method of service. If the action is based solely on a contract, one of whose terms specifies the manner of serving a claim form should the need arise, then the claim form *may* be served in this way.[51] This option, when applicable, essentially gives the claimant another choice when serving the claim form.

Alternative service

In many ways a claimant is spoiled for choice when serving the claim form; it is not often that at least one of the available methods of service will not work.[52] But it does happen sometimes, especially if a prospective defendant is elusive or actively evading service. So, if the court is persuaded that there is a 'good reason' to authorise service by 'a method or at a place not otherwise permitted' by the rules, it can make an order permitting service by an 'alternative method or at an alternative place.'[53]

The claimant's application to the court for such an order must be supported by written evidence, which would typically explain what attempts to serve have been made (or would have been) made were they not impractical, as well as what method of service is being put forward as more likely to bring the claim form to the defendant's notice. Dealing with cases fairly and efficiently and in keeping with the overriding objective will also be a relevant consideration for the court.[54] If the court makes an order for alternative service, it should go on to specify not only how service is to be effected, but when such service is deemed to be served and how long the defendant has to respond.[55] Alternatively, the court can order that steps which a claimant has *already* taken to bring the claim to the attention of the defendant, constitutes good service.[56]

51 CPR, r 6.11(2)
52 This was not always the case.
53 CPR, r 6.15(1). Absence of a bad reason is not necessarily a good one: see *Brown v Innovatorone* [2009] EWHC 1376 (Comm).
54 See, e.g., *Albon v Naza Motor Trading Sdn Bhd* (no 2)[2007] EWHC 327(Ch), [2007] 1 All ER (Comm) 813
55 CPR, r 6.15(4)
56 CPR, r 6.15(2)

It is also worth noting that this is a good example of an interim application which, out of necessity, would be made *without* giving the other side notice. If the claimant could serve the defendant for the purposes of the application, it is unlikely he would need the order at all!

Dispensing with service

In *exceptional* circumstances, the court may dispense altogether with the need to serve the claim form.[57] This might happen where there has been a very minor, technical fault with service, but it is no longer possible to try again to serve properly.[58] But the court will use this power very sparingly indeed; otherwise it would undermine the rules themselves. Service is not that hard to achieve, so it will be rare for the court to excuse a claimant for not managing to do it.

3. SERVICE OUT OF THE JURISDICTION

Usually proceedings in England and Wales are served on defendants *within* the jurisdiction. But what happens if the claimant is in the jurisdiction, but the defendant is not? Is it possible to bring proceedings here, and if so, how does one go about serving them on a foreign defendant? Answering these questions invites consideration of the rules about service *out* of the jurisdiction.

This, itself, is a complex area of procedure, and what follows is merely an introduction to the subject. Any practitioner dealing with such a case will simply have to delve into the detail, but will no doubt find this easier to do with a basic understanding of how the system works. At the time of publication, service out of the jurisdiction is not included on the BPTC syllabus for the Civil Litigation &

---

57 CPR, r 6.16(1)

58 As in *Cranfield v Bridgegrove Ltd* [2004] 1 WLR 2441

Evidence Assessment. However, it remains of particular interest to those training to become solicitors - since it is they who are principally the ones who issue and serve proceedings - and can come in handy for the pupil barrister, especially in a commercial set.

Before the coming into force of the Civil Jurisdiction and Judgments Act 1982 ('CJJA 1982'), permission of the court was always required when a claimant wanted to commence proceedings in the courts of England and Wales and serve them on a defendant who was out of the jurisdiction. The CJJA 1982 carved out a special system for those extra-jurisdictional cases 'with a European flavour', allowing a claimant to bring certain actions in England against defendants in Europe without *having to ask the court's permission*. The CJJA 1982, which made various international conventions between European states applicable in English law, has since been fine-tuned by later legislation and EU Regulation,[59] but the essential framework remains the same. For the sake of clarity I will refer to the countries who are part of this European system as 'participating states'.[60]

European system: permission not required

If a claimant living here wants to sue a defendant living[61] in another participating state, the European system applies. This essentially says that the defendant *must* be sued in the country of his domicile *unless* the CJJA 1982 confers jurisdiction on the courts of England and Wales,[62] either (i) exclusively or (ii) by virtue of an agreement between the parties conferring jurisdiction on our courts or (iii) because the case is one of those specified in the legislation where a person living in another participating state *may* be sued here, as an alternative to being sued in his or her own country.

This last category includes cases, for example, where a tort or other 'harmful event' is committed (or damage is suffered) here; the contract (or the principle

---

59 See CPR, r 6.30ff for detail.

60 In the rules they can, somewhat confusingly, be referred to variously as 'Regulation' or 'Member' States. Think in terms of members of the European Union, although the list of countries is actually a bit wider than this.

61 Strictly, the test is 'domicile', but that can be a technical subject in itself. Domicile is wider than, but includes habitual residence. See, e.g., CJJA 1982, ss 41-46.

62 Being another participating state. I am describing the system from the point of view of an English claimant, but it is actually formulated generically and not in terms of specific countries.

obligation under the contract) was to be performed here; the trust property which is the subject of the dispute is situated here.[63] What the specified cases have in common is they all describe situations where there would be sufficient *connection* with England and Wales to make it sensible to confer jurisdiction on our courts. It is important to note that with category (iii), suing the defendant here is an *alternative* to suing him in his own country. This is usually more convenient for a claimant living here; but assuming the conditions are met, it is the claimant's option. But a choice must be made: to bring the action here, there must be *no other pending proceedings* in respect of the action.[64]

The important thing to remember is that where a claimant brings an action in England and Wales against a European defendant by virtue of these rules, the claim form may be issued and served on the defendant in his own country *without the need for* having to ask the court for permission. The claimant must file and serve a notice with the claim form stating the basis on which the courts of England and Wales assume jurisdiction.[65] Translations will be necessary.

Outside the European system: service only with permission.

Where the defendant does *not* live within a participating European state, then the old principles apply and a claimant needs the permission of the court to issue and serve on a defendant outside the jurisdiction. The application is made without notice and must be supported by written evidence setting out the grounds of the application. There are three matters which the claimant must establish:

(a) There must be a 'good arguable case' that the court can assume jurisdiction within one of the 20 grounds set out in PD6B, para 3.1. Again, these grounds involve cases where there is sufficient nexus

---

63 Art 5, Jurisdiction and Judgments Regulation.

64 CPR, r 6.33(2)(a)

65 CPR, r 6.34

between the cause of action and England and Wales to make it sensible for the courts here to assume jurisdiction.

(b) There must be a reasonable prospect of success on the merits. This essentially means that trying the case is not a waste of time.[66]

(c) The court must be satisfied that England and Wales is the proper place to try the case. This again is a common sense consideration, requiring the court to ask itself where justice can be dispensed most fairly, efficiently and expeditiously. This involves looking at things like where the evidence is, the availability of witnesses, and generally the pros and cons of trying the case elsewhere.[67]

So, if the claimant lives within the jurisdiction, but the defendant does not, the first and essential question is: where does the *defendant* live? If the defendant is resident in Europe, think - the CJJA/European system. If the English courts must or may assume jurisdiction, no permission to issue and serve proceedings is necessary. If the defendant does *not* live in Europe, the CJJA/European system is not relevant, permission will always be necessary and different considerations apply. Where examined, professional assessments will test a basic understanding of this distinction, using obvious countries, like France v Mexico (sounds like the World Cup!). In practice, or in a take-home assessment, if you are not sure whether a country is covered by the CJJA or not, you will just have to look it up. But an unseen examination will not try and trick you by putting the defendant in the Channel Islands and leaving you to fret over whether they are part of the European system or not (they are not).

Note that where the claim form is to be served out of the jurisdiction, *whether in Europe or not*, it is valid for *six months* as opposed to the usual four. Service will be effected

---

66 See *Seaconsar Far East Ltd v Bank Marrkazi Jomhouri Iran* [1994] 1 AC 438

67 See, e.g., *Spiliada Maritime Corp v Cansulex Ltd* [1986] AC 460

68 See table set out at PD6B para 8

69 See generally below, Ch. 5

by reference to relevant international conventions and diplomatic channels. Basically, the more remote a defendant is from the English jurisdiction, the longer that defendant is given to respond to the particulars of claim.[68] A claimant who does not require permission to issue and serve proceedings out of the jurisdiction will, on the other hand, need permission to enter judgment in default, should that become relevant.[69]

revision tips

- Do not let the minutiae of the service rules overwhelm your essential understanding of the system. Get a grasp of the basics, and the rest will follow.

- Appreciate that, despite similarities, the rules for service of the *claim form* differ from the rules about service of other documents. Be confident about the essential nature of and reason for differences.

- Despite the various options for serving the *claim form* (in the jurisdiction), remember that this choice is sometimes constrained by the rules. It might help to remember what is sometimes called the 'hierarchy' of service by asking:

    (a) Is personal service required?

    (b) If not, has C been notified by D or his solicitors that service should be at the solicitor's address?

    (c) If not, has D given C another address for service (which is where he resides or carries on business)?

    (d) Even so, does C want to serve D personally (e.g. if time is of the essence)?

    (e) Otherwise, what is D's usual or (if reasonable attempts have been made but failed to find a current address) what is D's last known address?

- Be aware of the operation and implications of the *deeming* provisions, for both claim forms and other court documents. If doing something by 4.30 pm is mentioned, you can be pretty confident that deemed service of documents other than the claim form is (at that moment) being referred to.

revision tips *continued*

- Do not confuse the deeming provisions with the more general computation of time rules (CPR, r 2.8/9). As to the latter, know what is meant by 'clear days' and note that when computing short periods of time (5 days or less) for doing an act (e.g. giving notice), holidays and weekends are excluded from the calculation. For example, if an application must be served 3 clear days before a hearing date on Tuesday 14 October the 3 clear days would be the previous Thursday, Friday and Monday (assuming that this not a Bank Holiday), so the last day for service would be Wednesday 8 October. This is not the case for longer periods.

- Check your syllabus to see if Service out of the Jurisdiction is on it. If it is, just be sure to distinguish between the European system and the non-European system.

It is worth reading ...

Judgment of *Munby J* (as he then was) in *R (Lawer) v Restormel Borough Council* [2007] EWHC 2299 (Admin); [2008] HLR 20. This is not a mainstream case (it involves the Local Authority's obligation to house the homeless), but it is easy to follow the story. At this point it is the judge's comments about the without notice interim application (which was made over the telephone!) which you should take on board.

CHAPTER 5

Early judgment without trial

Even if matters are not resolved pre-trial and it is necessary to commence proceedings, it is still the case that most civil suits never get to trial. Some never even get to first base. Not only do the rules contain certain carrots to encourage the early settlement of cases with some merit, they also include several sticks to ensure that claims with no merit are thrown out well before the expense of a full trial. The most lethal of these sticks are *striking out*[1] and *summary judgment.*[2] These can be deployed against *both* claims and defences, and are draconian but important weapons in the court's armoury for keeping control over its proceedings and achieving the overriding objective. Where claims are thus lost, then of course to that extent the defendant wins and the claimant, as the loser, will usually have to pay both side's legal costs.[3]

Claimants have the *additional* procedural stick of obtaining *judgment in default* under CPR Part 12, which in effect penalises defendants who do not make clear their desire to defend a claim.[4] A claimant who succeeds through any one of these methods in defeating the defendant's case will get judgment (almost invariably with costs) without the aggravation and expense of a trial of the action.

Early judgment for the *claimant*

The two most common procedural devices claimants use to get early judgment without having to go to full trial are *judgment in default* under CPR Part 12 and *summary judgment.*

---

1 See Ch. 13
2 See below

3 See generally Ch. 18 on the costs rules

4 Judgment can be entered in default of compliance with other procedural requirements, but CPR, r 12.3 is the first opportunity for a claimant and is the form of default judgment discussed in this chapter.

1. DEFAULT JUDGMENT

Default judgment applies where a defendant does not want, or does not indicate a desire to contest a claimant's action. Since it would be silly to carry on any further in those circumstances, the claimant may in such cases obtain judgment 'in default' of the defendant's manifesting an intention to defend. Where the claim is for *money* only, default judgment is usually an *administrative*, not a judicial, process; it is available on request from the relevant court office by merely filling out a form. No application or appearance before a judge is needed. However, non-money claims (for example, injunctions), *always* require an *application to the court*.

Availability of default judgment

With some *limited* specialist exceptions (certain consumer credit cases, Part 8 claims, contentious probate cases), a claimant may obtain default judgment in respect of *any* sort of claim.[5]

Meaning of default judgment

It is important in this context to remember that the document to which the defendant must respond is the *particulars of claim*, and not the claim form as such.[6] When the particulars of claim are served, they must be accompanied by a 'response pack' containing forms of acknowledgement of service, admission and defence/counterclaim.[7] These give the defendant a range of options for responding to the claim. Silence is not really one of them!

Once the particulars of claim have been served, a defendant wanting to defend a claim should manifest this intention in one of two ways:

---

5   CPR, r 12.2/PD 12, para 1.2/3

6   CPR, r 9.1(2). You will remember that the particulars of claim can be put directly on the claim form, arrive with the claim form or be served within 14 days of service of the claim form (and in any event while the claim form is still valid for service). See Ch. 3.

7   CPR, r 9.2. See example in Sime, figure 6.3

1. by acknowledging service of the particulars of claim within 14 days of service and thereafter filing a defence (so long as this is within 28 days of service of the particulars of claim);

or

2. by skipping the acknowledgment stage altogether and filing a defence from the outset within 14 days of service of the particulars of claim. Defendants should file a defence at the outset i [8]

You will notice that filing an acknowledgment of service 'buys' the defendant a little more time to file his defence. It is worth noting also that the parties can agree to extend the time for filing the defence for up to (at most[9]) a further 28 days. The defendant should notify the court of the agreed extended period.[10]

Not surprisingly, default judgment is therefore possible in two basic situations:

(a) where the defendant has failed to file either an acknowledgement of service or defence in time (in effect, where there has been no response at all from the defendant);

or

(b) where, having filed an acknowledgement of service, the defendant has nevertheless failed to go on to file a defence in time.[11]

PROCEDURAL PREREQUISITES

The procedural requirements for entering judgment in default all have to do with ensuring that a defendant who intends to defend an action has had every opportunity, but has nevertheless failed to respond to the claim in an appropriate manner consistent with defending. First of all, the court must be satisfied that the defendant

---

8   CPR, rr10.1(3),10.3(1) and 15.4

9   Only the court could sanction a further extension. If the parties could agree to greater delay, this would impede the progress of the case and interfere with the court's duty to control the pace of proceedings.

10 CPR, r 15.5
11 CPR, r 12.3

has actually been served with the particulars of claim. If the court itself has not been responsible for effecting service, then the claimant will have to prove service by means of a certificate of service. Secondly, the time for filing an acknowledgment of service or defence, as the case may be, must have expired; obviously the defendant must be given the *entire* period in which to respond.

Finally, the defendant must have failed to file an acknowledgment of service or defence (as the case may be) *and* must not have either admitted the claim and asked for time to pay,[12] satisfied the claim, or applied for summary judgment.[13] Obviously it would be rather perverse to give the claimant judgment in default where (or to the extent that) the defendant was in the process of attempting to satisfy (or indeed had already satisfied) the claim, or had made an application to the court saying the claim itself is so groundless that it is the defendant and not the claimant who should get early judgment. In essence, if, in the allotted time, a defendant wanting to defend has failed to respond in a pertinent manner, the claimant may seek to enter judgment in default.

HOW JUDGMENT IS OBTAINED

On request

In money claims only (and this includes claims for delivery of goods where the claimant will accept money instead) default judgment is available 'over the counter', as it were, unless there are exceptional features (for example, claims against a child or protected party, who require a 'litigation friend',[14] a claim in tort against a spouse, a claim served out of the jurisdiciton).[15] In ordinary money cases, therefore, the claimant merely requests judgment on the prescribed standard form (including how and when payment of a specified amount of money is to be made where payment by instalments is acceptable). There is *no* hearing and *no* question of having to persuade

---

12 And provided relevant financial information

13 CPR, r 12.3/PD 12, para 4.1. If a defendant admits part of the claim and wants to defend part, this should be made clear by returning both the admission and defence forms.

14 See Ch. 17 for child witnesses

15 Permission must be sought in such cases (which are usefully summarised in Sime, 13.17): CPR, r 12.4

a judge to give judgment on the merits of the case; judgment will be 'entered' so long as the prerequisites mentioned above have been met, which only involves court staff checking that documents have or have not reached their relevant destinations[16].

Thus, in standard, everyday claims for *money* (whether for a specified sum or not) and/or claims for delivery of goods where the defendant is given the alternative of paying their value in *money*, entering default judgment is purely an *administrative* act. These account for the overwhelming majority of cases.

Note, however, that although entering judgment in such cases is administrative, it is *not* automatic, so unless and until a claimant enters judgment in default, a defendant can still manifest an intention to defend, even after the initial time for doing so has expired, thereby precluding judgment being entered. Thus a defendant who does not respond appropriately to the particulars of claim within the allotted time is *at risk* of the claimant's entering judgment against him; but the claimant actually has to *do* something to convert the risk into a reality.

On application

In money claims with exceptional features, and where the claimant is seeking a non-money remedy (for example, equitable relief), an *application* to the court is necessary. The reason for requiring an application in the latter sort of case is that equitable remedies are 'discretionary' and therefore require a judge to exercise his or her judgment on the merits. The view of the person at the court office is not good enough for this purpose!

Where permission is required, the application is made in writing and usually on notice in accordance with the Part 23 procedure for interim applications.[17] The application must be supported by written evidence relating to the nature of the claim and the meeting of the procedural requirements.[18] There will be a hearing and the court will give such judgment 'as it appears the claimant is entitled to on his

---

16 Or are taken to have reached: see the deemed service rules, discussed in Ch. 4

17 See generally Ch. 4

18 CPR, r 12.11/PD 12, paras 3-5

statement of case'.[19]   In other words, the court will consider the merits of the case, at least insofar as it appears on the pleaded case, and will otherwise act to ensure procedural fairness.

TYPES OF JUDGMENT IN MONEY CLAIMS

If the claim is for a '*specified*' amount of money (plus interest), judgment will be *final* as to both liability and quantum (including interest).[20]   Where the claim is for an '*unspecified*' amount of money (or 'damages'), or the claimant asks the court to decide the quantum or the interest, the judgment will be *partial* (sometimes called 'interlocutory' judgment).[21]   In other words, it will be final as to the defendant's liability to pay damages, but the *amount* to be paid will remain to be determined. The date of future hearings to decide this will be fixed (and relevant directions given) when judgment is entered.[22]

Under the old rules the distinction was made, not between specified and unspecified money claims, but between 'liquidated' and 'unliquidated' claims. A liquidated demand is one which is objectively ascertainable (usually by looking at the contract to which it relates) and not open to argument, although it might involve an element of calculation. Typical examples are debts and the price of goods sold and delivered. If you buy a Twix bar for 50p and find when you get it home that there is something basically wrong with it, in money terms your claim against the shop for a refund is for 50p - no more and no less - because that is what you paid for the Twix bar. It is a liquidated demand.

Unliquidated claims, on the other hand, are open to argument (even if nobody would bother) or require the exercise of judicial discretion in their assessment. Most claims for 'damages' are unliquidated: indeed the words are practically synonymous (although, confusingly, there is such a thing as 'liquidated damages'). Some claims

---

19   CPR, r 12.11(1)

20   CPR, r 12.5(2)

21   CPR, r 12.5(3)

22   CPR, r 12.7. Such will normally be dealt with at a 'disposal hearing'. These are apt to be short and not involve oral evidence: PD 26, para 12.4(1)

are obviously identifiable as unliquidated, for example claims for pain, suffering and loss of amenity or for future financial loss - so-called 'general damages'. But others can fool you. A claim for the amount paid to have a broken watch repaired or to buy a specially adapted car is also an unliquidated claim because the defendant may want to quibble about the amount which was spent. Maybe the claimant did not need a four-wheel drive Mercedes Benz with diamond encrusted wing mirrors! Just because a claimant can put a price tag on a damage claim does not make it liquidated, although in most cases price tags are accepted as fair and accurate.

Of course, to many people the words 'liquidated' and 'unliquidated' do not convey the meaning lawyers ascribe to them. So it is not surprising that in drafting the new rules an attempt was apparently made to update these expressions with more readily understandable vocabulary. But legal concepts and terms can sometimes be difficult to modernise. Possibly the descriptions 'specified' and 'unspecified' were intended to replace (and so translate into) 'liquidated' and 'unliquidated', but this is not what happened given how easy it is to 'specify' the amount of what is strictly speaking an unliquidated claim. The result is to place the burden on defendants to indicate if they take issue with, and seek the court's determination on, the amount of a claim, which although unliquidated is one on which the claimant has put a specific price tag.[23]

SETTING ASIDE DEFAULT JUDGMENT

Because of the non-judicial nature of most default judgments, it is not something which is subject to an appeal, as such. Instead, defendants who have had default judgment entered against them can apply to have it varied or 'set aside'. Such applications are made using the Part 23 procedure for interim applications.[24]

Default judgment will be set aside 'as of right' if it was wrongly entered. That is

---

23 Even so the distinction between liquidated and unliquidated claims comes up in other contexts, so it is useful to understand it.

24 The written evidence in support should address the matters which are relevant to the court's decision.

to say, it *must* be set aside if the court finds that the relevant procedural requirements of Part 12 were not met (for example, if the time for acknowledging service had not expired when judgment was entered).[25]

Otherwise default judgment *may*, and presumably will only, be set aside if it appears to the court on looking at the evidence in support of the application that 'the defendant has a *real prospect of successfully* defending the claim' *or* there is some other '*good reason*' for setting side or varying the judgment, or for letting the defendant defend the claim.[26] In either case, the court should take into account whether the application to set aside was made *promptly.*[27]

'Real prospect of success'

This is sometimes known as setting aside 'on the merits' of the case. Notice how the wording of the rule here intentionally invokes the summary judgment test, although in this context the burden of proof is always on the defendant.[28]

On the one hand, the court will not lightly let a defendant's case be lost simply because of an initial and isolated failure to comply with the timetable rules. Lord Atkin's sentiments expressed over 50 years ago in *Evans v Bartlam*[29] remain equally valid today:

> The principle obviously is that unless and until the Court has pronounced
> a judgment on the merits or by consent, it is to have the power to revoke
> the expression of its coercive power where that has only been obtained by a
> failure to follow any of the rules of procedure.

Recent cases confirm that at this stage the court's primary considerations ought to be, not procedural failings on the part of the defendant, but rather the nature of the defence, any prejudice to the claimant and, of course, the justice of the case. See,

---

25 CPR, r 13.2. In *Intense Investments Ltd v Development Ventures Ltd* [2005] BLR 478, for example, judgment was set aside as of right because it had been entered by the request method, in circumstances where an application to the court should have been made.

26 CPR, r 13.3(1)

27 CPR, r 13.3(2)

28 See discussion which follows

for example, *Thorn plc v MacDonald*, where the Court of Appeal set out the relevant principles in a helpful list.[30] An inadequately explained delay in applying to set aside may be indicative of a weak defence, but should not be taken as decisive.

On the other hand, there has to be some real point in carrying on with the case. It would be a waste of time and money to put the defendant's ship back on course when it would almost immediately - and inevitably - be sunk on the shoals of a successful summary judgment application.

'Some other good reason'

As we have seen, because of the deeming provisions, a defendant may be considered properly served with particulars of claim, even though it never in fact arrived. This is not a procedural defect, but it could amount to a 'good reason' to set aside any judgment in default entered as a result, despite there not otherwise being a real prospect of successfully defending the case. It would all depend on the circumstances. An example given by May LJ[31] was where the defendant would have paid up rather than having an embarrassing judgment entered against him. Unconscionable behaviour on the part of the claimant might also amount to a good reason.[32]

When a court in its discretion sets aside default judgment, it may impose conditions.[33] The most common is that the defendant pay the costs 'thrown away', since these will have been incurred as a result of a failure to follow the rules. Additionally, the defendant may be ordered to pay the whole, or some part, of the disputed sum into court before being allowed to continue defending the action. The court should not, however, impose a financial condition which the defendant cannot possibly meet, since this would if effect be a roundabout way of (re)giving judgment to the claimant.[34]

---

29 [1937] AC 480, HL
30 [1999] CPLR 660. These are summarised in Sime, 13.33.
31 In *Godwin v Swindon Borough Council* [2002] 1 WLR 997

32 See, e.g., *Roundstone Nurseries Ltd v Stephenson Holdings Ltd* [2009] 5 Costs LR 787
33 CPR, r 13.1(3)

34 The onus will be on the defendant to prove the impossibility of any financial condition. See also discussion of summary judgment below.

2.   SUMMARY JUDGMENT

SUMMARY JUDGMENT FOR THE CLAIMANT

It is relatively easy to manifest an intention to defend a claim; in the first instance this merely involves ticking a box on a form. Sometimes a defendant will go through the motions of defending - perhaps out of desperation or as a delaying tactic - when there is in reality nothing that can be said that would prevent the claimant succeeding at the end of the day. If this is so, it is really rather pointless to wait until the end of the day.

The rules provide two important means of ensuring that cases without merit are quickly laid to rest. One is the 'striking out' procedure. A defence must be set out with clarity and precision, and make clear where issue is being taken with the claim. Incoherent or meaningless defences would be liable to be struck out by the court.[35]

Summary judgment is a related, and to some extent overlapping, procedure.[36] It is used for situations where whatever a defendant says, however clearly or logically set out, it is incapable of succeeding as a defence (or is inherently implausible) and there is no other compelling reason why the case should continue on to trial. The point of summary judgment for the claimant, therefore, is to provide early judgment in those cases where the defendant has no realistic hope of success and any defence raised will merely have the effect of delaying the inevitable judgment for the claimant.

Availability of summary judgment for the claimant

With a *very few* exceptions (notably certain residential possession proceedings), summary judgment *for the claimant* may be given in any type of case.[37]

Claimant's application for summary judgment

Unless the court gives permission, the claimant may only apply for summary judgment

---

35   Claims can also be struck out: CPR, r 3.4(1) and see Ch. 13

36   Summary judgment and striking out can be applied for in the alternative: PD 3A, para 1.7. See, e.g., *Clancy Consulting Ltd v Derwent Holdings Ltd* [2010] EWHC 762 (TCC) where the court struck out certain paragraphs in a defence and then granted summary judgment in respect of the claim which, as a result, was no longer defended.

37   CPR, r 24.3(1)

after the relevant defendant has responded to the particulars of claim by filing an acknowledgement of service or defence[38] (a failure by the defendant to respond to the claim would, of course, mean that the claimant could seek default judgment as discussed above). An application by a claimant who has failed to comply with any relevant pre-action protocol will not normally be entertained until a defence has actually been filed (or the time for doing so has expired).[39]

Otherwise, such applications for summary judgment are normally made in the period between acknowledgment of service (which precludes a claimant entering default judgment) and the filing of the applicant's directions questionnaire.[40] Indeed the first question on the directions questionnaire specifically asks if a summary judgment application is pending. Certainly applications should be made as promptly as possible. The idea is to put a hopeless case down before unnecessary time and costs are wasted. Furthermore, a delay in applying, while not necessarily fatal, might show a certain lack of conviction on the part of the applicant.

The application is made in accordance with the rules on making interim applications under **CPR** 23, with relevant modifications. Thus the application is made in writing. Notice must be given to the respondent(s), although the notice period is *at least 14 days* before the hearing, rather than the usual three.[41] The written evidence in support of a claimant's application must identify concisely any point of law or provision relied upon and include a stated belief that there is no defence with a real prospect of success or other reason for a trial of the action.[42] A defendant's evidence in reply, geared to showing why there ought to be a full trial of the claim or issue, must be filed at least *seven* days before the hearing. If the applicant wishes to respond to this, further evidence must be filed within *three* days of the hearing.[43] Once the application by the claimant is made, a defendant may, but need not, file a defence before the hearing.[44] If the application is made before the case has been

---

38 CPR, r 24.4(1)
39 PD 24, para 2(6)

40 PD 26, para 5.3. See
    generally Ch. 8
41 CPR, r 24.4(3)

42 PD 24, para 2
43 CPR, r 24.5(2)
44 CPR, r 24.4(2)

allocated to a case management track, the application will be heard before the allocation is made.[45] If the matter arises at the allocation stage, the question of summary judgment can be dealt with at an allocation hearing.

Such applications are heard by a master (in the High Court) or a District Judge (in the County Court).

The hearing

For the claimant to succeed, the court must consider that the defendant 'has no real prospect of successfully defending' the claim (or an issue in the claim) *and* there is no other compelling reason to have a trial.[46]

'No real prospect of success'

We came across this part of the test earlier in the context of setting aside default judgment. It has been said that in order to have a real prospect of success a case must carry 'some degree of conviction' and be 'more than merely arguable'[47] If the defendant's evidence at best shows only a distinctly improbable case, then it will be right to grant summary judgment.[48] Having said that, it still remains the case that it is a serious matter to deprive a defendant of the right to put a defence case at trial, and so the 'standard of proof' at the summary judgment stage is a high one. In *Swain v Hillman*,[49] the architect of the CPR, Lord Woolf, said that the words 'no real prospect of success' are self-explanatory - 'real' means realistic, not fanciful; 'possible', not necessarily probable. He emphasised the need to keep summary judgment applications in proper perspective. They are not, he said, meant to dispense with the need for a trial where there are issues which should be considered and tested there (in other words, what used to be called 'triable issues'). If the defendant's case has some prospects of success, summary judgment should be refused.[50]

---

45 PD 26, para 5.3(2)

46 CPR, r 24.2

47 See, e.g., *Bee v Jenson* [2007] RTR 9, and *E.D. and F. Man Liquid Products Ltd v Patel* [2003] CPLR 384, at [8]

48 As in *Akinleye v East Sussex Hospitals NHS Trust* [2008] LS Law Med 216

49 [1999] CPLR 779

50 *Cotton v Rickard Metals Inc* [2008] EWHC 824 (QB)

Nor are summary judgment applications mini-trials. They are hearings to determine whether and to what extent there *ought* to be a trial, disposing in the process of cases with no realistic[51] prospect of success or other raison d'être. However it is described, given that justice is an integral part of the overriding objective, before granting summary judgment the court must be clear in its own mind that a trial would be a waste of time and money.

'No compelling reason for a trial'.

Sometimes the court may feel that the defence has little or no prospect of success, but there is some other compelling reason for a trial. This can arise if a case is very complex. It can also happen when the claimant's actions appear discreditable in some way. An infamous example is *Miles v Bull*.[52] In that case a farmer sold his farmhouse to the claimant while his estranged wife was still living in it. The wife had not registered her rights of occupation before the sale and so she was not protected as against the new owner, who wanted her out of the house. The new owner sued the wife for possession and applied for summary judgment. The wife did not really have a defence in law, but the court held that the husband and new owner had conducted their business in such a secretive, if not underhand, way that the wife ought to have access to all of the weapons of the litigation process to test the new owner's claim. In effect, the court felt that the claimant ought to be put to strict proof of the claim in order for justice to be done.

Burden of proof

CPR, r 24.2, unlike its predecessor, is not explicit about where the burden of proof lies in summary judgment cases. Assuming an application by the claimant,[53] the question is this: is it his job to persuade the court that the defendant's case has no

---

51   In E.D. and F. Man, *op. cit.*,
     Potter LJ at [6] said the
     terms 'real prospect' and
     'realistic prospect' were
     interchangeable.

52   [1969] 1 QB 258

53   Defendants can also apply
     for summary judgment, as
     discussed below.

real chance of success; or is it the defendant's job to prove that it does? The old rules clearly put the burden on the defendant, presumably because at that time he would have known more about his own case than the claimant. And while it may have been the original intention to replicate this in the new rules, there is not now anything in CPR, r 24.2 (or its accompanying PD) which says so explicitly. And what do the judges say? The question has never been directly decided, and it does not really keep anyone up at night since cases rarely turn on the point[54], but the weight of judicial observation indicates that the courts now interpret the rules as placing the burden on the applicant/*claimant* to show that the defendant/respondent's case is not worthy of trial.[55] One logical reason for this is that the applicant is the one asking for early judgment. When the defendant applies to set aside default judgment so that he can put his case at trial, the burden is on him to show his case has a real prospect of success.[56] It would seem to follow that when it is the claimant who is making the application, then the persuasive burden should be on him.

In any event, the judge will not test or weigh up the respective merits of the cases, which are typically set out in the parties' witness statements and exhibits, except to determine whether there is some point in having a trial. Cases which therefore tend not to be amenable to summary judgment are those where a substantive defence has been pleaded (for example, frustration), a specific answer to the claim has been raised (for example, a relevant exclusion clause), a point of law requires protracted argument and/or the relevant facts are disputed.[57] Negligence claims, for example, do not usually lend themselves to summary judgment once liability has been denied and the defendant has set out his disputed version of events. But every case must be looked at individually; in *Dummer v Brown*[58] summary judgment was granted against a coach driver who had previously pleaded guilty to a charge of dangerous driving in respect of the accident giving rise to the claim. Given the difference between the

54 See generally discussion of burden of proof at Ch. 17

55 In *E.D. and F. Man, op. cit.*, [at 9] Potter LJ said as much when contrasting the position with setting aside default judgment. Because that case was

about the latter, his view was strictly 'obiter', but other cases have taken similar approaches.

56 As discussed above

57 A lot of witness statements going back and forth in response to each other usually indicate a factual dispute worthy of a trial.

58 [1953] 1 QB 710. By way of comparison see *McCauley v Vine* [1999] 1 WLR 1977

criminal and civil standard of proof, it was almost inconceivable that the defendant could escape liability for negligence.[59]

It is important to remember, however, that the court is not liable to take every assertion made at face value; it will reject legal argument which is erroneous or evidence which is inherently implausible, irrelevant, self-contradictory or manifestly inconsistent with other believable facts. In short, the case of the party opposing summary judgment must appear to have a certain degree of credibility; for this reason summary judgment applications will often focus on the implausibility (or not) of the parties' allegations. In *Sandhar v Sandhar and Kang Ltd*,[60] for example, a respondent's assertion that he retained a beneficial interest in property was rejected as fanciful. No supporting documentary evidence had been exhibited, nor were the circumstances (including no provision for rental income or how his interest was to be realised) consistent with it. Summary judgment was granted.

POSSIBLE ORDERS ON CLAIMANT'S APPLICATION

At the hearing of the claimant's application for summary judgment, the possible orders of the master or District Judge are as follows.

Judgment for claimant

This is the appropriate order where no viable or believable defence is raised and/or there is no other compelling reason to have a trial. The claimant will normally get an order for the costs of the application.

Conditional order

This is an appropriate order where a defence cannot be ruled out altogether, but is 'shadowy' or of doubtful credibility; in other words where it appears to the court

---

59   See Ch. 17 on admitting previous convictions in a civil case.

60   [2008] EWCA Civ 238, LTL 14/2/2008

'possible that a defence ... will succeed, but improbable that it will do so'.[61] This is a safety net for cases where the court feels uncomfortable about giving summary judgment, but is only willing to let the defence continue on strict conditions, the most typical of which is that the defendant 'put his money where his mouth is' by paying part or all of the amount claimed into court, failing which the claimant gets judgment. The idea is that defendants should think hard about 'throwing good money after bad' if they have no real answer to the claim.[62] The court must not, however, impose a condition unless there is some prospect that the defendant can comply, since this would be tantamount to giving judgment for the claimant.[63] Having said that, the onus is on defendant to establish an inability to meet the condition 'were he really minded to do so'. Both of these principles were established in *Yorke Motors v Edwards*[64] where the appeal court reduced the amount the defendant was ordered to pay into court from over £30,000 to £4,000. The defendant wanted the condition lifted altogether, but the court felt that notwithstanding certain indicators of impecuniosity (including a legal aid certificate), a properly motivated Mr. Edwards (of whose defence the court was very sceptical) could lay his hands on the reduced amount. Requiring a defendant to take a particular step in the litigation (for example, filing a more detailed defence) may also be a condition. The usual costs order would be 'costs in the case'.[65]

Dismissal of application

This is appropriate where the defence clearly has a chance of success or there is some other compelling reason to have a trial. The defendant's means are irrelevant here. If there is a real prospect of success at trial, there is clearly a reason for a trial and that is that. Presumably the claimant should have figured that out, so in such circumstances the costs of the interim application will normally go to the defendant.

---

61 PD 24, para 4
62 In addition, when money is paid in under such an order, the claimant is a secured creditor for that amount in the event of the defendant's bankruptcy: *Re Ford* [1900] 2 QB 211

63 See, e.g., *Chapple v Williams* [1999] CPLR 731, CA

64 [1982] 1 WLR 444
65 This means that whoever wins at trial gets the costs of this interim application. See generally Ch. 18

When the claim or any part of it is proceeding to trial (that is, where the claimant's application is dismissed or a conditional order is made), the court will go on to give appropriate directions as to the future conduct of the litigation.

3.   EXPANSION OF SUMMARY JUDGMENT

The summary judgment procedure is not limited to use by claimants against defendants.   In giving the court effective case management powers, the CPR expanded summary judgment in two important ways.

(i)   Defendant's application

The first is that *defendants* may apply for summary judgment to attack hopelessly weak claims (or a particular issue in the claim). Thus, summary judgment *for the defendant* will be granted when the court considers that the claimant has no real prospect of succeeding on a claim or issue and there is no other compelling reason to have a trial.[66] Defendants' applications for summary judgment are possible in *any* sort of case and again are a useful adjunct to the power to strike out (which is also available against claimants). In this context, therefore, another possible order to be made by the court in summary judgment proceedings is the striking out or dismissal of the whole of, or some issue in the claimant's action. Otherwise, the same principles, procedure and range of possible orders discussed above applies to a defendant's application for summary judgment, adapted as necessary to the circumstances of the reversed roles. A *conditional order*, for example, would be most apt to involve some specified step which the claimant is required to make in the litigation before being allowed to proceed.

---

66   CPR, r 24.2

(ii) Court's initiative

Secondly, the court can fix a summary judgment hearing *on its own initiative*.[67] Thus, whenever, and as soon as it scents a weak claim or defence (usually at the allocation stage), the court can itself trigger a hearing, having given adequate notice to the parties. This procedure can also be used for the purpose of obtaining a summary determination of certain issues in a case where the court is satisfied that these do not require full investigation, thus reducing the complexity and length of any trial.

COUNTERCLAIMS, SET-OFFS AND SUMMARY JUDGMENT

Often defendants make claims against the claimant in response to the latter's claim against them. When these are included in the same proceedings as the claimant's action they are known as cross-claims or counterclaims. A 'set-off' is a special kind of counterclaim, which historically has had an important impact on summary judgment applications.

All set-offs are counterclaims ...

What makes a set-off special is its ability to operate as a *defence* (to the extent of the set-off). This can be highly relevant to the outcome of a summary judgment application by a claimant. Let us suppose, for example, that a claimant's claim is for £6000 and the defendant pleads nothing else except a (not inherently incredible) set-off to the value of £4000. There is thus a defence being raised up to £4000, but thereafter there is no answer given to the claim. So on a summary judgment application by the claimant, the proper order would strictly be: summary judgment for the claimant for £2,000 (the part that the set-off couldn't reach, as it were) and dismissal of the claimant's application as regards the £4,000, leaving the defendant free to continue his defence (or even get summary judgment *against* the claimant as regards the £4,000 if there is no real prospect the claimant will win on that issue).

---

67   CPR, r 3.3

It is important to know whether a cross-claim amounts to a set-off, because the particular magic about a set-off is its *defensive capability*. It is worth remembering that while *all set-offs are counterclaims, not all counterclaims are set-offs*! In essence there are three set-off situations:

(a) Mutual Debts

If D owes C £5,000 and C owes D £3,000 (both liquidated demands), then if C sues D for the £5,000, D can set the £3,000 which C owes him off against C's claim. Hence the expression 'set-off'! The amounts need not be debts strictly speaking, so long as ascertained amounts are owed.

(b) Supply contract set-offs

This applies where goods or services supplied under the contract in respect of which the claimant sues are claimed by the defendant to be defective. So where the claimant sues for the price of goods sold or services supplied (a liquidated demand), the defendant can set-off, in diminution of the price, any claim he has for defects in the quality of those *same* goods or services (usually an unliquidated claim).[68]

(c) The equitable set-off

This is a broad and somewhat nebulous category. In essence, a defendant's counterclaim will be treated as an equitable set-off where, even though it is not technically a set-off in law (or other accepted category of set-off), nevertheless it and the claimant's claim arise out of the same contract or transaction or are otherwise so inextricably linked that it would be unfair to uphold the one without taking into account the other. Equity in effect intervenes to treat such a cross-claim as a set-off.[69]

---

68 Purists will distinguish between sale of goods cases, where the set-off derives from the Sale of Goods Act 1979, s 53(1), and supply of services cases, where it derives, by analogy, from the case law, but the concept is identical.

69 See discussion in *Geldorf Metaalconstructie NV v Simon Carves Ltd* [2010] BLR 401

In the leading case of *Hanak v Green*,[70] for example, the claimant sued her builder for breach of contract for failing to complete works at her house. The defendant counterclaimed for (a) extra work done for the claimant by him outside the original contract; (b) loss sustained as a result of the claimant's refusal to let the defendant's workmen onto the premises; and (c) trespass to the defendant's tools. All three cross-claims were treated as equitable set-offs.

Another classic example of the equitable set-off arises in landlord and tenant cases. Typically, a tenant who has been sued by his landlord for arrears of rent will be allowed to set off against that claim a counterclaim for damages for breach of the same tenancy agreement (for example, the landlord's failure to repair).[71]

... but not all counterclaims are set-offs

Where the counterclaim is not a set-off (you might think of this as a 'mere' counterclaim), then it can have *no* defensive capability and cannot stop the claimant getting summary judgment. So, assuming the defendant is not raising any other defence, the claimant will get judgment. It may, however, be appropriate to delay, or 'stay' execution of that summary judgment (and so make the claimant wait for his money) until after the determination of the counterclaim. On the basis of the pre-CPR case law, this will be appropriate only where there is sufficient connection between the claim and the counterclaim, some unresolved issue between the parties and/or some other *compelling* reason to keep the claimant from the immediate fruits of his judgment. In determining whether a defendant's 'mere' counterclaim justifies a stay of execution, the court will have regard to:

(a) The degree of connection between claim and (mere) counterclaim (the closer the connection, the stronger the case for a stay)

(b) The strength of the counterclaim (the stronger the counterclaim, the

---

70 [1958] 2 QB 9

71 But cf *Bluestorm Ltd v Portvale Holdings Ltd* [2004] EWCA Civ 289, where the tenant's failure to pay rent had the intended consequence of impeding the landlord's ability to meet his obligations as landlord.

better the case for a stay).

and

(c)   the ability of the claimant to satisfy any judgment which the defendant might obtain on the counterclaim (any doubt on this matter strengthens the case for granting a stay).[72]

Effect of counterclaim on summary judgment applications

It can sometimes be difficult to distinguish between the equitable set-off (which, as a defence, can stop the claimant obtaining summary judgment) and the 'closely connected' counterclaim (which does not amount to a set-off, and so, strictly, cannot stop the claimant getting summary judgment, but which justifies a stay of execution of that judgment). You might say that one person's equitable set-off is sometimes another's closely connected counterclaim. Technically, and certainly historically, the outcomes are very different, and for this reason it is important (if only for the sake of argument) to understand how the legal effect of a set-off differs from that of a (closely connected) 'mere' counterclaim. Having said that, the practical result in both cases is much the same since in neither is any money paid over until after the trial (or earlier resolution) of the claim and counterclaim. Often, it is the practical rather than the technical result which matters.

Even predicting when a stay of execution will or will not be granted can be tricky. The Court of Appeal considered the 'lack of overall clarity' which existed under the old rules in *United Overseas Ltd v Peter Robinson Ltd*[73] and concluded that, all things considered it was a good thing because it gave the court useful room for manoeuvre in dispensing justice in individual cases. This approach, of course, is very much in keeping with the ethos of the CPR. Certainly, where fairness demands that no money passes hands until the defendant's cross-claim is resolved, the court will choose whatever route to that end best accords with the facts and the need to dispense justice proportionately and fairly.

---

72   See, e.g., *Mead General Building Ltd v Dartmoor Properties Ltd* [2009] BCC 510, and generally *Drake and Fletcher v Batchelor* (1986) LSG 1232 per Sir Neil Lawson

73   (unreported), March 26, 1991

THE CHEQUE RULE

Historically, one important exception to the rule about the defensive capability of set-offs has been the so-called 'cheque rule'. This is summed up in the maxim: *There is no defence to a bad cheque*. In effect, when you pay for something by cheque, you promise that the cheque is as good as cash. This is a second and *entirely separate agreement* to the one for the sale or supply of the thing being purchased. The implications of this are important. If you buy something with cash and later discover there is a fault with it, you can try and get your money back but you cannot prevent the money changing hands because the payment will already have been made! You are not meant to be any better off if you pay by cheque, so that not honouring a cheque which you have written is only very exceptionally treated as excusable by the civil courts. Thus where a claimant sues not on the original contract of sale/supply (sometimes called the 'underlying' contract), but *on the bad cheque*, then nothing the defendant can say about defects in the thing sold or supplied will be allowed to operate either as a defence or a reason to stay execution of the claimant's judgment on the dishonoured cheque, except in *very* limited circumstances. These involve situations where it is alleged either that the cheque was obtained by fraud or misrepresentation[74] or the underlying contract is void or voidable. If the underlying contract is effectively nullified, then no money should have changed hands in the first instance and the method of payment then becomes irrelevant. Thus allegations of fraud, illegality, invalidity and total failure of consideration can operate, exceptionally, as a defence to an action on a dishonoured cheque. The very limited nature of these exceptions was highlighted by Sachs LJ when he said that the court will not 'whittle away [this] rule of practice by introducing unnecessary exceptions to it under the influence of sympathy-evoking stories'.[75]

The cheque rule is a very old one. Of course, writing cheques these days is getting to be as rare as handwritten letters, but the rule applies to any form of promissory note, including direct debit mandates. It has both a legal and commercial rationale. Business

---

74 *Solo Indistries UK Ltd v Canara Bank* [2001] 1WLR 1800

75 *Cebora SNC v SIP (Industrial Products) Ltd* [1976] 1 Lloyd's Rep at 271. And see leading case of *Nova (Jersey) Knit Ltd v Kammgarn Spinnerei GmbH* [1977] 1 WLR 713, HL

people expect to be paid at the end of the period for clearing cheques and so forth, and the rule was formulated with the need to promote commercial stability in mind. Legally, its operation is explained by the existence of the two separate agreements. It is precisely because the claimant is suing on the *independent* contract about payment, to which there is rarely an answer, that counterclaims relating to the *underlying* contract of sale or supply will be ineffective in preventing summary judgment being given and enforced.

The fact that there is, as a rule, no defence to a bad cheque does not, of course, prevent the defendant complaining about the goods supplied or sold to him under the underlying contract. Indeed, it does not always prevent people stopping cheques as a bargaining tool when something has gone wrong with such contracts! What it does mean, however, is that such complaints will afford *no defence* to the *claimant's action* on the bad cheque, leaving any claim of defective goods or service to be pursued independently.

revision tips

- Be clear about the distinction - and relationship - between default judgment and summary judgment. The former rarely involves a hearing; the latter always does (as does an application to set aside default judgment). Part 12 default judgment is relevant when a defendant fails to manifest an interest in defending a claim; summary judgment against a defendant who *has* shown an interest in defending is appropriate when the claimant shows that the defence has no real prospect of success (and there is no other compelling reason to have a trial).

- Do not be fooled into thinking that a defence should necessarily be filed within 14 days after acknowledgment of service. A defendant who first acknowledges service has until *28 days after service of the particulars of claim* to file his defence. So a defendant who, for example, acknowledged service within four days would have longer from that point to file a defence than one who acknowledged service on day 12. Examiners like to test this point.

- A defendant seeking to set aside default judgment will have to convince the court that his defence has a real prospect of success or there is some other good reason to have a trial. The 'real prospect of success' test is effectively the same for claimants seeking summary judgment, although in such cases the burden is on the defendant seeking to set aside judgment to do the convincing.

- Know the significance of that special kind of counterclaim known as a set-off. Remember that all set-offs are counterclaims, but not all counterclaims are set-offs. Be able to recognise an obvious set-off and its effect in summary judgment applications.

- Don't forget the 'cheque rule'. Remember the maxim: *There is no defence to a bad cheque.* It will remind you that the principle only operates if the claimant sues on the bad cheque and not the underlying contract.

It is worth reading ...

Judgment of HH Judge Peter Coulson QC (as he then was) in *Khan v Edgbaston Holdings Limited* [2007] EWHC 2444 (QB). Not every judge guides you so methodically through a judgment - he even gives you a table of contents! The rules on sanctions have changed somewhat, but what you don't know about default judgment after reading this case, may not be worth knowing. So enjoy!

And for a creepy but fascinating case on summary judgment, read Males J's judgment in *Sargespace Limited v Natasha Anastasia Eustace* [2013] EWHC 2944 (QB). I doubt the former barrister-turned playboy (don't get any ideas!) will win any Prince Charming awards. Bet you can't read the first paragraph and not keep going to the end!

CHAPTER 6

Remedies without trial:
interim injunctions/payments

An important aspect of any case is the substantive remedy or relief sought by the claimant. Courts are limited in what they can do to put right wrongs which have occurred. No amount of money can actually replace a missing leg, for example, but it pays for services and other bills and so this is the remedy which claimants seek, for lack of any other. Another common remedy is an injunction, which is an order that the defendant do, or stop doing, something.[1] Usually it is not until the end of a case that such remedies are ordered; a judge would have to have heard all the evidence before deciding, finally, who was liable - and for what.

There are occasions, however, when the court will order this sort of relief as an *interim* measure, either where it is obvious the claimant will win at the end of the day and it would be unjust not to grant some part of his ultimate remedy at an earlier, pre-trial stage; or where, without an order pending trial, irreparable damage may be caused to the claimant. Interim injunctions[2] and interim payments are two important forms of this kind of pre-trial order, and it is useful to think of them conceptually as interim versions of the kind of substantive remedy which the claimant ultimately seeks.[3]

---

1 An order to do something is called a 'mandatory' injunction; an order not to do something, a 'prohibitory' injunction.

2 Somewhat confusingly, there are other specialised forms of injunction, which are also granted on interim applications but perform other functions. These are called not by the generic name, but by their more descriptive names, Freezing and Search Orders. See Ch. 7 below.

3 Not all interim remedies mirror the claimant's substantive claim. Most are aimed at assisting the progress of the litigation. But the rules lump them all together in one list at CPR, r 25.1, many of which are discussed in later chapters.

1. INTERIM INJUNCTIONS (GOING TO SUBSTANTIVE RELIEF)

Interim injunctions are temporary orders granted by the court to regulate the position between the parties to an action, pending trial. They are coercive in effect: a mandatory injunction requires the respondent to do some defined act(s); a prohibitory injunction restrains the respondent from certain specified conduct. Failure to obey is a contempt of court. Because the orders themselves, and the consequences of breach, are very serious, the *general rule* is that applications for interim injunctions are made to a High Court or Circuit Judge, *not* a master or a District Judge, unless the case is within the latter's limited County Court trial jurisdiction[4], or the parties agree.[5]

It is important to remember that injunctions are a remedy, not a right, and so applications must be founded on an identifiable cause of action (for example, trespass, defamation, breach of contract), over which the courts have jurisdiction. Most injunction cases involve actionable torts against named defendants committed in England & Wales. If appropriate, an interim injunction may be granted to prevent a threatened wrong before it actually occurs - these are known as quia timet injunctions. Very occasionally (for example, where some but not all of the defendants are known), interim injunctions may be granted against 'persons unknown'.[6] As with all forms of equitable relief, whether or not to grant an injunction (interim or final) is a matter within the *discretion* of the court, which should be exercised with justice and proportionality and the overriding objective in mind.[7] These aspirations are fairly easy to articulate; what is more difficult is understanding how the court, in each individual case, goes about making a decision which achieves these results.

A. GENERAL RULE: *AMERICAN CYANAMID* GUIDELINES

Given the pre-trial context, it is as well to think about what the judge is being asked

---

4   Mainly claims up to £25,000, on the small claims or fast track

5   There are some other specialist exceptions. See BCP Table 37.1

6   See, e.g., *South Cambridgeshire DC v Persons Unknown* [2004] EWCA Civ 1280

7   See Sime, para 42.26/7

8   [1975] AC 396. Balance of 'hardship' might have been a better description. It is more likely to be the case that a mandatory injunction will cause more, and irreparable, hardship than a prohibitory injunction, but there is no underlying difference in principle between interim applications for either kind of injunction: *National Commercial Bank Jamaica Ltd v Olint Corporation Ltd* [2009] UKPC 16, [2009] 1WLR 1405.

9   Before that case, the courts had always

to do when considering whether to grant an interim injunction. Assuming the application is made on notice and both sides are present, the judge is being asked to make a decision on written evidence alone, which is usually conflicting, some of which may be wrong, and neither of which may tell the whole story. There is no testing of oral evidence, as there would be at a trial. In effect the judge is asked to make a premature decision, on limited and untested written information, about a form of relief which even if temporary may cause one or other side enormous financial or other irreparable damage.

For this reason, the *general rule* is that so long as the action is not frivolous or vexatious, that is to say, so long as there is a 'serious' (as opposed to a silly) issue to be tried, a decision *at this interim point* is reached by considering the so-called 'balance of convenience': which party would suffer more irreparable hardship by not getting what it wants at this stage? This is the well-known guidance set out in the leading case of *American Cyanamid v Ethicon*.[8] According to that case, a detailed examination of the merits of the case ought to be left to the trial, where witnesses can be heard and their credibility properly evaluated.[9] Thus, except in the special circumstances set out below, it is only as a *last resort* (to help tip the balance in those rare cases where it does not obviously favour one or other party) that the court at this *interim* stage should consider the substantive merits of the case[10] and attempt to prejudge the ultimate outcome.[11]

Over time a sort of DIY guide to help judges apply this general principle was devised, which tends to be set out as a series of steps to take and/or questions which the court should ask itself, namely:

(i)   Is there a 'serious issue' to be tried?

This is a very low hurdle. The court will therefore only investigate the merits to

---

considered the merits of the case in some detail to try and predict the outcome at trial. Lord Diplock (at 407) made clear in *American Cyanamid* that this was not the right approach: 'it is no part of the court's function at *this stage*

of the litigation to try and resolve conflicts of evidence on affidavits … nor to decide difficult questions of law which call for detailed argument and mature consideration'.

10   Beyond checking that there is a 'serious issue to be tried'.

11   Lord Diplock's short judgment in the *American Cyanamid* case sets out in detail how the balance of convenience is to be weighed up and is well worth reading.

the limited extent of satisfying itself that the claimant's cause of action has some substance in reality. It does not matter at this stage whether the chances of success are 20% or 80%.[12] If there is no serious issue to be tried (in other words, the chance of success is effectively 0%), the injunction will be refused.

(ii) Would the claimant be adequately compensated in damages?

If there is a serious issue to be tried, the court will then consider whether the claimant would be adequately compensated in damages were the injunction not granted. This is a sensible early question, since injunctions are equitable remedies which should not in any event be awarded if damages would adequately compensate the claimant. Damages might well be an adequate remedy in some contract cases, but are often considered *not* adequate in circumstances where the damage is non-pecuniary (for example, nuisance, trade secrets, negative covenants), or difficult to assess, or where the loss is irreparable (for example, a loss of voting rights). It will also be *very relevant* when considering this question whether or not the defendant would be likely to be *able to pay* any damages which might be awarded.

So, if damages would be an adequate remedy for the claimant (and the defendant could pay), then, again, the injunction would likely be refused. If damages would not be adequate remedy, however, then the court would look at the same issue (money as compensation) from the defendant's perspective, and ask itself the next question.

(iii) Would the defendant be adequately protected by an undertaking in damages?

An undertaking in damages is almost always required when an interim injunction is granted. This effectively is a promise by the claimant to compensate the defendant (and any other relevant person) for any loss caused by the imposition of the injunction

---

12 For an amusing case
    which did not even get
    over this initial hurdle see
    *Morning Star Co-operative
    Society Ltd v Express
    Newspapers Ltd* [1979]
    FSR 113

if it later appears that it was wrongly granted.[13] Here it is the *claimant's* ability to pay which is an important part of the equation. So, if money would put the defendant right in such circumstances (or others affected by the order) *and* the claimant could pay any damage award, then normally the injunction would be granted.

You might think of questions (ii) and (iii) as the 'money questions'. They are specific aspects of ascertaining hardship, which are logically considered first since they are often easiest to answer. If the scales of hardship are still evenly balanced at this point (as is often the case), then the court will go on to the next step.

(iv) Other factors weighing into the 'balance of convenience'

Most cases tip at this stage, where the court effectively puts into the balance all other factors in a case which are relevant to deciding whether the grant or refusal of an interim injunction would cause 'uncompensatable disadvantage'[14] to one side, and to what extent. Each case will be different, but the sorts of matters which can figure into this part of the equation are: loss of employment, loss of goodwill in a business, loss of market share, disruption to non-parties, the public interest in the outcome, the length of time to trial, special factors and so on. These are essentially the sorts of things that money can't easily buy back.

If the scales are still evenly balanced at this stage, then the court may be assisted by asking itself the next question.

(v) What order would best preserve the status quo?

In *American Cyanamid*, Lord Diplock said: 'Where other factors appear to be evenly balanced it is a counsel of prudence to take such measures as are calculated to preserve the status quo'.[15] The status quo in this context usually means the state of affairs pertaining before the conduct complained of, unless there has been

---

13 See CPR, PD 25A, para 5.1(1) and 5.1A (protecting other persons)

14 See Browne LJ's useful articulation of the *American Cyanamid* guidelines in *Fellows & Sons v Fisher* [1976] 1 QB 22, CA, set out in WB, Vol 2, Sec 15-10

15 *Op. cit.*, at 408

unreasonable delay, in which case it would be the state of affairs immediately before the application for the interim injunction. Immediately should not be taken too literally[16] but the claimant should act promptly to prevent the defendant's offending behaviour itself from becoming the status quo.

(vi) Only as a last resort should the court consider the substantive merits

In a case to which the *American Cyanamid* guidance applies, only very rarely will the court be justified in considering the merits of the case in detail, but if this aspect of a case is clear, it could go into the scales with everything else. The remedy is discretionary, and at the end of the day the *American Cyanamid* guidance should be applied with sufficient flexibility to give effect to the overriding objective.[17]

B.   EXCEPTIONS TO THE *AMERICAN CYANAMID* APPROACH

It is important to understand, and be able to identify, the situations where the *American Cyanamid* test does *not* apply, either because of an historical exception,[18] the intervention of statute,[19] or because one or more of the assumptions underlying the decision in that case is missing. For example, there are two very different sorts of circumstances when the court will decide the interim injunction application on the apparent strength of the cause of action. One is where the facts are not disputed and the law is clear, and applying one to the other is easy. In such cases the court will, quite happily, decide the matter 'on the merits', as it is called, because it will be obvious whom they favour. A trial is really unnecessary. The other situation is where it looks as if there will in fact never be a trial of the action because the decision at this interim stage will in effect amount to the final outcome. In such cases, the courts will again decide the matter on the merits, but much less happily. So that you do not confuse these two, I will refer to them as the 'happy' and 'sad' merits

---

16 See, e.g., *Play It Ltd v Digital Bridges Ltd* [2005] EWHC 1001 (Ch)

17 See, e.g., Laddie J's observations in Series 5 *Software Ltd v Clarke* [1996] 1 All ER 853

18 E.g., defamation cases

exceptions, respectively.[20]

Let's look at some of these exceptions to *American Cyanamid* in more detail.

(i) Freedom of speech

(a) Defamation cases

The general principle here is that an injunction to restrain an alleged defamation will *not* be granted, or if granted without notice, will be discharged, where the defendant pleads (or intends to plead) justification, unless the alleged libel is obviously untrue.[21] This is an historical exception[22] to protect free speech. It pre-dates *American Cyanamid* and is unaffected by it.[23] In effect, the public interest in freedom of speech takes *absolute* priority over any personal right to protect one's reputation by injunction and the individual is left to his (often not inconsiderable) remedy in damages.

But note that this very strict and stark rule does not extend to trade mark infringement cases, even where the trademark is used in comparative advertising (which might be said to 'bad mouth' the competition), nor to claims for damage to reputation not based on defamation. In short, to get the benefit of this particular exception, the cause of action must be *defamation*.[24]

Bear in mind, however, that the courts will not protect purveyors of obvious falsehoods and will check to see that the justification plea is not inherently implausible. Otherwise there is no consideration of merits, no consideration of any balance of hardship; if the defendant's plea of justification is a legitimate one, then no injunction will be allowed, end of story. This ancient guardian of freedom of speech is thus extremely protective where interim injunctions are sought; even more so than the human rights legislation.

(b) Other cases

It is with cases *other than* defamation where freedom of speech under Art 10 of the

---

19 See, e.g., s 12(3) Human Rights Act 1998 and Trades Union and Labour Relations (Consolidation) Act 1992, s 221(2)

20 Discussed below

21 See, e.g., *Greene v Associated Newspapers Ltd* [2005] QB 972. Allied defences, such as fair comment on a matter of public interest or privilege can also trigger the rule.

22 Notice the date of the leading case of *Bonnard v Perryman* [1891] 2 Ch. 269

23 As confirmed in the amusing case of *Bestobell Paints Ltd v Bigg* [1975] FSR 421. Obviously it also pre-dates the Human Rights Act 1998.

24 *Boehringer Ingelheim Ltd v Vetplus Ltd* [2007] FSR 29

European Convention on Human Rights is at issue, that s 12(3) Human Rights Act 1998 comes into play.[25] This requires the claimant to show a case which will 'probably succeed' at trial before an interim injunction will be granted which interferes with freedom of expression.[26] This clearly involves close consideration of the merits of the case, and so is another exception to (or at least an adaptation of) *American Cyanamid*.

Applications based on a right to privacy under Art 8 can also present a conflict with Art 10. There is no cause of action for privacy, as such, and this is an evolving field jurisprudentially. Interim injunctions in such cases are determined by applying *American Cyanamid*, but specifically weighing into the balance the public interest element. In other words a court will ask itself, in each case, whether the desire to keep the information in question private ought, in the circumstances, to yield to the right to free speech under Art 10, bearing in mind that neither Art 8 nor Art 10 takes precedence over the other in principle. In *Douglas v Hello! Ltd*[27] for example, the court would have been a lot more sympathetic to the happy couple's claim that the defendant magazine's desire to publish photographs of their wedding infringed their right to privacy had they not already sold the right to do so to someone else (so in fact privacy was not really the point!).

(ii)   The common law 'merits exceptions'
(a) 'Happy' merits cases: clear cut restraint of trade and similar cases
Where the facts are not disputed and the law is clear (so that the right to the remedy is clearly established) it will be straightforward to apply the one to the other and the court will be 'happy' to grant the relief sought at the interim stage. In effect, there is no serious issue to be tried (or no need for a trial) since the outcome is obvious.[28] This is somewhat analogous to a summary judgment situation (and indeed this may sometimes be an appropriate alternative application). Typical sorts of cases falling

---

]25 See *ibid*, applying *Cream Holdings Ltd v Banerjee* [2005] 1 AC 253

26 *McKennit v Ash* [2008] QB 73

27 [2001] QB 967

28 *Office Overload v Gunn* [1977] FSR 39, CA

within this exception include: clear-cut breaches of prima facie valid restraint clauses (or other negative covenants); clear-cut cases of breach of confidence; clear-cut sale of land cases; and cases generally where there is no arguable defence. Lord Denning described restraint of trade cases as in a 'special category',[29] but they are really just a common example of the sort of case where the remedy sought is justified on its face, thus rendering any balance of convenience irrelevant.[30] But it is important to note that if the claimant's case is not 'open-and-shut',[31] then the *American Cyanamid* principles would apply (unless the case falls into the next category).

(b) 'Sad' merits cases: interim decision effectively final

Sometimes the outcome at the interim stage will effectively dispose of the action and/ or render a future consideration of the case pointless, at least as far as the injunctive relief is concerned. This situation commonly arises when something is scheduled to happen within a relatively short period of time (for example, the transmission of a TV programme), and either it will be stopped or not, depending on the outcome of the interim application. As a result, there is unlikely to be a later trial (on that issue) because by then the injunction issue will be history. Alternatively, a future trial may come too late to be of any use.[32] In such cases, the court is unhappy, but feels compelled to decide the application on the strength of the cause of action because if the case never goes to a full trial, it is 'now or never'.[33]

It is important to understand that where the courts, exceptionally, decide the application on the substantive merits under either of these two types of 'merits exception', there must be *far more* than a 'serious issue' to be tried in order to succeed, that is, claimants must have a much more 'overwhelming' case to get the injunction. Wherever the outcome at the interim stage effectively gives the claimant his final

29 In *ibid*
30 *Lawrence David Ltd v Ashton* [1991] 1 All ER 385, CA
31 As in *ibid*, per Balcombe LJ
32 See, e.g., *Cream Holdings*, *ibid*.
33 See, e.g., *Cayne v Global National Resources plc* [1984] 1 All ER 225, CA

remedy, there must be a compelling reason to deprive the defendant of the chance to put his case at trial.[34] Claimants usually do have cases of this strength when the 'happy' merits scenario applies (for example, clearly established breach of negative covenant or no arguable defence) and so they get their remedy and are also happy. But they do not have to work very hard for it because the strength of the case will be obvious. By contrast, claimants are rarely able to show such an overwhelming case in a 'sad' merits situation, which likewise makes them feel sad when they lose the interim application. This is the most difficult scenario for any claimant seeking an interim injunction.

(iii) Mandatory injunctions

It is pretty clear now that there is no underlying difference in principle between interim applications for prohibitory and mandatory injunctions, but generally speaking the latter is apt to cause greater 'inconvenience' than the former. So mandatory injunctions are harder to get on that account. But some acts are easier to perform than others, so much will depend on the circumstances of the individual case, as Lord Hoffmann made clear in *National Commercial Bank Jamaica Ltd v Olint Corporation Ltd*.[35]

C.   PROCEDURE

The application is much like any other under CPR, r 23. Useful summaries are found in BCP's Checklists 19 and 20. Such applications may be made in any sort of case (even one allocated to the small claims track) and are usually made *on notice*. Thus the appropriate form is issued and filed, and served on the other side at least *three clear days* before the hearing. A *draft order* should be attached, unless the case is very simple. The application should normally be supported by *written evidence*. *Skeleton arguments* are usually required, especially in the High Court, and *costs schedules*

---

34 *Per Eveleigh LJ, Cayne v*   35 [2009] 1 WLR 1405
     Global, ibid p.233

should be filed by both sides 24 hours before the hearing.

The only justification for applying for interim injunctions (of the kind we have been discussing in this chapter) without giving the other side notice is *urgency*.[36] Where the application is made without giving formal notice to the other side, all reasonable attempts should be made to tell the other side what is going on (with informal notice, the other side may be able to attend).

A claim form should also have been issued, unless the case is so urgent there was no time to do this either, in which case an application by a claimant pre-action can be entertained. Some latitude is given for cases of this degree of urgency, so that informal evidence may be relied upon. It would be very unusual for a prospective defendant to want to apply for an injunction pre-action, and they can only do so with the court's permission (they must normally wait until they have filed an acknowledgement of service or defence in an on-going case).

In the absence of the other side, full and frank disclosure[37] *must be made* to the court; the applicant must explain why formal notice could not be given, and set out what was done to give informal notice. The advocate should also make a note of the hearing. To grant an injunction against someone who has not had his day in court is very serious indeed. An order granted on a without notice hearing will only last for such limited time as is necessary for the application to be resumed after proper notice is given to the respondent.

It is especially important to be aware of the relevant *undertakings* which may be necessary when injunctions are ordered or agreed - more will be required if the application is pre-action and/or without notice.[38] The undertaking (to the respondent or an affected third party) as to damages and the undertaking to serve the order on the respondent are the most obvious, but it may also be necessary to give an undertaking to issue and serve the claim form, to serve the notice of application,

36 Compare the position here with Search and Freezing Orders. A very rare exception is the secret 'super injunction' see Sime, 42.66. Note also that search and freezing orders' bring different considerations into play, see Ch. 7.

37 See Ch. 4

38 See generally PD 25A, para 5.1

to serve on the other side the evidence on which the application was based. In effect, whatever an applicant was unable to do because of lack of time, he will have to undertake to do as part and parcel of any order he is granted. Draft orders, which are in standard form, reflect this distinction between urgent and non-urgent cases.[39]

2. INTERIM PAYMENT (OF DAMAGES)

Interim payments are a means by which claimants can get some of their money remedy ('damages, debt or other sum, except costs'[40]) 'on account' as it were, before the trial or assessment of damages. Where:

(i) the defendant has admitted liability;

or

(ii) the claimant has already got early judgment against the defendant (for example, default or summary judgment), damages to be assessed;

or

(iii) where the court is *satisfied* that (if the claim went to trial) the claimant *would* obtain judgment for *substantial* damages from the defendant,

- then the court may order the defendant to make an interim payment to the claimant.[41] Grounds (a) and (b) speak for themselves - as to (c), the claimant must show that he would actually succeed on his claim (or part of it) at trial *and* that he would obtain judgment for a substantial amount of money. Substantial means not negligible or nominal, and should be judged in the overall context of the case, but it means that interim payments are not appropriate for most small claims track cases.

---

39 PF 39 CH and PF 40 CH, for pre-action and post-issue applications respectively. A computer disc containing the draft order should also be made available to the court if possible, so it can use it, amended as necessary, for any order it might make.

40 CPR, r 25.1(1)(k)

41 See CPR, r 25.7. If C's claim is for possession of land, the court should be satisfied that if the case went to trial the defendant would be held liable to pay the claimant a sum of money for the occupation of that land whilst the possession action is pending: CPR, r 25.7(d).

Indeed most applications for interim payments are made in multi-track cases.

The standard of proving the claim would succeed is the balance of probabilities, but it will likely be more difficult for a claimant to achieve this standard on the limited written material available to the court at this interim stage than it would be at trial.[42] The idea behind the interim payment procedure is to make it possible for a claimant to be awarded at an early stage some of the money which it appears clear he will obtain at the end of the day, and where it would be unjust to make him wait that long. The court has a discretion, but if the conditions are made out it will usually make an order unless there is some good reason not to. Bear in mind that ordering an interim payment runs counter to the general notion that defendants should not have to part with any money until final judgment has been given - so it is important to get it right. Certainly no-one wants the claimant to have to sell his wheelchair because the interim payment made to him needs to be given back to the defendant.

Thus, in the context of a summary judgment application by a claimant, where that application is dismissed, and the case continues to trial, it would be inconsistent also to grant the claimant an interim payment award. The court cannot simultaneously be satisfied to the requisite standard that the claimant would succeed at trial for interim payment purposes *and* that the defendant has a real prospect of success at trial. It might, however, be possible to have an interim payment where the summary judgment application has been dealt with by way of a *conditional* order (although this would depend on how doubtful the court is of the defendant's defence); indeed the making of the interim payment could be the condition.

Interim payments thus help tide claimants over during what can sometimes be a long period until trial or assessment of damages.[43] And there can be a benefit for the defendant too - if, for example, an injured claimant uses the money for early rehabilitative treatment, this might well reduce the overall amount of the claim.

42 Tests Claimants in FII *Group Litigation v Commissioners of HM Revenue and Customs*(No 2) [2012] 1 WLR 2375

43 Liability may well be admitted, but calculating damages can be very complex.

Indeed, sometimes interim payments are made voluntarily for this purpose.[44] And of course an interim payment would reduce the defendant's liability to pay interest at the end of the day.

It is obvious that interim payments are particularly useful in personal injuries actions, but important to note that they *are not limited* to such cases. Examiners like to test students on this.

Stringman v McArdle[45] (a pre-CPR case) decided that a claimant does not have to show a need for the money as a pre-condition of getting the order; only that the procedural requirements have been met. On the other hand, the relevant practice direction specifically requires the claimant to include in the written evidence supporting the application what the money will be used for.[46] *Stringman v McArdle* may still be good law, but later cases stress the undesirability of making an interim payment order which effectively ties the trial judge's hands (or runs the risk of overpaying the claimant). The interim judge will have to be very careful (and conservative) in predicting the sort of order which the trial judge might make. One has to be especially cautious as regards future losses, particularly when these might ultimately be catered for, not with a single sum, but with a periodic payments order.[47] To this extent, therefore, need will be highly relevant both as to how much to order by way of interim payment and, if choices have to be made, *for what aspect* of the claimant's losses.[48]

Multiple defendants

Where there are two or more defendants, if it is clear to the court that a specific defendant will be liable to the claimant, then, assuming the other procedural requirements are met, the court can order an interim payment against that one identified defendant, regardless of the fact that there are other defendants named in

---

44 For example, as part of the PI pre-action protocol. See Ch. 2
45 [1994] 1 WLR 1653
46 PD 25B, para 2.1(2)
47 These are very common with catastrophic injury cases and involve regular payments over what is often a very long time. If a big chunk of money has been expended with an interim payment award (for example, to buy a specially adapted house), this might mean there is not enough capital left at the end of the day to fund a periodical payment award. In a sense the 'need' for the new house becomes a foregone conclusion by the time of the trial. Coulson J sets out the principles well in *Brewis v Heatherwood & Wrexham Park Hospitals NHS Trust* [2008] EWHC 2526 (QB).
48 See *Cobham Hire Services v Eeles* [2009] EWCA Civ 204

the proceedings. In other words, even where there are multiple defendants, if the claimant can establish that he would recover substantial damages from one of them, the court can make an interim payment order against that one, if it sees fit.

Where, however, there are multiple defendants and it is *unclear* against whom the claimant will succeed, then an interim payment may still be ordered, but *only* if it is established that:

- The claimant will succeed against at *least one* of the named defendants, even if it is not clear which;

and

- *all* of the defendants are *either insured, public bodies* or defendants whose liability will be met by, for example, the Motor Insurance Bureau. [49]

These additional requirements are intended to safeguard the position if the 'wrong' defendant is required to make the interim payment, which could easily happen if it is not clear who will be held ultimately liable to the claimant. Where *only* insurance companies and public bodies are involved, no great injustice will occur if one of the defendants has to reimburse another at the end of the day. Otherwise, the claimant has to point the finger of blame clearly at the defendant from whom he seeks an interim payment.

Amount of interim payment

It is important that the court does not order an interim payment greater than the amount ultimately awarded at trial. Thus an interim payment must not exceed a '*reasonable proportion*' of the likely amount of the final judgment.[50] The rules are no more specific than this, to allow the courts to exercise their discretion from case

---

49 See CPR, r 25.7(1)(e). The Motor Insurance Bureau (MIB) picks up the tab for uninsured drivers.

50 See CPR, r 25.7(4)

to case, although in practice the amount ordered will be apt to cover the special damage claim, plus (perhaps) some proportion of the general damage claim, taking care not to fetter the trial judge's options.[51] But the wording of the order is left purposely wide. Counterclaims/set-offs and allegations of contributory negligence will obviously have to be taken into account.[52] The idea is that at the end of the day, the claimant recovers *more* by way of total damages than was awarded by way of interim payment.[53]

Note that if an interim payment has been ordered, no *mention of it should be made to the trial judge until all matters of liability and quantum are decided.*[54] There is an obvious risk of prejudice if the trial judge knows that an interim judge thought the case so clearly favoured the claimant. This is a *very important* rule which is forgotten at the advocate's peril - such could result in a mis-trial and a personal costs order.

Remember, too, that unlike a Part 36 offer,[55] an interim payment has no costs implications. It is not an offer of settlement in any way. Nor is it a payment into court. Rather it is an order or agreement that a defendant pay out to a claimant *now* some of what the defendant will, or will almost certainly, have to pay out to the claimant at the end of the trial or other assessment of damage.

Procedure

This is a fairly typical Part 23 interim application. It is made on *notice*, with supporting *evidence in writing* to include the matters set out at PD 25B, para 2.1, which are specifically geared to the nature of the interim remedy.[56] This includes the amount sought by way of interim payment, what the payment is to be used for, what the likely total judgment will be, the reasons for believing the grounds for such an order are made out, and so on. Documents in support (including medical reports) must be exhibited - defendants in personal injuries actions should obtain and file a

51 As discussed above
52 CPR, r 25.7(5)
53 Though the court has extensive powers to make 'adjustments' if need be, including orders that the claimant reimburse the defendant. See CPR, r 25.8
54 Unless the defendant does not mind, which would be rare. See CPR, r 25.9
55 See below, Ch. 15
56 There is also a useful summary at BCP, Checklist 24.

certificate of recoverable benefits.[57]

An application for an interim payment cannot be made before the time the defendent is given to acknowledge service has expired[58] (but otherwise should be made as soon as the desirability of doing so becomes apparent).

The application (like a summary judgment application) must be served on the defendant at least *14 days* before the hearing. A defendant should serve any evidence in reply at least *seven days* before the hearing date, and any further evidence in reply from the claimant must be filed at least *three days* before the hearing.[59]

Second or further applications for an interim payment may be made in appropriate circumstances.[60]

INTERIM PAYMENTS VERSUS PROVISIONAL DAMAGES

Word of warning! Do not confuse interim payments with provisional damages
They sound as if they could be the same thing, but they are very different. Interim payments, which can be awarded in *any sort* of case, are about a claimant getting some of his ultimate damage award *before* the trial of the action. Provisional damage claims are limited to *personal injuries claims only*, and really focus on what happens (or might happen) *after* the trial (or settlement).

Damages are usually calculated on a one-off, once-and-for-all basis, immediately after liability is established or as soon thereafter as damages can be properly assessed. This is not well suited to situations where, at the time of assessing loss and damage, there is merely a *chance* that some deterioration in health (for which the defendant would be liable) will occur in future. If that chance is assessed on a once-and-for-all basis, it can only be calculated in percentage terms. This can result in the claimant either being over-compensated, if the disease or deterioration never happens, or (more problematically) under-compensated, when it

---

57 CPR, PD 25B, para 4.1   58 CPR, r 25.6(1)   60 CPR, r 25.6(2). See WB
                             59 CPR, r 25.6(3)-(5)   para 25.6.7

does happen, because the damages awarded earlier reflected merely the possibility, not the actuality. The problem is particularly pronounced in cases where there is a relatively small chance of some dreadful disease occurring.

To remedy this situation, the courts are given the power to make awards of what are known as 'provisional damages'. They work like this: in assessing immediate damages on a once-and-for-all basis, it is assumed that the *named* disease or deterioration in question will not happen, and so is *left out of account altogether*. But if it does occur within a *specified time*, the claimant[61] can come back to court and have that aspect of his losses accurately assessed.[62]

There are essentially four conditions:

(a) Condition 1: The claim for provisional damages must be set out in the *particulars of claim*.[63]

(b) Condition 2: The possible future disease or deterioration must be '*serious*' in nature. To be serious, the condition must be something beyond ordinary wear and tear. Conditions like osteoarthritis pose problems because we all are apt to suffer them with age.[64]

(c) Condition 3: It must be '*proved or admitted*' that there is a '*chance*' of the future disease or deterioration occurring. In other words, it is only *how* the loss is to be compensated which remains at issue, not the nature of the loss, nor the defendant's responsibility for it. The chance of deterioration is usually fairly easily established by the medical evidence.

(d) Condition 4: The future development or deterioration must be of the claimant's '*physical or mental condition*'. So, provisional damages are limited to this one, albeit important, aspect of a personal injuries claim. It does not apply to the chance that a claimant might lose his job or his

---

61 Or his dependents if the claimant has died. See Fatal Accidents Act 1976, s 3.

62 See, Senior Courts Act 1981, s 32A; County Courts Act 1984, s 51

63 CPR, r 41.2(1)

64 See, e.g., *Willson v Ministry of Defence* [1991] 1 All ER 638

house in future; if causally connected, these sorts of loss continue to be assessed on a once-and-for-all basis.

Even if these conditions are all met, it is still a matter of the court's *discretion* whether to make a provisional, rather than a conventional, damage award. Common sense considerations apply, including which form of judgment would dispense better justice and how easily it will be to know when and whether a serious deterioration has in fact occurred.[65]

If an order for provisional damages is made, it should specify both the nature of the disease or deterioration in question *and* how long a period the claimant has to make a future application to the court should the worst happen.[66] Provisional damages are hard enough on a defendant, without the time-frame being completely open-ended. Having said that, the period can be expressed to last for the claimant's life, in appropriate circumstances. A claimant making an application for the further assessment of damages must give the defendant or the defendant's insurers at least 28 days notice. Many years might have passed since the original order and it may take some time to find the files. Subsequent procedure is much like that for an interim payment, which conveniently brings me back to my initial warning: be sure you know the difference between interim payments and provisional damages!

---

65 *Ibid*

66 See generally CPR, r 41.2(2) and PD 41A, para 2.1. An example of a provisional damage award is given at the annex to PD41A.

revision tips

- The interim remedies discussed in this chapter mirror the claimant's substantive claim. Others are aimed at assisting the litigation process. CPR, r 25.1 lumps them all together in one list but it helps to make the distinction.

- You must be able to recognise both the guidance in, and the name of, the *American Cyanamid* case. It is worth reading Lord Diplock's judgment.

- You should have a good grasp of the main situations where the principles in *American Cyanamid* do *not* apply - and *why*. Check your syllabus to know which exceptions to focus on.

- Be clear about the *distinction* between interim payments and provisional damages. They sound similar, but they are very different.

It is worth reading ...

Lord Hoffmann's judgment in *National Commercial Bank Jamaica Ltd v Olint Corporation Ltd* [2009] UKPC 16, [2009] 1 WLR 1405. This is a Privy Council case, which might just get you feeling sorry for banks (if that is possible)! Lord Hoffmann's judgments are a pleasure to read - this one is short, and to the point, but no less enlightening for that. Note in particular what he has to say about without notice applications and the court's approach to granting (interim) mandatory injunctions. You should be getting the message now that the courts do not much favour applicants who do not give notice to the other side when (as is usually the case) they should.

The White Book's procedural guide to interim payments is clearly set out in summary form at D8-001 (Vol 1, Section D).

CHAPTER 7

Making litigation meaningful:
freezing and search orders[1]

There are some forms of interim injunction which are not geared to the claimant's ultimate remedy or relief, but which aim to make the litigation meaningful, either by ensuring the there are funds to enforce against if the claimant wins, or by preserving crucial evidence. These are known, respectively, as *Freezing* and *Search* orders, although the older case law will refer to them by their pre-CPR names of Mareva Injunction and Anton Piller Order[2]. It is important both to distinguish them from the more 'bog standard' type of interim injunction discussed in the last chapter, and also to appreciate just how draconian these forms of order are.

1. FREEZING ORDERS

Freezing orders are designed to stop defendants (or potential defendants) from wilfully turning themselves into paupers or hiding assets in order to thwart a claimant's ability, if he wins the case, to get his hands on them. If there are no assets, there will be no way to execute judgment[3] and the claimant will get no money! Freezing orders make litigation meaningful for a claimant because a 'paper' judgment is of little use. Freezing orders thus restrain defendants from 'disposing of', 'dissipating'

---

1 At the time of writing these forms of injunctions had been taken off the BPTC syllabus (for 2013/14). This could change in future years, so always check carefully what is being examined when revising for exams.

2 Named after the leading cases of *Mareva Compania Naviera SA v International Bulk Carriers SA* [1980] 1All ER 213 and *Anton Piller KG v Manufacturing Processes Ltd* [1976] Ch. 55. The CPR gave them more modern and descriptive names.

3 As to execution generally, see below at Ch. 19. It is usually claimants who seek freezing orders against defendants, and so I use those terms here, but anyone in a 'claimant-like' position can apply, e.g. a counterclaiming defendant or defendant against a third party.

or even 'dealing with' certain of their assets so as to frustrate the enforcement of any judgment the claimant may obtain against them. The amount 'frozen' should not normally exceed the value of the claim. It is, of course, very serious to stop people using their own money before they have been judged liable to pay some of it to another person, so such orders are not granted lightly. After all, maybe it will be the defendant who wins the case! So, although the granting of such orders, like all injunctions, is discretionary,[4] the conditions for obtaining freezing injunctions are very strict. They are as follows:

(i) Jurisdiction

The claimant must show a substantive cause of action over which the court has jurisdiction (or in respect of which it can act). An injunction is a remedy, and thus needs a cause of action to which it relates. The order cannot 'simply be made in the air'.[5] As a general rule, therefore, an applicant must be able to point to proceedings underway or about to be commenced, so as to show where and on what basis he expects to get judgment against the defendant. It is no longer strictly necessary to show that the substantive action is to be brought in the English courts,[6] although this will usually be the case.

(ii) Strength of case

The claimant must show he has a 'good arguable case'. This is a middling standard; higher than that required for an *American Cyanamid* type of injunction (which is about as low as it gets), but not as high as, say, summary judgment applications.

(iii) Assets

The claimant must show that the defendant has assets in (or exceptionally out of) the jurisdiction.

---

4   S 37(1) Senior Courts Act 1981 enables the court to grant interim injunctions where it appears 'just and convenient' to do so, and 'on such terms and conditions' as it thinks just.

5   Per Lord Mustill in *Mercedes-Benz A.G. v Leiduck* [1995] 3 All ER, PC, at 929

6   See CJJA 19882, s 25 and *Fourie v Le Roux* [2007] 1 WLR 320, HL

Assets come in all shapes and sizes: money, land, valuable things, like cars and jewellery. So long as the asset belongs to the defendant, or he can get his hands on it, then it can be the subject of an order. Normally, the assets must be in the jurisdiction, but in exceptional circumstances, the court will make a 'worldwide' order affecting assets both here and/or abroad.[7] The relevant assets must be identified with some degree of precision, so the court can make the order. Normally an order would freeze named assets up to a maximum value, not to exceed the most that the claimant could win in the case.

(iv) Risk of dissipation

The claimant must show that there is a 'real risk' of the dissipation or disposal of those assets so as to render judgment of no value. This is the *critical* requirement, and the most difficult to establish, in part because there is rarely direct evidence of such a risk. It is usually to be inferred from some conduct or attitude of the defendant's, but an expression of general apprehension on the part of the claimant will not be enough.[8] The ease with which a defendant could dispose of assets will be an obvious consideration, but the claimant's ability to enforce judgment is also key. Remember, too, that it is not the job of a freezing order to provide security for the claim;[9] its purpose is to obviate the risk that a defendant's actions might render himself 'judgment proof'. A useful list of factors relating to this aspect of freezing orders is set out at BCP, para 38.13.

Have a look at the standard form of freezing injunction annexed to PD 25, which includes a version for both domestic and worldwide orders, to get a feel for what the order typically sounds like.

---

7   These will only be ordered, effectively, when it is shown that there are no or insufficient assets in the jurisdiction and that there are identifiable assets out of the jurisdiction. See, e.g., *Derby v Weldon (No 1)* [1990] Ch. 48. CA

8   See, e.g., *O'Regan v Iambic Productions* [1989] 139 NLJ (Sir Peter Pain)

9   The order does not put the claimant in any better position than any other creditor. But note that the fact that a defendant has a dubious credit history does not in itself justify the making of an order: *Mobile Cerro Negro Ltd. V Petroleos de Venezuela SA* [2008] 1 Lloyd's Rep 684 (Walker J at para 36).

on an application for a search order, it is always incumbent on a claimant to have considered whether some less draconian measure would suffice.[14]

In any case, remember that a search order is *not* a search warrant. It is directed to a named person, not a place. The defendant can refuse entry, and no one should be kicking in doors or otherwise forcing entrance. It is not a police operation! Having said that, a failure to comply with a search order would amount to a contempt of court and itself could be rather damning evidence against the defendant in the upcoming trial to which the order relates.

Given the harsh nature of search orders, there are a host of *safeguards* and rules designed to ensure that they are carried out properly and fairly, and that any property belonging to the defendant is returned as soon as its evidential value has been preserved (for example after photocopying). These are set out very clearly at PD25A, paras 7.2 to 7.11. In addition, an example of a search order is annexed to the practice direction. Take a careful look at these. Note especially the possibility of including what are sometimes called 'ancillary orders' which augment a search order. These typically require the defendant to disclose relevant information, either as regards the evidence in question or the cause of action itself. None of these are unusual in themselves, since they may be required or ordered in the ordinary course of litigation. In the context of a without notice search order, however, they become part and parcel of the draconian nature of the injunction.

As you might appreciate, there is an uncomfortable interface between search orders and an individual's privilege against self-incrimination, that is, the right to refuse to answer any questions, or produce any document or thing, if to do so would expose that person to criminal sanctions.[15] Although in one sense rather damning to assert this privilege, the consequence of relying on it has been to

---

14 E.g., order to produce or deliver up documents, order to inspect, etc. See generally list at CPR, r 25.1.

15 See, e.g., wording of Civil Evidence Act 1968, s 14(1) which is declaratory of the common law: *Rio Tinto Zinc Corpn v Westinghouse Electric Corpn* [1978] AC 547, p. 636.

thwart the execution of many a search order, given the types of cases in which such orders tend to predominate.[16] As a result, the right to rely on the privilege was *removed by statute* in cases involving *intellectual property and passing off*, although any incriminating evidence obtained *cannot be used in any related criminal trial*.[17] In other sorts of cases, the threat or risk of self-incrimination has been successfully removed by the promise, in writing, not to use the evidence obtained in any criminal proceedings - a sort of contractual version of the statutory provision which can, as appropriate, be included in the order.[18]

There are some points to note about *both* freezing and search orders:

(i) Secrecy

In both cases, the application is almost invariable made *without notice*, because *secrecy* is essential. Given that the claimant is effectively saying to the court "*If the defendant knows I am asking for this order he will hide his money or destroy the evidence*", then giving notice of the application would defeat its purpose. The situation may also be urgent, but the key is secrecy. Usually applications are made *after issue* of proceedings, but *before* those proceedings have been *served* (because of the secrecy aspect). In urgent cases, the application can be made 'pre-action', that is before proceedings have even been commenced.

(ii) Level of Judge

Historically, these applications could generally only be made to a *judge* in the *High Court*. Only rarely is the County Court or any interim judge empowered to grant freezing or search orders. Since April 2014, however, *nominated* Circuit Judges in the County Court can made freezing orders in any sort of case.[19] This is a logical adjunct to other increases in the County Court's jurisdiction and

---

16 The right at common law to rely on the privilege was upheld by the House of Lords in *Rank Film Distributors Ltd v Video Information Centre* [1982] AC 380

17 Senior Courts Act 1981, s 72

18 See, e.g., *AT and T Istel Ltd v Tully* [1993] AC 45, HL

19 County Court Remedies Regulations 2014 (SI 2014/982)

workload brought in at that time. Search orders, however, remain essentially the purview of High Court judges only.

(iii) Full and frank disclosure

The claimant must make *full and frank disclosure* of any facts which militate against the order being given. This is the general rule where without notice applications are concerned, but is particularly important where such severe injunctions are at stake. Any failure to make full and frank disclosure will result in the order being discharged.

(iv) Affidavit evidence

Written evidence in support of such applications is made by way of *affidavit, not* witness statement. This is a rare example of where affidavits are mandated by the rules.[20]

(v) Draconian orders

These orders are both very draconian, and you want to be aware of the various principles and *safeguards* which protect defendants as far as appropriate. These are clearly set out in both the White Book and BCP. So far as freezing orders are concerned, be aware of the limitations and *various grounds of variation or discharge.* With search orders, be aware of the safeguards in *execution.*

(vi) Undertakings

The various *undertakings* that a claimant gives when such orders are granted are very important. The undertaking as to damages is even more crucial with these sorts of injunction than with a 'normal' interim injunction - the more harm the order

---

20 PD 25A, para 3.1

21 See, e.g., *Columbia Pictures v Robinson, op.cit.*

may cause, the more assurance the court will need that the claimant's undertaking in damages has substance. The various undertakings that might be needed in any given case are set out in the sample orders appended to PD 25.

Bear in mind that, however exciting these forms of injunction are, freezing and search orders are to be treated as *exceptional*. Most litigation is able to proceed without them. They are different from the average interim injunction, and different from each other, although they share some common features and both give litigation value to a claimant by preserving evidence for trial or assets for enforcement. The fact that one of these exceptional orders may be appropriate in a case, does not mean that the other will be - but it is not unheard of for both orders to be made against the same, very mad or very bad defendant. [21]

revision tips

- Both the White Book and BCP have some useful procedural summaries to help with revision. BCP's Checklist 19 reviews without notice procedure generally. The WB's procedural guides D 17.1 and 17.2 deal specifically with Freezing and Search orders.

- Be sure you can distinguish between 'normal' interim injunctions and these exceptional forms of order (and that you can distinguish between freezing and search orders).

- Try 'grading' on a scale of 1 to 10 the strength of cause of action required for the various interim applications we have been discussing so far. Assuming 10 to be the highest, summary judgment applications would be right up at the top and *American Cyanamid* cases would be right down at the bottom. The rest are somewhere in between- freezing orders might be about a 5; search orders about an 8?

It is worth reading ...

Another Hoffmann (J as he then was) judgment in the case of *Lock International plc v Beswick* [1989] 1 WLR 1268. Well written as always. This was in the days when the search order was called an Anton Pillar order, but what the judge had to say about the strength of case required and the draconian nature of the order still holds true.

PART TWO

on to trial

CHAPTER 8

Track allocation and case management

Once it seems clear that a case will proceed towards a trial, it will have to be allocated to (and managed on) one of three tracks: (1) the small claims track (this is essentially citizen's justice); (2) the fast track (for basic, no-frills litigation) or (3) the multi-track (for more complex or 'needy' cases and/or where the trial will last more than one day). Most defended actions will be able to proceed along a predictable path, with directions in more or less standard form (fine-tuned for any particular need of a case) and given without the parties having to attend court. This leaves case management (and other) hearings for the more complex and important issues.

Once a defence is filed[1] a court official will *provisionally* allocate the case to a suitable track (largely based on the value of the claim), and serve on each *party a notice of proposed allocation*. This notice will require the parties to file a completed *directions questionnaire* and serve them on each other by a specific date, which in small claims track cases will be no less than 14 days (and in other cases no less than 28 days) after service of the notice.[2] If a party is unrepresented, the court will send such person the appropriate directions questionnaire - otherwise the notice will simply 'inform' the parties how to obtain it (by downloading it off the internet, basically). If the case looks suitable for the fast or multi-track, the notice will also require that the parties *file proposed directions* by the date specified in the order. The notice may also require

---

1   If there is more than one defendant, then this will happen when the last defendant has filed his defence, or the time for doing so has expired: CPR, r 26.3,(2).

2   CPR, r 26.3(1)(b) and 26.3(6)

other tasks to be completed by dates specified in the order (in multi-track cases this might include the filing of costs budgets or a disclosure report[3]) and will give the appropriate court address for doing so.

If a party fails to file a completed directions questionnaire in time, then if the claim is an ordinary County Court money claim, then a reminder will be sent, but further non-compliance (usually within a further seven days) will result in the claim or defence (as the case may be, depending on who failed to comply) being *automatically* struck out.[4] For other sorts of cases, the court will make such order as it sees fit in the circumstances, which can range from simply giving further directions to striking out.[5] The defaulter normally picks up the tab.

Once the completed questionnaires have been filed, the *procedural judge* (that is, a master or District Judge) will make an 'official' allocation. If, before this happens, the parties are before the court on a different matter (for example an application for summary judgment), it may take the opportunity to deal with allocation at that hearing and/or dispense with the need for directions questionnaires and/or give appropriate case management directions at that time. This is just common sense - if the parties are already there, it is an efficient use of court time to complete as many tasks on that occasion as possible.[6]

Not surprisingly, the information on the directions questionnaires is geared to making sure the case ends up on the right track. The parties should consult and cooperate on allocation issues, but it is the claimant who pays the allocation fee. Note that allocation will be deferred where a 'stay'[7] has been requested or ordered to allow for early settlement of the action.[8] If the court thinks it necessary, it can hold an allocation hearing, but it will *often deal with track allocation and give directions without* doing so, in which case it will notify the parties in writing by means of a *notice of allocation.*[9]

---

3 See below
4 CPR, r 26.3(7A)
5 See Ch. 13

6 See generally PD 26, para 2.4.
7 A temporary halt to the proceedings which can effectively become permanent. See Ch. 13

8 CPR, r 26.4
9 CPR, r 26.9

The track to which a case is allocated should reflect both its value and its case management needs (often the latter follows from the former). When assessing the former, the court will disregard interest, costs and any amount not in dispute; as to non-financial considerations, rational factors apply - for example, the nature of the remedy, the complexities (legal or factual) of the case, the importance of the outcome to persons not directly involved, the extent of oral evidence required and so on. Note that the court is entitled to allocate a claim to a track higher or *lower* than its financial value alone would indicate, having regard to such considerations.[10] Money isn't everything!

The overriding objective requires that cases are dealt with fairly and cost-effectively, and the three track options are designed to facilitate this. A brief summary of the attributes of each is set out below.

1. THE SMALL CLAIMS TRACK

Broadly, the small claims track is designed to provide a proportionate procedure for the simplest of cases. It is the normal track for defended claims not exceeding £10,000.[11] There are, however, refinements or exceptions in certain kinds of cases, including claims raising allegations of dishonesty, certain landlord and tenant cases and personal injuries claims where the value of the pain, suffering and loss of amenity element exceeds £1,000, in which case the normal track will be the fast track (even though the total claim does not exceed £10,000).[12]

There may, of course, be other reasons why a claim falling within the value range of the small claims track is not allocated there. These might include the

---

10 There used to be a veto on going lower, but this was lifted in April 2013. See CPR, r 26.7/8.

11 This figure was recently raised from £5,000: CPR, r 26.6(3)

12 See CPR, r 26.6(1)-(4) and r 26.7(4).

complexity of the case, the nature of the allegations or the need to make use of the more standard features of litigation, which are missing from this most basic track. The hallmarks of the small claims track are as follows:

- On allocation, a date for a hearing (and its length) will be fixed and *directions* given, usually in *standard form*. Directions differ according to type of cases, for example holiday cases, building disputes and so on, but common to all are standard directions about exchanging only the *documents which each party will by 'relying on'* in the case,[13] bringing original documents to the hearing, and an obligation to *inform the court if the case settles*.[14] If necessary, special directions can be given and/or a preliminary appointment fixed.
- *Other common features of litigation are missing*, including wider orders for disclosure, most interim remedies (except interim injunctions), most case management directions, most evidential rules, Part 36 offers, and the traditional approach to the conduct of the proceedings. The hearing is conducted on an *informal* basis, usually in the District Judge's room. If the parties agree (or if space is at a premium), the hearing will be conducted in private. Evidence is not generally given on oath.[15] Crucially, *no expert evidence*, either written or oral, may be given without the court's permission.[16]
- The small claims track is designed to be navigated by the lay person, and so the scope for recovering *costs is severely constrained*. They are essentially limited to disbursements (for example, court fees) and out-of-pocket expenses. In particular, the idea is to exclude lawyers (who are expensive), and so the cost allowed for legal assistance is almost

---

13 This is more limited than for the other tracks. See generally Ch. 9.

14 See generally Appendix A and B to PD 27

15 See generally CPR, r 27.8

16 CPR, r 27.5

non-existent (if the court felt it was important that a party be legally represented, this would be a good reason to allocate to the fast track). Appeals, however, are now dealt with in the same way as any other case.[17]

2. THE FAST TRACK

The fast *track is the 'Easyjet'* of the system, providing a no-frills, value-for-money route to justice for relatively inexpensive, straightforward and predictable claims. It steers a middle course between the bare necessities on offer on the small claims track and the more complex handling of cases on the multi-track, although it resembles the latter more than the former. Most defended claims falling within the £10,000 to £25,000 monetary band, and where the trial will take *no more than one day*, will be allocated to the fast track.[18] Its hallmarks are:

- Few or no interim hearings
- Standard directions
- Speedy timetable with a virtually immutable trial date fixed by the court when the case is allocated
- Limited numbers of experts
- Single joint expert evidence (on any one issue) admitted by means of a written report is the norm
- One day trial
- Trial costs are 'fixed'; 'summary assessment' of other costs[19]

---

17 See Ch. 19   18 CPR, r 26.6(4) and (5)   19 See Ch. 18 on costs

On the fast track, the case will be actively managed to a *tight timetable* usually lasting no longer than *thirty weeks*.[20] This usually allows enough time to get the essentials completed, but little scope for embellishment. Case management directions will generally only be given at *two* stages: when the case is *allocated* to the track and once the parties have filed *pre-trial checklists*.[21] As on all the tracks, many directions are predictable and so are given using a standard form,[22] but they are not given on a 'one size fits all' basis. The court will 'tweak' the form as necessary to produce directions which are able to meet the requirements of the case at hand.

Directions on allocation

This first set of directions, which follows the (official) track allocation of the case, will lay down the case management *timetable*, including setting the trial date or 'window'.[23] Typically the matters to be dealt with in this first instance will include the identification and exchange of various items of evidence: documentary evidence, witness statements, expert evidence.[24] The court will have looked at the parties' statements of case and considered the information included on the directions questionnaire (that is what it is for!). Its main concern at this point is to equip the parties with the means (by reference to exchanged evidence) to identify and narrow the issues.[25] It will hold a hearing only if necessary.

Pre-trial directions

The second stage for giving directions occurs after pre-trial checklists have been filed, or dispensed with.[26] Again standard form directions will be tailored to the circumstances of the individual case. At this point the focus is on checking compliance with previous directions which have been given, and on the impending trial. Typical issues and directions at this stage include how evidence is to be received at trial,

---

20 CPR, r 28.2(4)

21 These were previously known as listing questionnaires. See CPR, PD 28, para 2.1

22 Model standard form directions are set out in the Appendix to PD 28.

23 Like any 'window of opportunity', this is a given period of about three weeks during which the trial will take place, the precise date to be determined closer to the time. See typical timetable in Sime, table 28.1

24 Usually to be exchanged in that order. See generally PD 28, para 3 (para 3.12 contains the typical timetable).

25 PD 28, para 3.3

26 PD 28, para 7

agreeing and filing bundles of documents and so on. More complex cases may need more sophisticated directions about the time to be allowed for examination and cross-examination of witnesses and so forth - it is, after all, only meant to be a one day trial. The parties should seek to agree such directions between themselves, which the court can then endorse (or make a different order) if it sees fit.[27] The claimant must pay a listing fee (which is not refundable) and a hearing fee (which is refundable in whole or in part if the case settles before trial).[28] If the fees are not paid, a reminder will be given, and if they remain unpaid, the claim will be struck out. Not less than two days before the trial, both parties should file a statement of costs.

In fast track cases, the court will attempt to limit the giving of directions to these two occasions, and so will normally give directions *without the need for a hearing*. A crucial feature of this track is that the trial date, or 'window', is practically set in stone, so applications must be sought *promptly* if different or other directions are required. Strict adherence to the timetable is encouraged. The parties can agree among themselves to do things in a different order or at a different time, but *only* so long as none of the following *three* key dates is altered or adversely affected:

(i)   the date for returning the directions questionnaires;

(ii) the date for returning the pre-trial checklists; *or*

(iii) the trial date/window.

The date for these three case management events can *only* be changed (or 'varied' as the rules put it) with the court's *permission*.[29] In particular, the court will not allow a failure to comply with directions to lead to the postponement of the trial 'unless the circumstances of the case are exceptional'.[30]

A fast track trial should only last one day. Were it to run over, the judge will

---

27 PD 28, para 7.2

28 See Sime, para 28.10

29 CPR, rr 26.3(6A) and 28.4(2)

30 PD 28, para 5.4(1). An exceptional circumstance might, for example, include unforeseeable problems with the evidence or an unexpected change of solicitors. See CPR 26.3(6A).

normally sit the next day to finish the case off. Remember, too, that the trial judge may depart from the procedural judge's directions as to the conduct of the case. No doubt most witness statements will stand as the evidence-in-chief[31] and, given that the natural or designated time for speeches and cross-examination will be limited, it will be necessary for advocates to be very focused in their questioning.

As regards costs, the normal rule is that on the fast track these will be dealt with summarily at the end of the trial. This means the judge will decide there and then how much the loser will have to pay toward the winner's costs, assisted by the various statement of costs submitted by the parties before the trial. As to the trial costs themselves, these are fixed by reference to the value of the claim.[32]

3. THE MULTI-TRACK

The multi-track is for the more complex and time-consuming cases, in other words those where more than £25,000 is claimed and/or those requiring closer management and/or those requiring a trial lasting more than one day. Part 8 claims and specialist proceedings (for example TCC cases) are usually treated as appropriate for the multi-track. Many of the same 'classic' directions given in fast track cases are also relevant in multi-track cases, but the time frame may need to be more generous, or additional and more focused directions given. Multi-track cases are particularly prone to rack up costs, which is why the Jackson reforms have concentrated on these in the drive to ensure that they are managed efficaciously. Hard choices may sometimes be required. The idea is that (for cases commenced on or after 1 April 2013) if a direction or order applied for is not considered proportionate to the case or relevant issue, it should not be given, however reasonable it might otherwise be.

---

31 See below, Ch. 17

32 See CPR, r 28.2(5) and see generally Ch. 18

As with the other tracks, once a case is allocated to the multi-track, the court will give directions (which might include a requirement that the parties consider ADR) and hold such procedural hearings as may be necessary.[33] If the court cannot set a trial window/date at this stage then it should do so 'as soon thereafter as is practicable' - a usefully elastic description.[34] Directions must be case-sensitive on the multi-track, which must be capable of meeting the needs of claims from £25,000 to £25,000,000. Thus some multi-track cases will proceed much like those on the fast track; others will require more robust intervention.

'Docketing' has been introduced to ensure judicial continuity, especially for those cases which need continual and consistent supervision. The idea is that such cases are allocated not just to the multi-track, but to a specific procedural judge, who will then be primarily (but not necessarily exclusively) responsible for overseeing the management of the case and giving appropriate directions.[35]

Effective case management means that the court will intervene only as, and to the extent necessary. The parties are encouraged to do their part by agreeing case management directions, and submitting these to the court for approval (thus avoiding the need for a hearing, and so reducing costs).[36] When giving or agreeing any case management directions, both the parties and the court should use the relevant standard direction template as a *starting* point. At the allocation stage, for example, the court will only ratify agreed directions if they include the essentials as a minimum, namely by setting out a timetable by reference to calendar dates, including a proposed trial date (or window), and providing for the exchange of documentary, factual and expert evidence.[37] The procedural judge will consider proposed agreed directions carefully, and use them if appropriate, but at the end of the day it is the court which has ultimate responsibility for the management of the case.

Thus some case management on the multi-track can be done 'on the papers'

---

33 See PD 29, para 4 for the range of options for allocation directions on the multi-track.

34 CPR, r 29.2

35 This is a sensible aspiration, although how well it works in practice remains to be seen.

36 CPR, r29.4

37 CPR, PD 29, para 4.6/7. See also Sime fig 15.2 for directions template.

based, like those on the fast track, on completed directions questionnaires, pre-trial checklists, proposed directions and so forth), but where this is not possible, then one or other of the following may be necessary:

A.   CASE MANAGEMENT CONFERENCES (CMC)

This is the *principal device for keeping more complex litigation focused and on track*, and can be held immediately upon allocation and thereafter *as necessary* to monitor and further the progress of the case. The purpose of these hearings is to ensure that the real issues are identified and directions given so that each case is managed according to its needs.[38] Notice is given to both parties (at least three clear days), but in practice it should be possible to anticipate the need for such hearings.

Before the first CMC in multi-track cases, the parties must now file and serve:

(i)   In non-personal injury cases, disclosure reports [39]
(ii) Proposed directions (agreed if possible)
(iii) Costs budgets (agreed if possible)

Those attending a CMC need to be well versed with the case, and all relevant documents should be brought to court (in a case management bundle). If legal representatives are not adequately informed, prepared or capable, a wasted costs order will normally be made.[40] It may assist to provide the court with case summaries.

At the CMC, the court will review the statements of case, allocate the case to a track (if this has not already happened), check compliance with any previous orders or directions, review any costs budgets (and make any necessary revisions), record any relevant agreement on the conduct of the case, and make any directions needed to move the case along. It is always incumbent on the court to promote the use of

---

38 See generally PD 29, para 5   39 See Ch. 9   40 PD 29, para 5.2(3)

ADR, and if appropriate a stay may be granted to allow the parties to engage in such a process, although the court will be careful that these do not become unproductive delays disguised as attempts to settle.

Typically, either by (court sanctioned) agreement or at a CMC, directions (with deadlines) will cover the usual sorts of management needs,[41] including:

- the scope of disclosure of documents required
- the nature of the expert evidence, and how it should be obtained; experts on both sides will be more common on the multi-track
- disclosure of witness statements
- filing of pre-trial checklists
- whether it is possible to fix a trial date

Directions in a multi-track case might also include things like amendment of statement of case, use of witness summaries, and orders for inspection of relevant property. Parties should always attempt to deal with all case management needs at a scheduled CMC. This clearly saves money! If something arises which is not necessarily dealt with as part of case management (for example, application for an interim payment), and it is clear that the application is opposed, the claimant should issue and serve notice in time for it to be heard at the scheduled CMC. The more unusual the application, the more notice should be given, so the opposing party can made effective representations.[42]

B.   COSTS MANAGEMENT

Costs management is a new invention of the Jackson reforms. These new rules have been amended once already since April 2013, so let's hope that's it for a while.

---

41 PD 29, para 5.3

42 See, e.g., *Norbrook Laboratories Ltd v Carr* [2010] EWCA Civ 1108

All Part 7 multi-track cases commenced after 22 April 2014 are governed by the *costs management regime* set out in CPR, r 3.12-3.18 *unless* (a) the claim is for or worth an amount in excess of £10 million; or (b) the claim (unusually for such cases) is subject to scaled or fixed costs.[43] This is obviously the large majority of multi-track cases. Note also that it is always possible for the court (on a case by case basis) to decide to apply costs management to any case (which would otherwise be ineligible), or to disapply it in any case, if it so chooses.[44] The regime does not apply to Part 8 claims.

The idea behind *costs management* is that, in appropriate cases, this will go hand in hand with *case management*. Because costs at the end of the day are usually awarded to the party who succeeds, there has been a tendency for litigants to 'throw money' at cases, thinking this will help them win and thus recover from the loser at the end of the day whatever they have spent in so doing. This, not surprisingly, drives up costs overall. The idea behind costs management is to set an overall budget, proportionate for the needs of a case, and then make case management decisions based on that budget. Thus projected costs budgets are prepared by the parties and either agreed or approved by the court. These budgets are then used as a basis for making case management decisions. It's like putting in a new kitchen - you need to keep your requirements and financial outlay in balance.

Costs management can itself generate costs, so it will not be appropriate for absolutely every case - certainly not if the case is very complex or unpredictable. The idea is to impose budgetary restrain on those cases where this would be both feasible and effective to keep costs proportionate. Cases subject to a fixed costs regime don't need it and the exceptionally expensive cases won't benefit.

Where costs management applies, what essentially happens is this:

---

43 An example is a claim in the Patents County Court: CPR, r 45.30ff

44 See CPR, r 3.12 (as recently amended). The expression 'unless the court orders otherwise' is a common and useful discretionary power in the CPR.

(i) The parties prepare and exchange litigation budgets. There is a standard form for this purpose.[45] If costs do not exceed £25,000, only page one of the form must be completed. If the costs exceed £25,000, then all five pages must be completed. As you might expect, the budget must be verified with a statement of truth.

(ii) Unless the court orders otherwise, any party who fails to file a costs budget as and when ordered to do so by the court, will be treated as having filed a budget comprising *only the applicable court fees*. This is a draconian sanction,[46] no doubt intended to keep solicitors on their case management toes (litigants in person do not have to file costs budgets). The idea is that when this happens, they race back to court to be excused from this punishment and with a proper budget, so that proper case management can at least be achieved from this point.[47]

(iii) Costs budgets should be *agreed by the parties* (one of whom will probably have to pay those costs at the end of the day, so both so should be on their guard). In the absence of agreement, the court will review the budgets, and only approve such budgets at each stage of the litigation as is *proportionate.*

(iv) Costs management orders record the parties' agreed costs budgets, or (where these are not agreed) the court's approved costs budget.[48]

(v) So far as possible, thereafter the case is managed *in accordance with* the approved budget. In making directions (for example at a CMC), the judge should have regard to the available budgets, which may lead him or her to substitute a more proportionate direction than that proposed. In particular, parties are required to give an *estimate of the cost*:
- of any disclosure directions sought in a disclosure report[49]

(which may lead to a more limited disclosure order if the budget requires), and

---

45 See example in Sime, fig 16.1

46 See, e.g., *Mitchell case*, discussed in Ch. 13

47 As to 'relief from sanctions' see Ch. 13

48 CPR, r 3.15(1)

49 See Ch. 9

  - • when seeking permission to rely on expert evidence[50] (which
    may lead to some restrictions on the number of experts to be called).

(vi) As the case progresses, amended budgets may be filed and (if
proportionate) approved. This should typically be done at a *costs
management conference*, which (in order to keep costs down) can be dealt
with in writing or by telephone. It will be quite important for solicitors
to learn not only to get budgets right in the first place, but to keep a
close eye and seek amendments as soon as the situation arises. It is
early days and there will be a steep learning curve.

(vii) Finally, at the end of the litigation, the recoverable costs of the winning
party are assessed in accordance with the approved budget.[51]

C.   LISTING HEARING[52]

These are not all that common. If there are matters outstanding following the filing
of pre-trial checklists, which usually happens after evidence has been exchanged
but before the case is set down for trial, a listing hearing may be necessary. These
hearings concentrate on matters affecting the trial *date* and are useful where it is
proving difficult getting a case ready for trial. The main focus will be listing the
case for trial.

D.   PRE-TRIAL REVIEW

Typically a pre-trial review, if needed, will take place about eight to ten weeks
before the trial. This gives the court the opportunity to see that earlier orders have
been complied with and make relevant directions as to the *conduct* of the trial - in
particular, how the evidence is to be adduced and what time limits will be placed on
cross-examination, speeches and so forth.[53]

---

50 CPR r 35.4(2) and see
Ch. 17

51 See Ch. 18

52 These are hearings
pursuant to CPR, r 29.6(4).
Pre-trial checklists used
to be called 'listing
questionnaires', and so
these hearings came to be
called 'listing' hearings.

On the multi-track, again the parties may between themselves and by mutual consent agree to vary the case timetable so long as doing so does not affect or make it necessary to change the dates of any of the following *five* key case managements events, namely the date set for:

(i)   the return of directions questionnaires,

(ii) any case/cost management conference

(iii) any pre-trial review,

(iv) return of pre-trial checklists *and*

(v)   the trial date/window.[54]

If any of these dates would be affected, the permission of the court must be sought.[55] As you might expect, the court will be very reluctant to vacate these dates, especially if the only excuse is a dilatory litigant!

---

53 CPR, r 29.7

54 On the fast track it is three case management events which may not be varied without the court's permission; the multi-track rule includes these same three, but adds two more multi-track features, making five altogether

55 CPR, r 29.5

revision tips

- In mainstream litigation, provisional allocation by a court official is followed by completion of directions questionnaires and then *formal track allocation* by a procedural judge.

- Remember that the allocation procedure essentially applies to case where liability is contested.

- Remember the basic values for the tracks, but do not forget that other aspects of a case (complexity or public interest) can affect where it will be allocated. Cases can be allocated to a track *below as well as above* that indicated by its value. You did not use to be able to go lower, so the examiners might test you on that.

- Where possible (even on the multi-track) directions are given without a hearing. This save money!

- Costs management now applies to Part 7 multi-track cases (unless the costs are fixed/scaled, the value exceeds £10 million or the court decides otherwise). This is all very new and has been refined once already since 2013, so watch this space in future years. Come back to this topic when reading Chapter 13 on sanctions, and especially the severe sanction for failing to file a costs budget as required.

- Think in terms of the 'big three' (fast track) and 'big five' (multi-track) case management events which may not be affected or changed *without the court's permission*.

It is worth reading ...

The content of the Directions Questionnaire. This is Court Form N181 (Form N180 is especially for small claims track cases) and it is available on the WB on-line service which you can access through Westlaw. It is only 5 pages long and will tell you a lot about what issues the court needs to deal with as, and after, it allocates a case.

CHAPTER 9

Documents and things:
disclosure/inspection/further information

Once a case has been allocated to a track, it is into the second half of the litigation process, which is dominated by disclosure of documents and related processes by which the parties - to the extent that they have not done so already - acquire relevant information about the nature of the case against them. This allows the parties to assess (or re-assess) the true strengths and weaknesses of their respective cases and so helps to narrow the issues and encourage settlement. Much of this exchange of evidence should in fact now happen during the pre-action phase.

An order for disclosure of *documents* heads the list of the (often standard) directions given on all of the tracks (unless it is thought to be unnecessary),[1] although on the small claims track disclosure will generally be much more limited than on the other tracks.[2] It is hard to think of a case which would not involve at least some documentary evidence (invoices, receipts, letters, records, wage slips and so on). So, documents come first - but they are not the only things with evidential value. Parties also acquire relevant information by means of requests or orders that relevant *things* be preserved, inspected, and examined for the purposes of litigation. It might be the car, whose brakes failed and caused an accident; or the equipment an employee was

---

1   Because, for example, disclosure has already taken place. See below and PD 28, para 3.2

2   See below and PD 27, Appendix B

using when she was injured at work. If it is appropriate for an expert to look at these things and give an opinion on what went wrong, the expert will need access to them.

Parties can also request straight out *information* from their opponents, if the circumstances warrant it. These used to go by the somewhat sinister name of 'interrogatories' and could stop a case in its tracks by the sheer volume of (often feigned) curiosity; but the CPR now ensures that only legitimate requests will be sanctioned. If used properly, they can be very effective in ferreting out a weak case.

One thing to notice in the discussion which follows is that each of these types of orders is a typical (and usually uneventful) part of the normal litigation process. There are times, however, when such orders are made even when there is no relevant litigation going on (yet), or against people not involved in ongoing litigation. In such cases, special rules apply.

1. DISCLOSURE OF DOCUMENTS

Disclosure of documents is the longest standing, and one of the most important ways in which relevant evidence is exchanged in litigation. When he took on the task of re-wiring the country's civil litigation system in the 1990s, Lord Woolf recognised the essential value of what then went under the rather nautical term 'discovery'. But he put much of the blame for the length and costs of litigation on a process which at the time required a very wide range of documents to be disclosed.

Typically, this was the stage where cases 'went to sleep' under the old rules (which were open to tactical exploitation of various kinds). Lord Woolf referred in particular to the 'curse' of the photocopier (now we have the curse of the internet). Not surprisingly, it was felt that excessive disclosure led to an expensive, unwieldy and time-consuming process, often to little evidential purpose. For this reason, the CPR rules (on what was re-branded 'disclosure') are aimed at keeping this aspect of litigation *focused and proportionate* - and under court control. Further refinements were added in April 2013.

Orders for disclosure of documents form part of the normal litigation process. They can also, exceptionally, be ordered against parties who are not (at that moment anyway) being sued. It is important to distinguish between these two situations.

A.   IN THE NORMAL COURSE OF LITIGATION

(i)   Fast Track and Multi-Track Disclosure

The idea behind the disclosure rules is to ensure that the process is effective, yet proportionate, and able to adapt to the variety of cases which can come before the courts. To this end, disclosure in fast track and multi-track cases can take *one* of two pathways:

(a)   in fast track claims, multi-track personal injury claims[3], and other multi-track claims where the court so directs, disclosure is governed by CPR, r 31.5(1), which starts from the premise that parties should give *standard disclosure*;

(b)   all other multi-track cases (for example, complex commercial cases and such like) are governed by the new '*menu-option*' procedure laid down in CPR, r 31.5(3)-(8), added by the Jackson reforms.

(a) Standard Disclosure

Standard disclosure requires each party to disclose in advance of trial the *existence* of every disclosable *document* which they have, or have had, in their *possession, power*

---

3   The litigation needs of
     personal injuries actions
     are pretty predictable
     whatever their value/track.

or control. This is usually accomplished by *exchange of disclosure lists.*[4] Further, each side must allow the other side to inspect such of those documents still in their possession which are not privileged or otherwise protected from inspection. Once written notice of the desire to inspect such documents has been given, inspection should be permitted within seven days.[5]

It is important to appreciate that this is actually a two-stage process - *first, disclosure* by list, followed by *inspection* - although sometimes the word 'disclosure' is used to refer globally to both aspects. Orders for disclosure are generally made on allocation or at a case management conference. Compliance is usually straightforward, so applications to the court will not often be necessary. Inspection can take place either by giving a party the opportunity to come and look at the documents, or by sending photocopies to them. There is a right to request the latter, if reasonable copying costs are paid.[6] Inspection can even take place by electronic means. What is sensible varies from case to case and essentially depends on how many documents there are and what form they take.

Thus unless the court orders otherwise, the usual order for disclosure in cases governed by rule 31.5(1) is an order to *give standard disclosure.*[7] This requires[8] a party to disclose only:

   (i)   the documents on which he *relies;*

and

   (ii) the documents which could -

        - adversely affect his own case;

        - adversely affect another party's case;

        - support another party's case;

and

   (iii) the documents which he is required to disclose by a relevant practice direction.

---

4 CPR, r 31.10. The parties can agree in writing to disclose without making a list.

5 CPR, r 31.3/31.15. There is a right to inspect documents which are not protected by privilege and so on, and so if one party, for no good reason, (and despite reminders) forces another to have to apply to the court for an order to inspect, then that party will no doubt pay for their intransigence in the form of the costs of the application.

6 CPR, r 31.15(c)

7 CPR, r 31.5(1)(a)

8 CPR, r 31.6

In a nutshell, *(i)* and *(ii)* amount to all documents which either help or hurt[9] your own case, or help or hurt another party's case. They come close to, but do not exactly equate to all documents which are 'relevant' (so do not use that term when describing standard disclosure in an examination) - for example, it has been held that these categories do not cover documents relevant only to credibility.[10] As regards *(iii)*, relevant PDs are those governing pre-action conduct and PD 31B on electronic documents. The latter seeks to ensure effective disclosure without parties getting hopeless mired in cyberspace.[11]

So-called 'train of inquiry' documents (those on the 'far end of the spectrum of materiality' which are not themselves relevant, but which could contain information which may lead to such documents) were the bane of the old system, and it is important to note that they are very intentionally *not* part of *standard* disclosure. It is possible to ask the court for such an extended order, but it would take some very effective advocacy to persuade it to do so.[12]

Remember too that standard disclosure can be *limited* or *dispensed with*, either by the written agreement of the parties or by court order.[13] This would happen, typically, where disclosure has effectively taken place already, usually in the pre-action phase. It is very important to realise, however, that parties *may not agree* between themselves to *widen* the ambit of disclosure. *Only the court* can order this[14], which it will only do if proportionate and necessary to achieve the overriding objective. This will be rare, even on the multi-track.

(b) Menu Option Disclosure

Standard disclosure was an improvement over the old rules, and it works well to keep the process within bounds, up to a point. Some multi-track cases, however, are so complex and document-driven, that even standard disclosure can be overwhelming.

---

9 Practitioners sometimes have to explain the purpose of these rules to their clients (who may baulk at 'helping' the other side) usually by pointing out that it is a two-way street.

10 *Favor Easy Management Ltd v Wu* [2011] 1 WLR 1803

11 PD 31B gives detailed guidance on the maintenance, preservation and exchange of disclosable e-documents. See WB, para 31.6.5. for details.

12 See, e.g., discussion at BCP at 50.14, referring to Coleman J's comments in *O Co. v M Co.* [1992] 2 Lloyd's Rep at 350-1

13 CPR, r 31.5(1),(b),(c)

14 CPR, r 31.5(1)(a)

It was thus felt necessary to create more scope for making proportionate and bespoke orders, on a case-by-case basis. Hence the introduction of menu option disclosure.

In *non-personal injury multi-track* claims, the menu option system applies, unless the court orders otherwise.[15] Menu option disclosure breaks down into three stages, which is focused around the case management conference ('CMC').

Disclosure report

Not less than 14 days before the first CMC, each party must file and serve a disclosure report, verified by a statement of truth, which should describe relevant documents, where they are (including details of storage of electronic documents, and completed electronic questionnaires if appropriate) and the estimated the costs of giving disclosure (which should tally with the party's costs budget[16]). It should also set out what disclosure directions are sought. The disclosure report is a way of getting the parties (as well as the court) to think carefully about this part of the process, knowing that time is money and costs are budgeted.[17]

Agreed 'proposal' for directions

Not less than seven days before the first CMC, the parties must seek to agree a proposal to put to the court about disclosure, which is in keeping with the overriding objective of dealing with cases justly and at proportionate cost. The parties can meet in person or by telephone. Any proposal must be filed with the court, which *may* approve the proposal without a hearing. If it does, this is a bit like DIY disclosure orders. It could save a lot of court time and expense!

---

15 CPR, r 31.5(2)   16 See Ch. 8   17 There is an example, in
                                                Sime, fig. 31.2

CMC disclosure direction (from the menu)

If the court does not make disclosure directions without a hearing, it will do so at the CMC, *choosing from the menu of options.* Standard disclosure is one of the options; so too is a form of 'train of inquiry' disclosure. Other options include (i) that a party disclose the documents on which it relies, and at the same time request any specific disclosure it requires from another party and (ii) that where practicable disclosure be given by each party on an issue by issue basis. Not surprisingly, the court can also make any other order it thinks appropriate or dispense with (further) disclosure altogether.[18] The point here is that the court should make an order having regard to the overriding objective, the available costs budgets, and the need to act proportionately and limit disclosure only to what is really necessary to deal with the case justly.

Note also that the court may at any point give directions as to *how* disclosure is to be given, including what searches are to be undertaken, whether lists are required, whether disclosure should take place in stages and so forth.[19]

Whatever pathway a case is on, and whatever the extent of disclosure ordered, it is important to remember some key points:

Not just paper

The first point is that 'documents' are *not limited to paper,* and include 'anything in which information of any description is recorded' - for example discs, audio tapes, video cassettes, computer programmes, electronic data bases and so forth. Only one copy need be disclosed, although copies with *significant* modifications will be treated as *separate* documents.

---

18 The menu is set out at   19 CPR, r 31.5(8)
    CPR, r 31.5(7)

(b) Possession or control

Secondly, a party's duty to disclose documents is limited to documents which are or have been in that party's *control*, that is, if -

- it is or was in his physical possession;
- he has or has had *a right* to possession of it (just as, for example, UK patients are entitled to their heath records by virtue of the Access to Health Act 1990);

or

- he has or has had a right to inspect or take copies of it.[20]

(c) Reasonable search

Note also that although parties are now generally required to disclose a narrower, more focused range of documents than once was the case, the disclosing party must make a *'reasonable search' for all disclosable documents.* What is reasonable will depend on common sense factors (for example, the number and significance of documents involved, the nature of the proceedings, the ease and expense of retrieval), the circumstances of the case and the overriding principle of proportionality.[21]

(d) Disclosure statement

A *disclosure statement* must be included on the exchanged list, indicating an understanding of and compliance with the duty to disclose, as well as making clear, where relevant, when and why it has not been reasonable to search for a document. These statements must normally be signed by the *parties personally* (since they have the primary responsibility to make full disclosure,) *not* their solicitors (who nevertheless should have explained early on to their client about the need to preserve documents for disclosure).[22]

---

20 CPR, r 31.8(2)

21 See CPR, r 31.7/PD 31A, para 2. The court may give directions on searching in menu option cases: r 31.5(8)(a).

22 There are exceptions where a party is not an individual (in which case a human representative will sign the statement) or the electronic disclosure questionnaire is used. CPR, r 31.10(6)-(9), Annex A to PD 31A and PD 31B.

(e) List in three sections

The exchanged list sets out disclosable documents in three discrete sections, which effectively tells the other side: (1) these are the documents I still have and which you may see; (2) these are documents which I have but you may not see and (3) these are disclosable documents I used to have but do not have them any more.[23] The second section typically includes *privileged* documents. They go in the list because their existence needs to be disclosed (although usually this is done in very vague terms), but the other side is not, at this stage anyway,[24] entitled to see them. The most common privilege claim in this context is legal professional privilege.

Finally, note the following points about disclosure in the normal course of litigation:

(f) Immediate inspection of certain documents

A party may ask *at any time* to see a document which has been *'mentioned in'* a statement of case, witness statement, affidavit or (to some extent) an expert's report.[25] This is a common sense rule. Obviously, if the document in question has been mentioned in one of these other documents, its existence is known and so there is no need to wait for the exchange of disclosure lists. Inspection can follow immediately.

(g) Possible limitations on inspection

The court can impose terms on the ambit of inspection (for example, limiting inspection of confidential documents to a party's medical and legal advisors) or agree that inspection may be disproportionate to the issues involved and so need not take place.[26] In *Webster v Ridgeway Foundation School Governors*, for example, inspection of a redacted version of the school's data base recording the behaviour of pupils was a huge task and regarded as disproportionate.[27]

---

23 See example in Sime, fig 31.1
24 An expert's report, for example, may be privileged from inspection at this stage, but will ultimately have to be exchanged if it is to be used at trial. See below Ch. 17.

25 CPR, r 31.14. A document is mentioned if specifically or directly alluded to. *Rubin v Expandable Ltd* [2008] 1 WLR 1099

26 See CPR, r 31.3(2). It is for the party who does not want to allow inspection to flag up the matter in the disclosure list and apply for the appropriate order if necessary.

(h) Specific disclosure

Sometimes litigants omit to list all pertinent documents in their disclosure list. If a party can identify a document or a class of documents missing from the other side's list (perhaps because it was referred to in one of the other documents that had been disclosed) then an application may be made to the court for disclosure and/or inspection of that particular document(s).[28] This is known as *'specific'* disclosure/inspection. Application is by notice, specifying the order sought and the facts which lead the applicant to believe the document (which must be described with reasonable precision) is disclosable. Where the document sought should have been covered by standard disclosure and/or its disclosure is in keeping with the overriding objective, then specific disclosure will usually be given (and vice versa). Such orders are not limited to inadequate disclosure lists; they can come in handy at various stages of the litigation process. Specific disclosure also forms part of one of the menu-option directions.[29]

(i) Use of disclosed documents

There has always been an important principle that a party inspects documents on the understanding, express or implied, that they will only be used for the purposes of the litigation in which they are disclosed, and not for a 'collateral purpose'. However, once the documents have found their way into the public domain, for example by being read out in open court, any such undertaking ceases to be of effect, *unless* the court orders otherwise. Further, even if a document has not been made public, the court has power (although it would use it sparingly) to sanction its use for a collateral purpose.[30]

(j) Penalties for non-disclosure

The court will impose penalties on a party who fails to make proper disclosure and/or inspection. One of the most serious would be to order that the party in

27 [2009] EWHC 1140 (QB)
28 CPR, r 31.12
29 See, e.g., *Dayman v Canyon Holdings Ltd* (2006) LTL 11/1/2006 and see menu-option in CPR, r 31.5(7)(b).

30 See generally CPR, r 31.22. This is a complex area, but the rules attempt to tread a middle ground between ensuring disclosed document are only used for the immediate litigation purpose, thus limiting their negative impact on the disclosing party; and, recognising that, when documents (and the information in them) have become public, it is hard to justify stopping the one party who may most need to use the document from doing so.

default *may not* rely on the documentary evidence in question, unless the trial judge gives permission.

(ii) Small claims track disclosure

Don't forget that in small claims track cases, different rules apply. Parties there are only required to disclose those documents on which they intend to *rely* at trial, such documents to be exchanged by the parties no later than 14 days before trial.[31]

B. EXCEPTIONAL DISCLOSURE ORDERS (AGAINST NON-PARTIES)

Disclosure of documents is a litigation tool and so an *important general rule* has been that it is *only* available against a party to litigation. You cannot go wandering up and down your street seeking disclosure of documents from people you are not suing! Of course, nowadays, as pre-action disclosure is seen as a way of achieving fair settlement of claims without the need to litigate, so the exceptions to this rule have increased. In many ways the exceptions are close to becoming the rule. Nevertheless, it is still helpful to look at them from this perspective.

In one sense, disclosure under the pre-action protocol procedure is clearly an exception to this general rule, since no action will have been officially commenced at that point. Indeed, the whole point of the pre-action protocols is to avoid the need for proceedings. But it is part of a formal pre-action procedural process, so might be viewed as widening the rule (or the notion of litigation) to include not only the act, but also the foreplay.

In addition, there are some important, and more long-standing, exceptions to the rule that disclosure is only available against a party to the litigation to which it relates. It is important not to confuse them - examinations often test the novice's ability to distinguish between them.

---

31 CPR, r 27.4(3)

(i)   The rule in Norwich Pharmacal

This is a common law exception, which provides a procedure for getting disclosure of the *identity of wrongdoers*, so that a claim can be made against them.

To paraphrase Lord Reid in the leading case of *Norwich Pharmacal Co v Commissioners of Custom & Excise*:

> If, whether through any *fault of his own or not*, a person gets mixed up in the transactions of others so as to facilitate their wrongdoing, he comes under a duty to assist the person who has been wronged by giving him full information and disclosing the identity of the wrongdoers.[32]

The key component of the test[33] is that the person who may be required to disclose the information must have *facilitated*, whether unwittingly or not, the *wrongdoing* of others.[34] It is the *identity* of those others which must be disclosed. It is very important to understand that *mere witnesses* to an event come under *no* such duty and *cannot be made* to disclose what they saw *before* an action has even been commenced (they can of course be compelled to come to court to give evidence at trial).[35] It does not take much involvement to be a facilitator, but being a mere witness is not enough.[36] In addition, the information sought must not be protected by privilege.[37]

Remember, too, that the facilitators need not *necessarily* have done something wrong themselves – in the *Norwich Pharmacal* case itself, the defendants were so-called 'innocent facilitators'. In lots of cases, however, facilitators have committed their own wrongs. Applicants must have a legitimate interest in the information, and not merely wish to satisfy their curiosity. Typically, but not exclusively, that interest will be the desire to pursue a legal claim against the wrongdoer once they find out who they are. But remedies can be sought 'by court proceedings or otherwise'.[38]

Norwich Pharmacal orders are only available from the High Court because they

---

32   [1974] AC 133, at 175, HL (my emphasis).
33   In its pure form. There have been some extensions at the margins. See discussion at BCP, 50.98
34   The principle was extended in *Murphy v Murphy* [1999] 1 WLR 282 where an order was made against a person who created a discretionary trust to disclose to a potential beneficiary the names of the trustees so that the former could contact the latter to discuss a possible distribution to him. There was no suggestion of wrongdoing, as such, on the part of the trustees, although the applicant might have wanted to challenge their actions with trust property. Some think this a generous interpretation of the principle, but

derive from its inherent jurisdiction. They are not limited to disclosure of documents, and can include answering questions or providing a 'narration of facts'. The remedy, however, is *discretionary* and even if all the other requirements have been satisfied, the court may refuse the order if, for example, there is some public interest in doing so.[39]

This is a kind of *pre-action* disclosure, because until the name of the wrongdoer is known, no action can be brought against him. But it is known by the name of the leading case, so be *very careful* not to confuse it with the procedure discussed below. In a nutshell, a *Norwich Pharmacal* application is appropriate when *the applicant knows he has a good claim against someone, but does not know who that someone is.* It will be for the 'facilitator' to supply that information. There have been cases extending the ambit of this form of disclosure to include, additionally, information to help the applicant assess the strength of and even the nature of the case against the wrongdoer. If this trend continues, there may be an eventual merging between this form of pre-action disclosure and that discussed in (b) below. *But it is important to be able to distinguish between them.*

The procedure for making the application is a little involved since it derives from the common law, and varies depending on whether the facilitator is innocent or not. If the former, the applicant issues a *claim form* against the 'facilitator', seeking disclosure of the identity of the wrongdoer. An interim application is then made *on notice* (to a master in the QBD, a judge in the ChD), unless urgency or secrecy justifies not doing so, for example, where the order is to be annexed to a Freezing or Search Order.[40] Once the identity of the wrongdoer is disclosed, the proceedings against the facilitator have achieved their objective and so come to a natural end - a fresh claim can now be brought against the newly identified wrongdoer. Remember: if you already know the identity of your wrongdoer, you do not need a *Norwich Pharmacal* order!

---

the relief needs to be 'flexible' so that it is 'capable of adaptation to new circumstances': per *Lightman J, Mitsui & Co Ltd v Nexen Petroleum UK Ltd* [2005] EWHC 625.

35 See Ch. 17

36 See, e.g., *Harrington v Polytechnic of North London* [1984]

37 See Ch. 17

38 For example, by dismissal from employment or deprivation of pension rights. See, e.g., *Ashworth Hospital Authority v MGN Ltd* [2002] 1 WLR 2033

39 See, e.g., *Interbrew SA v Financial Times Ltd*, The Times, 4 January 2002 (at first instance)

40 See Ch. 7

If the claimant is also suing the 'facilitator' for his own wrongdoing, as is commonly the case, the application for this special form of disclosure is made as an interim application in that action. Once the (other) wrongdoers are identified, then they can be joined to the action or new proceedings brought against them.

It is the applicant who pays the costs of these applications, but these may be recovered from the wrongdoer at the end of the day.[41]

(ii) Statutory pre-action disclosure (from a 'likely' future defendant)
This form of pre-action disclosure is governed by statute and is available in both the High Court and County Court.[42] Somewhat confusingly for beginners, it is known as 'pre-action disclosure', as if it were the only one, so be sure you are able to distinguish it from the *Norwich Pharmacal* order. Statutory pre-action disclosure is appropriate where the applicant *knows* who the defendant would be, but does not know whether the case is strong enough to make it worthwhile pursuing the claim.

Over the years this kind of pre-action disclosure has evolved from being very limited in its scope[43] to being generally available in any sort of case, but not often necessary. Before the days of pre-action protocols and access to medical records, a typical situation where such an order was sought might be one where the applicant went into hospital with a minor complaint and came out with a serious medical condition. Until the applicant (and his advisors) got a look at his notes to find out what went on in the hospital, it was difficult to gauge whether the suspicion that the doctors had been negligent, and so could be successfully sued, was supported by the evidence. This is what the statutory pre-action disclosure allowed him to do. Pre-action protocols now generally serve this purpose, but of course the application may still be required if, for example, the protocol is not complied with or a hospital does not comply with a request under the Access to Health Records legislation. Most

41 Assuming the wrongdoer loses. See generally Ch. 18

42 Senior Courts Act 1981 ('SCA 1981), s 33 and County Courts Act 1984 ('CCA 1984'), s 52.

43 For many years it was only available in personal injuries and fatal accident cases.

44 I am paraphrasing. See the actual wording of CPR, r 31.16(3)(a) & (b). The applicant cannot really become a party to the subsequent proceedings unless he or she does something to instigate them.

45 CPR, r 31.16(3)(d)

46 CPR, r 31.16(3)(c). So any and all documents sought under this form of pre-action disclosure must be documents which would in due course be subject to standard disclosure: *Hutchison 3G UK Ltd v O2 (UK) Ltd* [2008] EWHC 55 (Comm).

cases nowadays involve commercial transactions.

Thus, the courts have power to make an order for disclosure of material documents against the respondent where both that person and the applicant are 'likely' to be parties to 'subsequent proceedings'.[44] It is therefore available against a *future* defendant whose identity is known and who is in *possession* of *material* documents, the early disclosure of which will *save costs or encourage settlement*.[45] The application is made by way of interim application in the anticipated litigation (that sounds weird, I know). Such disclosure is limited to *documents* which would be disclosable in the ordinary course of litigation.[46]

Over the years there has been judicial consideration of what 'likely' means in the context of the rule (the wording of which has changed somewhat over the years).[47] Lord Denning's broad interpretation (of the original wording) that it amounts to being able to say that a claim 'may well' be brought by the applicant against the defendant, depending on the outcome of the disclosure,[48] has come under some threat from time to time.[49] If, however, the applicant has to show too strong a case at this point, it would defeat the purpose of the remedy, and it now seems clear from *Black v Sumitomo Corporation*[50] that there is no requirement to show that the claim is likely to be brought, as such; just that if it were brought, the applicant and the respondent will be the likely parties, and in this context 'likely' means 'may well' rather than 'more probably than not'. Generally, therefore, the court will not look deeply into the merits at this stage, although if the case is weak on its face, this would militate against an order being made. In any event, such disclosure should not be used as a 'fishing expedition' (or a 'speculative punt' as we now say) or to force disclosure of a document, the need for which is not made out.[51] And, as you would expect, any application will be determined in keeping with the overriding objective. Even if the court has the power to make the order, there is still a discretion to refuse to do so if,

---

47 Before the CPR the wording included reference to whether a claim was 'likely to be made', but this was dropped from the current rule. There are still lots of 'likely's in CPR, r 31.16, but they refer to parties, not claims. So the pre-CPR cases are not binding, as such, but still give useful guidance. After all, you cannot have parties if you do not have a claim. See discussion in leading case of *Black and others v Sumitomo Corpn and others* [2002] WLR 1562

48 *Dunning v Liverpool Hospital Board* [1973] 1 WLR 586

49 As in *Burns v Shuttlehurst* [1999] 1 WLR 1449, where it was said the applicant had to show a reasonable basis for the claim.

50 *Op.cit.*

51 See, e.g., *Alan Kneale v*

for example, it is oppressive or otherwise not in the public interest.

So this form of pre-action disclosure *differs* from the *Norwich Pharmacal* order in several respects, namely:

- It derives from statute.
- It is *limited to disclosure of documents* which would be subject to *standard disclosure* in due course.
- It caters for the situation where a (prospective) claimant knows who his defendant would be, but he does not know, until he sees the documents, whether the case is worth pursuing.

The costs of applying for these types of pre-action disclosure order are usually borne by the person seeking the order, although if the court takes the view that the respondent forced an application unnecessarily (because it was obvious the court would make the order), it may award costs to the applicant.

(iii) Orders against 'strangers' to on-going litigation

Once a case has commenced, a party may be able to get an order for the production of relevant documents by a 'stranger' to that litigation, in other words, someone who is *not* one of the *parties* to it. This is allowed where the non-party has control over documents which assist the applicant's case and disclosure would help fairly dispose of the action and/or save costs.[52]

This is not a form of pre-action disclosure, but it is an exception to the general rule we started with because the person against whom the disclosure is sought is not a party to the proceedings to which the disclosure relates. If the court did not have this power, the only way a party to litigation could get access to

---

Barclays Bank plc (trading as Barclaycard) [2010] EWHC 1900 (Comm).

52 See SCA 1981, s 34/CCA 1984, s 53, which grant the power, and CPR, r 31.17(3)

53 A person can be required, by means of a witness summons, to attend court to give oral evidence and/ or to produce documents. See CPR, rr 32.2-32.7

54 See, e.g., *Re Howglen Ltd* [2001] 1 All ER 376 where an *application* made in very general terms for disclosure against a non-party bank for records and interview notes resulted in a very

specific order limited to three specific interviews identified in the written evidence accompanying the application.

55 E.g., under Data Protection legislation.

relevant documents in the hands of a non-party would be to require the latter to attend as a witness at trial, along with the document.[53] Not only would this be a very roundabout and expensive way to achieve disclosure, but it would happen far too late for the desired purpose.

As you might expect, the order will not be made just to annoy the non-party or as a speculative venture, and it will be limited as appropriate.[54] Again, there may be other ways a litigant can get the information, thus rendering the application unnecessary.[55]

The application is made by way of interim application in the on-going proceedings, on notice and supported by written evidence. The order must specify what documents are to be disclosed and can ask the respondent to indicate where such documents are, if they are no longer in his possession or control.[56]

2.   INSPECTION AND SO ON OF RELEVANT PROPERTY

Like documents (usually, of course, it is what is contained *in* the document which matters), *objects* can provide useful evidential information. Such things are referred to in the rules as 'relevant property'. To get evidential value from such things, one might need to look at them or take samples from them, perform tests on them and so on. To do that, it may be necessary to preserve the property for one or other of these purposes. To that end the courts have power to make orders giving one party (or his advisors) access to relevant things in the possession of another party. Again, the general rule applies - such are normally available only against parties to the litigation in question. But, as ever, there are exceptions.

---

56 See CPR, r 31.17(4) and (5)

A.   IN THE NORMAL COURSE OF LITIGATION

Preserving relevant property for inspection, testing and so forth is commonplace in litigation, and unexceptional. Parties are usually able to arrange this between themselves. If, for example, a claimant sues her employers because she was injured by a machine she was required to operate at work, it may be important to allow those who are qualified to pass judgment on the state of the offending machine a chance to inspect it while in the same condition it was in when the claimant was injured (or near enough). The machine is the 'relevant property' and an order, where necessary, would typically allow for the 'preservation' of the machine,[57] and access[58] to it so that it can be examined and so forth by a person who knows how such machines are supposed to work (an expert, in other words).[59]

A analogous situation arises when seeking orders relating to the medical examination of a claimant in a personal injuries to be conducted by the defendant's expert.[60] As the claimant is a human being and not a machine, the court cannot force the claimant to do this - it would be an infringement of personal liberty. However, the court can achieve much the same result by the indirect method of ordering a halt to proceedings if the claimant *unreasonably* refuses such a m edical examination.[61] Whether or not a stay is granted is entirely within the discretion of the court - the facts of the individual case and a party's reasons for seeking, or resisting, the proposed medical examination, are all matters to be taken into account. There is a balance to be struck between the claimant's human rights and the defendant's litigation rights. A medical examination which might harm the claimant's health would, of course, pose special difficulties, which would need to be weighed in the balance.

Sometimes claimants are only willing to submit to a medical examination on conditions. Those which are personal to the claimant (for example, payment of fares getting to the examination, the presence of a friend,[62] an assurance the doctor

---

57 The idea is that the machine is examined before any defects have been put right or repairs carried out.

58 It may well be at the defendant's premises.

59 See CPR, r 25.1(c) and Ch. 17 for experts.

60 It is fairly typical to have experts on both sides in a personal injuries action of any complexity.

61 *Edmeades v Thames Board Mills Ltd* [1969] 2 QB 67, CA

62 But see *Whitehead v Avon County Council,* The Times, 3 May 1995, CA, where the Court of Appeal upheld a decision that the claimant's action be stayed unless she submitted to a psychiatric examination without a friend or relation being present.

will not discuss the case with the claimant except insofar as medically necessary, a request for a doctor of a particular gender if the examination is of an intimate nature) will usually be uncontroversial. However, conditions which in effect amount to attempts to choose the defendant's expert for him (unless there are doubts about the competence or honesty of the choice of doctor) or interfere with the purpose of the examination will be more apt to be considered unreasonable.[63]

Applications for such orders (whether to gain access to inspect things or people) are made on notice,[64] supported by written evidence which speaks to the need and relevance of the order. They are, however, often rendered unnecessary by the other party's willingness to give access, because it is so obvious that this is precisely what the court would order.

B. EXCEPTIONAL ORDERS (AGAINST NON-PARTIES)

The exceptions to the general rule that orders for the inspection, experimentation and so on of relevant property are available only against *parties* to the relevant litigation, mirror those statutory exceptions discussed above relating to disclosure of documents. Indeed, they too are statutory.[65] Thus it is possible, where the object in question may become relevant to the subject matter of *subsequent* proceedings, to get an order for inspection and so on before those proceedings have been started. Similarly, it is also possible to get such orders against a 'stranger' to on-going litigation, where that non-party is in possession or control of property which is relevant to the subject matter of that litigation.

When such an order is necessary, the application is again generally made on notice, supported by written evidence identifying the property in question and the need for the order. If the order is, *exceptionally*, made not only pre-action,[66] but also (doubly exceptionally) without notice, it is called a Search order.[67] Thus it is that a

63 See also *Starr v National Coal Board* [1977] 1 WLR 63, CA

64 CPR, r 25.3. Typically such orders are sought at the track allocation stage.

65 See SCA 1981, ss 33 and 34/CCA 1984, ss 52 and 53

66 Or pre-service of proceedings.

67 See Ch. 7

'search order' is really just a dramatic and surprising version of something which can otherwise be quite ordinary.

3.   REQUESTS FOR FURTHER INFORMATION

One can, of course, get evidential information by requesting it. Not surprisingly, perhaps, these are called 'requests for further information'. Sometimes a party might be vague about aspects of his case or something might be mentioned in a witness statement which requires clarification. Before the CPR, the former situation was dealt with by something called 'Further and Better Particulars' (which was limited to asking parties to be more specific about the allegations made in their statements of case); and the latter was dealt with by 'Interrogatories' (a request for answers to questions where these would help fairly 'dispose of the action or save costs'). These two old procedures were rolled into one, so that a 'Request' for further information under CPR, r 18.1 can be used to seek clarification of any matter in dispute, or get information about any such matter, whether or not it is contained, or referred to, in a statement of case.

This litigation tool (and it is a litigation tool - no exceptions here) can be very useful in exposing weaknesses in the case against you. It can reveal an inability to make, much less prove a specific allegation. Having said that, requests will only be ordered where they are reasonably necessary, proportionate and concise; they should not be used as a delaying tactic, nor as a hit and miss expedition 'fishing' for factual ammunition. Their function is to enable the requesting party to 'prepare or know the case to be met'[68]

So, if a party looks at an allegation and thinks *"Well, like what?"*, or *"In what way?"*

68 PD 18, para 1.2

69 It is also a good way of testing your own drafting skills to ensure you have been as specific as possible in drafting the statement of case before it is served.

70 CPR, r 18.1(1)

or *"How exactly?"*, this is an indication that an early request for further information about that allegation may well be appropriate.[69] Or the need for clarification may happen further down the litigation road, for example after evidence has been exchanged. The court can also use the procedure on its own initiative, for example, to help narrow the issues or for case management purposes.[70]

Such requests should be made as soon as practicable after the need arises. The party seeking further information should first serve a written request [71] on the party from whom it is sought, leaving an appropriate time for responding. The request is a formal document and, if practicable should be served by e-mail.[72] It is *only* in the absence of a proper response (or if the respondent objects to the request), that an application to the court will have to be made. Such applications will be determined by reference to the principles of proportionality and in accordance (surprise, surprise!!) with the overriding objective.

Responses should mirror the format in which the request was made and must be verified by a statement of truth.[73]

71 The format is very precisely set out in the rules: PD 18, para 1.6. See example in Sime, fig 18.1

72 PD 18, para 1.7

73 PD 18, paras 2 and 3 and example in Sime, fig 18.2. The request itself is just a series of questions and is thus incapable of being true or false. So, it does not need to be verified by a statement of truth, unlike other documents containing answers, allegations and so on.

revision tips

- Be clear that *standard* disclosure is the normal direction in fast track cases and personal injuries actions on the multi-track (small claims have their own, much narrower form of order).

- Other multi-track cases (think big commercial cases) are now governed by the new *menu-option* procedure, which allows for more focused and tailor-made orders. This will no doubt also be on the menu of options for exam questions, so make sure you understand it!

- Review what is meant by standard disclosure and how it unfolds - BCP's procedural guide 25 is a useful summary. Know the key words in the rules (e.g., 'reasonable' search, 'specific' disclosure).

- Be clear about how disclosure orders against non-parties *differ* from those made in the normal course of litigation.

- Be clear about the distinction between *Norwich Pharmacal* orders and statutory pre-action disclosure of documents. This is typical fodder for examinations.

It is worth reading ...

The judgment of Lord Donaldson MR in *X Ltd v Morgan-Grampian (Publishers) Ltd* [1991] 1 AC 1, HL. It is an interesting case about disclosure of journalist's sources, and in particular how the Contempt of Court Act 1981, s 10, fits into the *Norwich Pharmacal* equation. As you will see, journalists and judges don't always see eye-to-eye on the public interest.

The judgment of Flaux J in *Alan Kneale v Barclays Bank plc (trading as Barclaycard)* [2010] EWHC 1900 (Comm). Unlike some such cases, the facts are very straightforward. The applicant was applying for disclosure of a document that it appeared he wanted, rather than needed, which did not motivate the court to make the order. It is a very clear review of the case law and there is an interesting couple of paragraphs on the costs of such applications.

PART THREE
efficiency and control

CHAPTER 10

Limitation of action

The courts have never been sympathetic towards dilatory claimants - even less so are they under the CPR. The ethos of the current system is that litigation is to be avoided where possible, through well-informed pre-action conduct, ADR, and costs disincentives. If, however, litigation becomes necessary, actions should be commenced promptly, and in any event within a specified amount of time, known as the 'limitation period'. Once the claim form has been issued, it should be served in good time - negotiations can follow or continue once those two straightforward procedural steps have been taken. Amendments made late in the day can be problematic, and will only exceptionally be allowed once a relevant limitation period has expired. Finally, tight case management by the court will force the pace of litigation, so that once started, cases get to trial efficiently and speedily.

Limitation is the subject of this chapter; the other aspects of court control referred to above will be considered in those immediately following.

The general rule is that actions must be brought within the relevant limitation period or face (or risk facing) the impregnable defence that the action is 'time-barred'. The latter is a *procedural* defence and it is for the *defendant* to raise it - it must be specifically set out in the defence.[1] It will not be raised by the court on its own initiative, nor should the claimant anticipate it in the particulars of claim.[2] If

---

1 PD 16, para 13.1

2 The claimant, or his legal advisors, may well anticipate the 'risk' that a defendant might raise limitation, and might even make an application to the court about it, but no pre-emptive strikes of a 'just in case you mention *limitation in your defence*' kind are ever made in the particulars of claim.

a claimant does not discontinue an action which is time-barred, the defendant can apply to have the case struck out as an abuse of process.

It would be very hard on defendants if they were perpetually at risk of being sued - memories fade and evidence can degrade over time. And so the purpose of limitation periods is to put a reasonable but finite limit on the time during which actions can successfully be pursued, and to stop unduly stale claims (that is, claims a defendant did not expect to have to meet) being litigated.

Fixed limitation periods have been laid down for different types of cases[3], but a certain amount of flexibility has been built into the system over the years, in particular to help people who may for some considerable time be unaware that they have suffered harm.

The result of an action being time-barred is to extinguish the claimant's remedy.[4] In the case of adverse possession of land and conversion, expiry of the limitation period has the additional effect of extinguishing the claimant's title.[5] Actions must be 'brought' in time to avoid limitation problems. The date the court issues a claim form usually tells us when the case was commenced, but if the claimant has done all he needs to do in time (by delivering all the relevant documents and fee to the relevant court office), then he will have 'brought' the claim before limitation expired even if the court did not actually issue the claim form until after the time had expired.[6] If things are getting that close to the wire, however, it is a good idea for the claimant (or his representative) to go to the court personally to issue proceedings.

The *important thing to remember* is that what must happen during the limitation period is that the claim is *issued/brought*; service can come later (but not much later). Third party claims are deemed to be commenced on the date the Third Party/Part 20 claim form was issued.[7] Counterclaims and set-offs are deemed to have been commenced on the same date as the original action - they are, as it were, 'back-dated' to that date.[8]

---

3   Most are set out in the Limitation Act 1980 ('LA 1980'). The periods vary because different types of cases bring with them greater or lesser degrees of urgency, depending on things like how ephemeral the evidence is likely to be, what can be expected of claimants in such cases and/or the nature of the conduct alleged. For example, breach of trust claims brought by beneficiaries against trustees alleging fraud or conversion of trust property have no limitation period at all: LA 1980, s 21(1). This is partly because what is being alleged might well amount to a criminal offence.

4   Strictly speaking the cause of action still exists, but cannot effectively be pursued.

5   LA 1980, ss 3 and 4

1. KNOWING WHETHER AN ACTION IS TIME-BARRED

Determining whether the relevant limitation period has expired in any given situation is basically a *two-stage process*. It involves asking yourself two questions: how long is the limitation period in this case, and when did it start to run? Once these questions are answered, in most cases it can easily be determined whether an action has been, or can be, brought in time.

As to the first question, most time periods are laid down in the Limitation Act 1980, as amended. The important ones are conveniently set out at BCP, table 10.1. Remember that personal injury and fatal accident claims[9] can arise in contract as well as in negligence actions; generally speaking 'personal injuries' describes the nature of the damage caused by a breach, not the cause of action.[10]

As to the second question, time ordinarily runs from the (first full day after the) date the cause of action 'accrues', as it is called, although statute has provided alternatives in some cases. The *nature* of the cause of action will normally dictate when it accrues and time starts to run.

A. LIMITATION PERIODS

Thus, looking at both questions together, as they relate to the general run of cases:

(i) Non-personal injuries claim founded on simple contract

The limitation period is six years. Time runs from date of breach. This can vary depending on the nature of the contractual obligation which has been breached.

---

6 See *St Helens Metropolitan Borough Council v Barnes* [2007] 1 WLR 879 and WB, Vol 2, Sec 8-3.1

7 LA 1980, s35(1)(a). As to Third Parties generally, see Ch. 3

8 LA 1980, s35(1)(b). And see also amendment outside the limitation period at Ch. 11 below.

9 A fatal accident is an extreme personal injury, so these two appear in the rules as something of a twin-set. Therefore (unless I indicate otherwise) when I refer to the latter I include the former.

(ii) Non-personal injuries claim founded on common law tort (not including defamation)

The limitation period is six years. Where the tort is actionable per se (that is, without having to prove damage, as with trespass), time runs from the date the tort is *committed*. Most tort actions, however, are only actionable on *proof of damage*[11] (as is the case with negligence, nuisance and so on) and in those cases time runs from the date of *damage*, unless the Latent Damage Act 1986 provides an alternative.

(iii) Personal injuries and fatal accident cases

Here several special rules apply. First, the limitation period is shorter, that is, *three* years. Time runs from the date the cause of action accrues (for example, the date of damage, if a negligence action) or, to deal with those cases where the claimant does not realise he has been injured until much later, from the 'date of knowledge'. Analogous provisions apply to fatal accident cases (fatal accidents being the ultimate personal injury).[12] Further, even if time has expired, the court has a further discretionary power to allow such cases to continue, nevertheless.

Date of knowledge

This is specifically defined in the Limitation Act 1980.[13] It is important to remember that the requirements are *conjunctive*. There are three (sometimes four) components. In a nutshell, the date of knowledge is the first date when the claimant knew *all* of the following:

- that the injury is significant (in other words, worth suing over),

and

- that the injury was caused by the alleged act or omission,

and

- the identity of the defendant.[14]

---

10 See wording of LA 1980, s 11. At one time it was thought that physical or mental injuries caused by intentional trespass to the person (as opposed to unintentional trespass or negligence) were not personal injuries as defined by LA 1980, but this (at best, tortuous) distinction was declared false in *A v Hoare* [2008] 1 AC 844.

11 Sometimes easier to describe than to identify. See, e.g., *Khan v R M Falvey and Co* [2002] EWCA Civ 400, BCP para 10.9

12 LA 1980, s 12 and 14

13 LA 1980, s 14. See detailed discussion in WB or BCP

14 If the act or omission of someone other than the defendant is relevant, as is common in vicarious liability cases, then the identity of that person also needs to be known.

In essence, if you were to date stamp each individual part of this knowledge puzzle, the date the last piece fell into place (or the latest date recorded) is the date of knowledge.

Note too that date of knowledge is all about the date certain *facts* became known. Knowledge of law, or the legal implications of those facts, is irrelevant.[15] In addition, claimants will be expected to act reasonably (given their situation) in acquiring knowledge for these purposes, for example by making such inquiries and seeking such expert advice as the circumstances warrant.[16]

The date of knowledge provisions were first introduced in the 1960's to assist miners who had suffered damage to their lungs while down the pits, but were unaware of any injury until their disease (pneumoconiosis) manifested itself many years, often decades later. However, there were still some litigants who failed to bring a claim in time even once they had the requisite knowledge - some had taken poor advice from the employers who had caused the harm! As a result, further provision was passed, now s 33 Limitation Act 1980, giving the court a *discretion*, where it thinks it *equitable*, to let a personal injuries action proceed notwithstanding that it is out of time. In exercising the discretion the court does *not extend* the limitation period, but, rather, overlooks the fact that it has expired. For this reason it is inelegantly known as 'disapplying' the limitation period.

Sec 33 Discretion

Sec 33(3) says that the court should have regard to '*all of the circumstances*' of the case when deciding whether to exercise its discretion, and 'in particular' those factors contained in a relatively long list at s 33(3)(a)-(f). These are largely a matter of common sense and include things like the length and reason for the claimant's delay in bringing the action, the effect of the delay on the cogency of the evidence,[17] the behaviour of the defendant after the cause of action arose, how promptly the

---

15 LA 1980, s 14(1)

16 See LA 1980, s 14(3) and *Adams v Bracknell Forest Borough Council* [2005] 1 AC 76 and generally relevant commentary in WB or BCP

17 Ss 33(3)(a) and (b). The relevant delay for these purposes is that between the end of the limitation period and commencing the action. See e.g. *Long v Tolchard* [2001] PIQR P2, CA. Delay during the limitation period would be material to other of the factors.

claimant acted once time (as extended by the date of knowledge provision) began to run and so on. It is worth having a look at this list yourself – but remember *it is not* exhaustive. The specific matters mentioned there are 'exemplary, not definitive'. The discretion is unfettered.[18]

What the court must do is *balance* the prejudice to the claimant in not being able to pursue the personal injuries action on the one hand, against the prejudice to the defendant in having to meet a stale claim. These days 'forensic' prejudice (the state of the relevant evidence) is an important part of this equation - the loss of the ability to meet the claimant's claim on its merits will weigh more heavily than the loss of a procedural defence, as such (and what that might mean financially to the defendants). The overriding question is one of justice: would it be fair, in the circumstances, to let the case continue?

It is for the claimant to convince the court that it is equitable to disapply the limitation period - how difficult or easy that will be will very much depend on the facts of the particular case[19]. Factors not specified in the s 33(3) list which might also be relevant include how long the defendant has known about the claimant's claim (the earlier the notification the better for the claimant), the reason for not pursuing the claim from the outset, and whether the claimant has an alternative claim in professional negligence against his or her legal advisors. Note however that the latter, while obviously pertinent, is not necessarily decisive. There are several drawbacks to suing your own solicitors (not least of which is that you might like them!), so it should not be viewed as an easy option. Indeed, if there can still be a fair trial against the original defendants, there is a lot to be said for allowing the case to proceed against them, as the ones who (allegedly) caused the damage in the first place! As it was put in *Cain v Francis*, a tortfeasor only deserves to have his obligation to pay damages removed if the passage of time has significantly compromised his

---

18 *Nash v Eli Lilly & Co* [1993]
    4 All ER 383, at 402 (CA).
    And see discussion in WB,
    Vol 2, para 8-92ff.

19 See *Sayers v Hunt* [2013]
    1 WLR 1695

ability to defend the claim.[20]

Applications under s 33 are usually made to a High Court or Circuit judge (although in the Country Court application may be made to the District Judge if the case is within his or her trial jurisdiction), usually as an interim application, but sometimes as a preliminary issue to be determined before trial. The court may need to hear oral evidence in order to exercise its discretion properly, as for example where there are allegations of child abuse or psychological damage.[21]

At one time it was held that if an action had been commenced within the limitation period, but the claim had not progressed to trial because of a 'self-inflicted' wound resulting, for example, in the case being struck out,[22] s 33 could not be used to start a second, identical claim.[23] These were the so-called 'second action cases'. However, this (rather artificial) restriction was removed by *Horton v Sadler*,[24] and such cases will be determined like any other, although why the first action was 'lost' may well be relevant to the court's decision.

(iv) Claims under the Latent Damage Act 1986 (LDA 1986)

Just as with injuries to people, sometimes other sorts of damage (for example, to buildings from poor construction) happen before it is noticeable. Thus, where damage (*other than* for personal injuries) is latent, not patent, a claim in the *tort* of negligence[25] may be brought under this Act, which inserted ss 14A and 14B into the Limitation Act. Two alternative limitation periods are offered: six years from the date of damage or a shorter period of *three years*, to run from the earliest date when the claimant *knew*, in effect, that damage worth suing over was caused by an identifiable defendant. This is known as the 'start date', and these provisions are clearly analogous to the date of knowledge in personal injuries actions.[26] You might think of them as applying to injured buildings, rather than injured people, but bear

20 [2008] EWCA Civ 1415, quoted in BCP para 10.20
21 See *R v Nugent Care Society* (Practice Note) [2010] WLR 516, CA.
22 See Ch. 13
23 *Walkley v Precision Forgings* [1979] 1 WLR 606
24 [2007] 1 AC 307
25 Contract based actions are not covered under this legislation.
26 Discussed above.

in mind that the LDA 1986 can also apply, for example, to tort-based claims against solicitors and financial advisors for negligent advice.

There are, however, two *important* aspects in which such cases of latent damage *differ* from those involving personal injuries: one is that there is a so-called 'long-stop' preventing LDA 1986 cases being brought after 15 years from the negligent act.[27] The other is that there is no discretion to 'disapply' the relevant limitation period as there is in personal injury cases. Examiners may well want to test you on this difference!

B. FURTHER INSTANCES OF COMMON LIMITATION PERIODS

(v) **Contribution claims**

The limitation period here is *two* years, but time only begins to run from the *date of judgment or settlement* of the main action. Most contribution claims are made by way of an additional claim (for example, third party claim) under Part 20 and are dealt with at the same time as the main action.[28] If this has not happened, then a defendant has a further two years after liability is established (or admitted) to bring his contribution claim.

(vi) **Recovery of land cases**

The limitation period here is twelve years. There are detailed provisions set out in Schedule 1 of LA 1980, but (very) broadly, time runs from the date of dispossession or, if later, from the date when the claimant's interest in the land vested.

(vii) **Judicial review**

This time period is more analogous to lodging appeals.[29] Such claims must be

---

27 LA 1980, s 14B. See generally Sime, para 21.45-48

28 Third party proceedings are discussed in Ch. 3

29 Judicial Review is not an appeal mechanism as such, but rather a challenge to and review of public law functions. It is a very complex area. See Ch. 19

made *promptly* and in any case within three *months* after the grounds for making the application arose.[30] The time for making the application can be extended by the court if there are good reasons.

This is a very basic summary of some of the more common limitation periods (the detail in Schedule 1 of the Limitation Act 1980 goes on for four pages!); it is the sort of entry level of knowledge and understanding that an unseen assessment will test. If and when a limitation problem arises in practice (or in a take-home exam), then clearly you will need to check the detail in the relevant statute and/or case law to identify and advise on the issue.

C. FACTORS WHICH PREVENT TIME STARTING TO RUN

Be aware, too, of the various circumstances which can stop the limitation period from *starting* to run when it otherwise would. They include:

(i) Children and protected persons

This is a common situation. Where the claimant was a 'child' when the cause of action otherwise arose, the limitation period does *not start to run until* the child becomes 18 years old.[31] As we saw in Chapter 3, a person who has not yet attained the age of majority is said to be acting under a legal 'disability'. So too is a 'protected person' who lacks the mental capacity [32] to conduct proceedings. Like the litigant who has not yet turned 18 years of age, if at the time the cause of action would otherwise have arisen, the clamant is of unsound mind (possibly because of the injury suffered), then time will not begin to run until the mental incapacity has ended. Be aware, however, that once time has started to run, *later* mental incapacity *cannot* stop it again.[33] It's a bit like a horserace - a legal disability can keep the starting gates from opening; but once

---

30 CPR, r 54.5(1)
31 LA 1980, s 28
32 Within the meaning of the Mental Capacity Act 2005. See LA 1980, ss 28 and 38(2).

33 It would be very awkward for a defendant if it could, since he would have to keep checking up on the claimant's mental health to know if limitation was running or not. It is easier with the claimant's age, since once you become 18 there is no going back.

This is not necessarily true of mental health.

they have and the horses have got out, there is no stopping them until the race is over.

(ii) Misconduct

Misconduct on the part of the defendant can have a similar effect. If, for example, the action is founded on an act of *fraud* by the defendant, or if the defendant has *deliberately* concealed a fact relevant to the right of action, time will not start to run until the claimant has, or could reasonably have been expected to have discovered the fraud or concealment.[34]

(iii) Mistake

Similarly, where the claimant's action is for relief from the consequences of a mistake,[35] time will not start to run until the mistake is, or, with 'reasonable diligence', could have been discovered. A good example of this is *Peco Arts Inc v Hazlett Gallery Ltd.*[36] In that case, the claimant had, on advice of a specialist, bought a drawing from the defendants. It was an express term that the drawing was an original, signed by the artist. Six years later, the drawing was re-valued, and no doubts were cast on its authenticity at that time. Five years after that, it was found to be a reproduction (obviously a very good one). The claimant sued for return of the purchase price as the money had been paid under a mutual mistake of fact. It was held that 'reasonable diligence' is a matter of fact in any given case, and here it meant acting like a prudent buyer of valuable art, which is what the claimant had done. He was thus able to recover.

Two final points to note generally about limitations. The first is to remember that limitation time periods do not, as such, apply in respect of claims for *equitable* relief.[37] These will, of course, be defeated by 'delay' and 'acquiescence'[38] in deciding

---

34 LA 1980, s 32(1)(a) and (b). Re the latter, see examples in *Cave v Robinson Jarvis and Rolf* [2002] UKHL 18, [2003] 1 AC 384. Unlike the situation with the mentally incapable claimant, a deliberate concealment by the defendant after time has started to run can operate to 're-set' the clock, as it were: *Sheldon v R.H. Outhwaite (Underwriting Agencies) Ltd* [1996] AC 102 – in such cases the defendant has control over his own behaviour!

35 In the legal sense.

36 [1983] 1 WLR 1315

37 LA 1980, s 36(1). Sometimes ordinary time limits can assist the court by analogy.

38 Specifically preserved by LA 1980, s 36(2).

which the court has a wide discretion - as is in the nature of equity!

Finally, a note of caution: the relationship between the pre-action protocols and problems of limitation must be watched closely. As regards personal injuries actions, to an extent the s 33 discretion is an arguable fallback if proceedings are brought out of time. Having said that, it is a matter of simple common sense that a limitation period should *never knowingly* be allowed to expire. Indeed, the notes of guidance to the PI protocol indicate that if a claimant is in the middle of the protocol and the relevant limitation period is about to expire, *'protective proceedings' should be issued*, giving the other parties as much notice of the intention and need to issue proceedings as is practicable.[39] The parties could then invite the court to extend time for service of statements of case, or allow a stay in proceedings, while the recommended steps in the protocol are followed or completed. This must be of general application.

---

39 Para 2.11

revision tips

- Make yourself a table of the mainstream limitations periods: when time starts and how long it lasts. Be clear about the different permutations so that you can *recognise a limitation scenario when you see one* in an exam. Watch out especially for personal injuries actions involving children - there may be quite a few variables to consider.

- Remember that the discretion under s 33(3) LA 1980 to disapply the limitation period in personal injuries actions is *unfettered*, and not limited to the factors in the statute. The case law tells us this. What are sometimes referred to as non-statutory considerations (although the statute does say "all the circumstances"!) include the possibility of a fair trial, early notification and possible alternative claims open to the claimant. But every application must be judged *on its own merits*. There is nothing 'off-the-peg' about the s 33 discretion.

It is worth reading ...

Judgment of *Jackson LJ in Sayers v Hunter* [2013]1 WLR 1695. Easy to follow and a good review of the case law. Note what he says about the costs so far, and the 'glitzy' ads which united the claimant with his (not very impressive) solicitors.

CHAPTER 11

Amendment of statement of case

In the course of litigation, a party may wish to amend the wording of a statement of case[1] after it has been filed or served. This is a common occurrence, which often happens after disclosure of documents or other evidential information comes to light. Amendments can range from the correction of minor 'slips' to more significant adjustments to the presentation of a case. A claimant who wants to add a claim based on a new cause of action or to join a new defendant, for example, will have to amend the claim form as well as the particulars of claim. A defendant may want to amend the defence or add a counterclaim.

As a general proposition, the overriding objective of dealing with cases justly means that if made in good time, amendments of this kind are often uncontroversial and allowed almost as of right (if not by agreement). It is important that the real issues in any given case are litigated and it would be very harsh if a mistake or omission in a statement of case could not be put right, so long as the other parties are not prejudiced by the correction. However, problems can arise if a party seeks to amend very late in the day and it poses *real* difficulties if a relevant limitation period has expired.

---

1   'Statement of Case' is a generic description for the typical documents setting out a party's case in any litigation, i.e. the claim form, particulars of claim, defence, reply, additional claim forms and any further information given in relation to any of these: CPR, r 2.3.

1.   AMENDMENT *BEFORE* EXPIRY OF A RELEVANT LIMITATION PERIOD

The following points provide a summary of the position.

A.   AMENDMENT *BEFORE* SERVICE

A party is allowed to amend a statement of case at any time *before* it has been *served* on any other party.[2] *No permission of the court is required*, but a court could later disallow the amendment.[3] Such amendments are obviously made quite early on,[4] given that the exchange of statements of case is one of the first things that happens in any litigation. It makes sense to say that if the other party has not even seen it yet, it is no big deal to make changes to the document before they do.

B.   AMENDMENT *AFTER* SERVICE

However, if the statement of case has *already been served*, as often happens, it can only be amended either with the *written consent* of the parties or the *permission of the court*,[5] *unless* the amendment involves a *change of party*, in which case the court's *permission is always required*.[6] This special requirement about amendments involving a change in party is sensible when you think about it – the court is happy for the named parties to sort out the nature of the allegations between themselves, but if *new* or different parties are to become involved, the court would like to know about it. Otherwise it might go a long time thinking the case is Bob v Alice, when in fact it has become Bob and Carol v Ted and Alice (I am showing my age here). Like any host, the court wants to know who is invited to the party! More to the point, it wants to have a say about the guest list. The main consideration in any decisions to add, substitute, or indeed remove a party

---

2   CPR, r 17.1(1)
3   CPR r 17.2. An application to disallow such an amendment should be made within 14 days of service of the amended document.
4   Either between issue and service of the claim form (which can be as long as four months) or between filing (with the court) and service (on other parties) of other statements of case, which is usually a very short period of time. We are not, of course, talking about the several drafts it might take counsel to carry out the solicitor's instructions properly. The amendment rules are all about changing documents which have come to the attention either of the court or the other parties.
5   CPR, r 17.1(2)
6   CPR, r 19.4
7   See generally CPR, r 19.2
8   CPR, r 19.4(4)

(where there is no limitation problem) is whether the amendment is 'desirable' to ensure that all relevant issues in dispute can be resolved.[7] This ultimately is for the court to decide. As you might expect, however, nobody can be forced to be a claimant.[8]

C.   GENERAL PRINCIPLES

In determining an application for permission to amend generally, the courts should, in accordance with the overriding objective, decide where the justice of each case lies. Certainly significant amendments very late in the day can be more problematicthan those made relatively early on,[9] although with effective case management this situation should not now often arise. But so long as the amendment is required to determine all of the relevant issues, and is not tactical or foolish, then the justice of the case will almost always, if not inevitably, lie with the person seeking to amend- unless the other party or parties can show that they will be prejudiced *over and above* the fact that time and expense will be incurred in redrafting their own statements of case in response to the amendment, which can usually be dealt with by way of an order for costs against the amending party. Over a hundred years ago, Brett MR in *Clarapede v Commercial Union Association*,[10] put it like this: 'However negligent or careless may have been the first omission, and however late the proposed amendment, the amendment should be allowed if it can be made without injustice to the other side. There is no injustice if the other side can be compensated by costs.'

Nowadays we are more sophisticated (and less tolerant of foolishness), and the courts recognise that not all amendments can be 'paid for' in this way. In the modern era, the courts are 'much more conscious that in assessing the justice of the case, the disruption caused to other litigants by last minute adjournments and last minute applications have also to be brought into the scales'.[11] In particular, amendments sought

9   See, e.g., *Kettleman v Hansel Properties Ltd* [1987] AC 189. In that case the defendants were about to lose on the merits of the case at trial and sought to amend at the very last minute to plead a limitation defence, which no doubt could have been pleaded much earlier on. The House of Lords agreed with the Court of Appeal in saying that the amendment should not, in the circumstances of that case, have been allowed.

10 (1883) 32 WR 262

11 *Worldwide Corporation Ltd* v GPT Ltd [1998] EWCA Civ, per Waller LJ, who also referred to litigants (and no doubt the court) feeling 'mucked about'. Applied in *Swain-Mason v Mills & Reeve* [2011] 1WLR 2735

once the trial is underway may invite a greater degree of scepticism than those sought earlier, since by that time it may be apparent that a claim or defence is without merit or that the amendment will serve no useful purpose or that it represents such a departure from the pleaded case that it comes across simply as an act of desperation.[12] It also helps, as Lloyd LJ wryly observed, if a very late amendment is to be made, that the amended text should at the very least satisfy the basic 'requirements of proper pleading'. [13]

D.   THE COSTS OF AMENDING

The *usual order for costs* is that the party *making the amendment* must pay the *'costs of and arising from' the amendment*.[14] Having said that, if a party unreasonably failed to consent to an amendment and in effect forced an unnecessary application to the court, it might be ordered that the amending party pay the costs occasioned by the amendment (since these arise either way), but leaving the recalcitrant party to pay the costs of the avoidable application to the court.[15]

E.   SEEKING PERMISSION

Permission to amend is sought by application notice. Where a party is to be added or substituted, written evidence should be included setting out the new party's interest or connection with the claim.[16] Otherwise, such evidence may not be necessary if the purpose of any changes is clear from the proposed amended statement of case, which must be filed with the application.[17] The rules do not strictly require it, but traditionally *both* the original and amended text (in red) is shown – otherwise it is difficult for the court to know what was being proposed! Multiple further amendments will result in a very colourful display, since with each change a different colour is used.[18] Such applications are normally dealt with by a master or District Judge, as part of the court's case management function, although

---

12 As in the *Ketterman* and *Swain-Mason* cases themselves.

13 *Swain-Mason, op. cit.*, at [73]

14 PDs 17 and 19

15 See BCP, para 31.5

16 CPR, PD 19A, para 1.3

17 PD 17, para 1.2(2)

18 There are alternative ways of doing this in the electronic age. See e.g. PD 17, para 2.2(2)

applications may if necessary be made to the trial judge.

So amendments are not often controversial because, most of the time, they are sought early and payment of costs can compensate for the time and trouble they cause. There is one especially important situation, however, where no costs order could ever compensate for the injustice caused by a proposed amendment, and that is where a relevant limitation period has expired. Thus, if an amendment would deprive a party of the defence that an action is statute-barred (which cannot be compensated by any costs order), it will *not ordinarily* be allowed.

2. AMENDMENT *AFTER* EXPIRY OF RELEVANT LIMITATION PERIOD

An amendment to add or substitute a new party or cause of action is deemed to be a separate claim which is commenced on the *same date as the original claim*.[19] This is a purely practical provision, designed to achieve predictability and uniformity. You can see, however, that if the original action was brought *within* the relevant limitation period, but the amendment is made *after* it has expired, the effect of this rule would be to deprive the new defendant (or the original defendant defending the new cause of action) of a limitation defence. No amount of money by way of costs can make up for that. In this situation, therefore, the *general rule* is that a party may *not* amend *once a relevant limitation period has expired*. The idea is that once limitation has expired, a party should not be able to achieve something by way of amendment, which could not be achieved by actually bringing a separate action.

As always, there are *exceptions*, which essentially fall into *three* types of amendment, discussed below.

19 LA 1980, s 35(1). This is sometimes referred to as 'relate-back'

20 Note that it says 'may', not 'must'. There is still a discretion to say 'no' if justice requires it.

21 Not all proposed amendments do this necessarily. Some may just simply resolve obvious mistakes. See e.g. *Evans v CIG Mon Cymru* [2008] P.I.Q.R., p 17, where the claimant considered suing her employers both for an 'accident at work' and 'abuse at work'. She decided not to pursue the bullying allegation. The particulars of claim sought remedies for an 'accident at work' but because of a typing error, the claim form referred to remedies for 'abuse at work.' After limitation had expired, the defendants attempted to get the particulars struck out because they were irrelevant

A. AMENDMENTS HAVING THE EFFECT OF ADDING A *NEW CLAIM*

As an exception to the general rule, the court *may*[20] allow an amendment, even after the expiry of the limitation period:

(i) To add or substitute a claim/cause of action[21] if it arises out of the *same or substantially the same facts as are already in issue* on any claim previously made in the original action.[22] An obvious example might be a claim in breach of statutory duty being added, after limitation had expired, to an existing claim in negligence, relating to the same accident and facts as already pleaded in the particulars of claim. The court should look at the 'essential facts' as already drafted (or otherwise in issue, perhaps by reference to the defence version of events) and compare them with those of the proposed amended pleading.[23] But whether it decides that such amendments involve the 'same or substantially the same' facts as those already in issue will always, to some extent, be a matter of impression, degree, mood and motivation. Every case is different.[24]

(ii) To add or substitute a new *personal injuries* claim when the limitation period has been *disapplied under LA 1980, s 33*.[25] Obviously it would be a bit strange if the court could allow a personal injuries action to continue alone, but not in addition to some other existing action.

(iii) To allow a party to an existing action to raise a *counterclaim or set-off* for the *first* time.[26] Counterclaims are deemed to have been commenced on the same date as the original claim,[27] so it makes sense that the court may allow an amendment to plead a counterclaim which, were it not for this deeming provision, would be out of time. But it must be an 'original' counterclaim (we are *not* talking about amending an existing counterclaim). So long as the party proposing the amendment has not

---

to the claim form. The claimant applied to amend the claim form so as to substitute 'accident at work' for 'abuse at work'. The Court of Appeal (no doubt sensing that there really were bullies at work here) held that the amendment should be allowed and

the particulars not struck out. It said that whether a proposed amendment has the effect of raising a new claim had to be determined by looking at the entire claim as pleaded up to that point, not the claim form alone. What was involved in that case was not the raising of

a new claim, but a clerical error.

22 LA 1980, s 35(5)(a) and see also CPR, r 17.4(2). The rule is worded more narrowly than the statutory provision (it does not use the more expansive phrase 'fact already in issue' but instead refers to amending

previously counterclaimed,[28] then this exception will apply. But, again, the court can exercise its discretion to refuse to make the amendment, which it will do if it believes the proposed counterclaim is being used for tactical or other reasons not in keeping with the overriding objective.[29]

B.   AMENDMENTS HAVING THE EFFECT OF ADDING A *NEW PARTY*

As an *exception* to the general rule, an amendment to add or substitute a new party, once the relevant limitation period has expired, may[30] be allowed where:

(i) The court has exercised its *discretion under s. 33 to disapply* the relevant limitation period in *a personal injuries* action.[31] Exercising this discretion can result in the addition of a new party, as much as a new claim (or both simultaneously).

(ii) The amendment merely alters the (legal) *'capacity* in which a party *claims*, so long as that new capacity is one which that party had when the proceedings started or has since acquired'.[32] A typical example would be where a person who has brought the claim as an individual, wants to amend to carry on as a trustee (or vice versa). In a sense the party does not change, so much as their legal status. If such an amendment were to have the effect of adding or substituting a party (in addition to changing the capacity of an existing party), then one or other of the exceptions set out in this section would have to apply.[33]

(iii)   The amendment is 'necessary'.[34] An amendment to add or substitute a party, once the relevant limitation period has expired, will *only be necessary* where:

(a) (the original party has died, or been declared bankrupt, and his interest or liability has passed to the new party.[35]

---

a claim which has 'already' been made). But the courts have said that the more expansive words should be read into the rule. Thus, for example, if a defendant makes claims or allegations in the defence, they become facts 'in issue' and so give scope for an amendment

by the claimant under this provision: *Goode v Martin* [2002] WLR 1828.

23 *P and O Nedlloyd BV v Arab Metals Co* [2006] EWCA Civ 1300, [2007] Ch. 182

24 Compare, e.g. *Law v Society of Lloyd's* [2003] EWCA Civ 1887

(amendment refused) with *Senior v Parsons and Ward* (2001) LTL 26/1/2001 (amendment allowed) and the other examples at BCP, para 31.23.

25 See generally Ch. 10
26 LA 1980, s 35(3)
27 LA 1980, s 35(1)/(2)
28 And is on the opposite

(b) the amendment is *legally* necessary to maintain the action.[36] This exception corrects highly technical defects and is assumed to cover a very narrow range of circumstances such as used to be explicitly set out in the old rules, but which were not replicated in the CPR.[37] It covers things like needing to join the Attorney-General before the case can continue because the proceedings should have been brought as a relator action; or needing to add a co-clamant to maintain an action vested jointly in two people. For assessment purposes, you don't need to know much more about this exception than the fact that it exists. If it arises in practice, or a take home exam, you will just have to look it up.

(c) there has been a *mistake in naming a party* to the original action.[38] This is a rather vexed, and vexing, area of procedure, not least because aspects of the relevant legislation[39] and the pre-CPR rule[40] have been sprinkled about in two different places in the rules: Part 17 which deals with 'Amendment' and Part 19 which deals with 'Parties'. As the subject matter at hand is the addition or substitution of parties by amendment, it is perhaps not surprising that this 'division of labour' might have happened, but the relationship between the provisions in CPR, r 17.4(3),[41] and those in CPR, r 19.5(3)[42] has caused no end of judicial headache.

Mistaken name

The main problem is that both sets of rules contain different aspects of the one previous rule, which was stated to allow an amendment to 'correct the name' of a party (even if, in one sense, this resulted in the 'substitution' of a new party) if the court was satisfied that the mistake was a 'genuine mistake' and was not 'misleading

---

side of the record to the defendant to the (proposed) counterclaim.

29 See, e.g., *Law Society v Wemyss* [2008] EWHC 2515 (Ch)

30 Again, this is 'may', not 'must'.

31 LA 1980. S 35(3) and CPR, r 19.5(4)

32 CPR, r 17.4(4) My emphasis

33 *Roberts v Gill* [2009] 1 WLR 531

34 CPR, r 19.5(2)(b)

35 CPR, r 19.5(3)(c)

36 CPR, r 19.5(3)(b)

37 See e.g. Sime, para 22,33ff

38 CPR, r 19.5(3)

39 LA 1980, s 35

40 This was RSC 0 20, r 5.

41 The title to CPR, r 17.4 is 'Amendments to statements of case after the end of a relevant limitation period'; r 17.4(3) allows an amendment to 'correct' a mistake as to the name of a party.

or such as to cause reasonable doubt as to the identity of the person intending to sue or, as the case may be, intended to be sued'.[43] For some reason, the notion of 'correcting' a mistake but only if it was 'genuine' and caused 'no reasonable doubt' about the 'identity' of the party to be substituted made it only into CPR, r 17.4(3), but the idea of the actual 'substitution' of one party for another who was 'named in the claim form in mistake' is really all that appears in CPR, r 19.5(3). You might think the neatest solution would be to say that if the substitution is necessary under the latter rule because of a mistake in name, this would then send you back to CPR, r 17.4(3), which sets out the additional requirement of its needing to be a genuine mistake and so on.[44] But you would (at least so far) be wrong.

There was also a lot of case law under the old rule, in particular about just what kind of 'mistake' was correctable once limitation has expired and how misleading or not a correction of such a mistake might be. It was fairly clear that where, for example, the right person had been sued but called by the wrong name, this was correctable; but if a person had been sued by mistake for another, this was not. In what was then the leading case,[45] Loyd LJ commented that the notion of the 'identity' of the person intending to sue or intended to be sued was a concept which is 'not at all easy to grasp, and can be difficult to apply to the circumstances of a particular case …' He added that 'in one sense a (claimant) always intends to sue the person who is liable for the wrong he has suffered. But the test cannot be as wide as that. Otherwise, there would never be any doubt as to the person intended to be sued, and leave to amend would always be given. So there must be a narrower test.' He went on to suggest that where the party is named 'by reference to a *description* which was more or less *specific* to the particular case',[46] then this was the sort of mistake which was correctable without causing reasonable doubt about who was the intended party. So, for example, if in suing a defendant, the claimant gets the right description (for

---

42 The title to CPR, r 19.5 is 'Special provisions about adding or substituting parties after the end of a relevant limitation period.'

43 RSC 0rd 20, r 5

44 These two sections do cross-refer to each other, although the reference back to CPR, r 17.4 from CPR, r 19.5 is admittedly less compelling than that going in the other direction.

45 *The Sardinia Sulcis* [1991] 1 Lloyd's Rep 201

46 This became known as the 'Sardinia Sulcis* test' and see useful list of examples in WB, para 19.5.8.

example, employer, landlord and so on) but the wrong name, Lloyd LJ thought that there 'is unlikely to be any doubt as to the identity of the person intended to be sued. But if he gets the wrong description, it will be otherwise.'[47]

So, along came the new rules. CPR, r 19.5(3) does not specify the need for the mistake to be genuine and not misleading to the person whose name is to be substituted.[48] But CPR r 17.4(3), the old rule, and all the existing case law, does. So where does that leave us?

Trial and appeal judges have been grappling with this problem for some years now, with varying degrees of success. This has occasionally resulted in different, sometimes conflicting solutions, which are then either endorsed or overruled. Some have approached it by saying the two rules are entirely separate, and only r 19.5 is relevant to a 'substitution' of one name for another as a result of a mistake.[49] At one point, the Court of Appeal said[50] (and I am paraphrasing) 'Forget what the old rule said and the related case law, let's just start afresh with the new rules.' This approach (which did not really help with some aspects of the problem) was rejected in what is now the leading case of *Adelson and another v Associated Newspapers Ltd.*[51] The *Adelson* case held that pre-CPR case law *was* relevant to applications to amend out of time to add or substitute a new party. It also approved of the notion that CPR, r 19.5 deals with mistakes in naming parties which requires a new party to be *substituted,* leaving CPR, r 17.4 to deal with cases where there has been a mistake in setting out the name of a party, which needs *correcting.*[52] It also sets out the following principles about applications under CPR, r 19.5(3):

- The court must be satisfied that the person who made the mistake, directly or through an agent, was the person responsible for issuing the claim form;
- The applicant must show that had the mistake not been made, the new party would have been named in the claim form;

---

47 *Op. cit.*, p. 207
48 Neither does LA 1980, s 35, but that was so before the CPR.
49 Leaving r 17.4(3) for things like correcting spelling mistakes. See e.g. *Lockheed Martin Corporation v Willis Group Ltd* [2010] EWCA Civ 927

(the appeal was determined on another point, so the comments are obiter).
50 *Morgan Est (Scotland) Ltd v Hanson Concrete Products Ltd* [2005] 1 WLR 2557. The next appeal court to deal with the point felt bound by this case and so began to postulate (quite

understandably) a new 'test' (*"Can you change the name of the party without changing the claim?"*), which was in fact not a millions miles away from the *Sardicia Sulcis* test. But the latter was about to be rehabilitated in any event.

- The mistake has to be as to the name, *not the identity* of the party, thus endorsing the *Sardinia Sulcis* test. This can still be a very tricky point to decide - the line between the two can be quite hazy. Often there will be some corporate connection between the named party and the one to be substituted.[53] How lenient or harsh a court will be in deciding this aspect of a case can also depend on other factors in a case, which can sometimes be rather quirky.[54] Some, including *Adelson* itself, were applications by claimants to change their own names (when you might think they would know who they were from the outset!), and in those cases the court is more apt to think there has been a change of mind about who should sue, rather than a mistake in naming that party. In other cases, whatever the nature of the mistake, it was made by lawyers, against whom an action for professional negligence could be brought. This also tends to make judges more, shall we say, judgmental. One can usually imagine the sort of mistake in naming a party which the court would clearly allow to be corrected, even if by way of substituting a new party, as well as the sort of mistake which the court would clearly not allow - it's the situations in the middle which can be a lot more difficult to call.

- No injustice should be caused if the application is granted. This is how the court can factor in questions about the genuineness of the mistake and whether the substituted party has been misled, without actually referring to CPR, r 17.4(3).[55] If there are concerns, especially if the party to be substituted would be completely taken by surprise by the amendment, then the court can exercise its discretion (remember the rule says 'may', not 'must') to refuse to allow it.

---

51 [2007] EWCA Civ 701, [2008] 1 WLR 585

52 As decided in *Gregson v Channel Four Television Corporation* (2000) CP Rep 60. It may still, at times, be difficult to distinguish between these two.

53 As in *Adelson* itself.

54 In the *Lockheed Martin Corporation* case, op.cit., there was no cause of action against the defendant whom the claimant wanted, by amendment, to proceed against!

55 So problem solved? Watch this space – I would not be surprised if the Supreme Court had a go at it ... or maybe the CPR rules committee might beat them to it.

Finally, note carefully that *pure additions are not allowed* by operation of either CPR, r 17.4(3) or CPR, r 19.5(3)(a) - *only substitutions are possible.* The former merely allows for the correction of an existing party's name: the wording of the latter, is explicitly limited to substituting one party for another.[56]

C.   AMENDMENTS HAVING THE EFFECT OF ADDING A NEW DEFENCE[57]

Here the *emphasis is different* because limitation periods basically concern claimants, not defendants. Thus, amending a defence after the action's limitation period has expired is not usually a problem.

So here, the general rule is that the court *will* allow a *defendant* to amend the defence, *even after the limitation period* has expired, *unless* the claimant can show that he or she would be *prejudiced by it in a way which cannot be compensated in costs.* This would be the case, for example, where a defendant suddenly blames another person whom the claimant cannot now sue because the action against that person is statute-barred. In *Cluley v RL Dix Heating*,[58] for example, the claimant sued the defendants for breach of contract. The original defence admitted the contract but denied breach. After the limitation period for the contract action had expired, the defendants sought to amend their defence to deny the contract, and alleged that the claimant should have sued other parties. The amendment was not allowed, because it was now no longer possible for the claimant to sue any other parties, because limitation had expired, and the defendants must have known much earlier whether they had a contract with the claimants or not. In this sort of situation, the position can be summarised in this way:

A defendant *will* be allowed to amend his pleadings to raise a new defence allegation, even after the relevant limitation period has expired, *unless*:

---

56 *Broadhurst v Broadhurst* [2007] EWCA 1828. Somehow, Lord Phillips in the *Adelson* case managed to turn 3 claimants into 1, but disallowed the amendment on other grounds.

57 This is sometimes called amendments affecting accrued rights (i.e. the right of defendants to plead a limitation defence).

58 (2003) LTL 31/10/2003

59 *Weait v Jayanbee Joinery Ltd* [1963] 1 QB 239

60 As in *Turner v Ford Motor Co* [1965] 2 All ER 583. There is a useful, short exposition of these two cases at BCP, at para 31.24.

- the effect of the amendment is to blame another party whom the claimant cannot now sue,

and

- it is the defendant's fault in not seeking to amend earlier.59

However, if on a closer look, it turns out that the claimant knew all along of the facts giving rise to the defence amendment, that amendment may be allowed.[60]

revision tips

- Be confident in differentiating between:

  (i) amendments sought before versus after the limitation period has expired, and

  (ii) amending to add/substitute a party versus amending to add/substitute a cause of action – both before and after limitation has expired.

- Check the facts of any question carefully so you know what is being asked (for example, is the limitation period still current? Is it a change of party or cause of action which is needed?). Examiners love to test you on these differences.

It is worth reading ...

Neubeuger J's (as he then was) judgment in *Charlesworth v Relay Roads Ltd* (No 2) [2000] 1 WLR 230. In this case judgment had been given but not officially drawn up. Limitation had not expired, but talk about a last minute application to amend!!

CHAPTER 12

Renewal of claim form

In Chapter 10 we looked at the prescribed time periods for bringing proceedings, after which, with certain exceptions, a defendant will have an unanswerable limitation defence. To avoid a case being time-barred, therefore, a claimant should bring the action before the relevant limitation period has expired. An action is commenced when the claim form is issued. Once this happens, the next step is to *serve* it on the defendant while the claim form is still valid for service.[1]

The claim form is valid for service for *four months* if it is to be served within the jurisdiction - time runs from the day after the date the claim form is issued. Where it is to be served *outside* the jurisdiction, which can be more time-consuming, the period of validity is extended to *six months*.[2] The defendant does not need to receive the claim form during the period of validity, but the claimant must have *completed the steps* required by the rules to effect the chosen method of service.[3] The claimant has until midnight on the last day of the period of validity to do this.[4]

A claim form must be served while it is valid. If a claimant has a reason for not being able to do this, an extension may be granted either with the consent of the party to be served[5] or by the court. Extending the period of validity is sometimes referred to as 'renewal' (like a library book), and as we shall see, the rules are very strict (like some librarians). If the limitation period in the action has not

---

1   CPR, r 7.5
2   CPR, r 7.5(2)
3   See generally Ch. 4 on service.
4   CPR, r 7.5(1). Assume, for example, an action founded on contract (with a 6 year limitation period) with service to take place within the jurisdiction. If the claimant used both (limitation and validity) time periods to the full, in theory the defendant need not be served until 6 years plus 4 months from the breach. But it is never a good idea to leave these things to the last minute, unless unavoidable. The courts hate this.

5   Only written consent will be effective in these circumstances: CPR, r 2.11 and *Thomas v Home Office* [2007] 1 WLR 230.

yet expired, there is no huge reason to panic since an alternative to renewal would be to issue fresh proceedings.[6] *It is where the relevant limitation period has expired that serious problems arise.*

When the court serves the claim form, renewal should not often be necessary. But where claimants choose to serve the claim form themselves, there is scope for trouble. The key to understanding renewal is to see the *relationship* between the limitation period in the action and the period during which the claim form is valid for service - but *not to confuse the two.*

1. RENEWAL APPLICATIONS *DURING* THE PERIOD OF VALIDITY

Renewal is typically sought when a claimant is having difficulties serving a defendant. The general rule is that an application for an extension of the claim form's validity for service should be made *before* the claim form expires.[7] In such cases, sometimes referred to as 'prospective applications', the court has a *general discretion* to renew. The court will exercise the discretion in accordance with the overriding objective; allowing the renewal if it can do so justly, but mindful of the importance of ensuring that cases progress expeditiously. In particular, the court will look closely at the *attempts* made to serve (both when and how) and the *reason* for the need to renew - the better the reason, the more likely they are to allow the renewal: *Hashtroodi v Hancock*.[8] If there is a good reason, it has been said that the courts should also consider the balance of hardship between parties in either granting or refusing the extension of time.[9] This would be particularly important if the limitation period has (by this time) expired. It would also be relevant to consider the implications of the claimant's merely issuing fresh proceedings were the application to renew to be

---

6 There would be a price to pay, because you would have to pay to start fresh proceedings, but all would not be lost.
7 Or as specified by court order: CPR, r 7.6(2)

8 [2004] 1 WLR 3206
9 *Cecil v Bayat* [2011] 1 WLR 3086

10 See e.g. *Hoddinott, Hoddinott and R.G. Hoddinott Ltd v Persimmon Homes* (Wessex) Ltd [2007] EWCA Civ 1203 where this was one factor among many.

refused.[10] The main thrust of the court's approach to renewal has always been that a claimant should issue *and s*erve proceedings promptly. This is neither expensive (in the scheme of things), nor difficult. If any hiatus in proceedings is desired, it can occur *after* service of the claim form, not before.

So what amounts to a good enough reason? Not much, is the short answer. Historically, under the old rules, reasons which were *not* thought to be good reasons included: negotiations in progress, a strong case, an honest mistake, difficulty in obtaining evidence, and delays by the claimant in applying for public funding (although delays in the granting of funding might amount to a good reason).

Reasons which *were* considered to be good reasons under the old rules included a defendant evading service, or otherwise being obstructive, a defendant explicitly asking not to be served, or saving a defendant costs. Note the theme here: either the defendant is behaving badly and/or making service difficult, or the claimant is doing the defendant a favour. The cases under the CPR have continued in this vein.[11]

Remember that decisions in individual cases are merely a *guide* to the outcome of any given renewal application which has been made prospectively, although the reasoning can be enlightening. Every case is different and courts have a complete discretion. Having said that, the cases confirm a generally *restrictive* approach even in these cases. The overriding objective is, of course, overriding in such situations.

2. RENEWAL APPLICATIONS MADE *AFTER* EXPIRY OF THE CLAIM FORM

This is a much more difficult scenario. Where the application to renew is made *after* the claim form has *expired* (sometimes called a 'retrospective' application), the court's

---

11 Compare, for example, *Hoddinott* case (delay in receiving the expert's report on quantum was not a good reason; the claimant should have served the claim form and sought an extension of the time for serving the particulars of claim instead) with *Imperial* *Cancer Research Fund v Ove Arup & Partners Ltd* [2009] EWHC 1453 (TCC), June 23, 2009, (the claimant's need to evacuate the premises, investigate a water leak and obtain a expert's report on the liability of the defendant, and possibly others, was a good reason, especially since the defendants had been slow to disclose plans and documents when asked). The WB has a good summary at para 7.6.2.

discretion is severely constrained by the fact that it must be shown that (a) the claimant has taken 'all reasonable' steps, but failed (or the court was unable) to serve the claim form in time *and* (b) the application was made promptly.[12] Although not contained in the rule, giving reasons why the application was made after (rather than before) the claim form expired would not go amiss, either. In any event, this is an *exceedingly narrow* set of criteria, really focusing *only* on failed attempts to serve.

Furthermore, there is virtually no escape from the confines of CPR, r 7.6(3). In a line of cases,[13] the Court of Appeal decided that CPR, r 7.6 constitutes a *complete code*, so that recourse may not be had to other powers[14] under the CPR, nor even it seems the overriding objective, to mitigate the severity of the rule - except in *very exceptional* circumstances. The possibilities are:

(i)   To apply retrospectively for an order for alternative service;[15]

(ii) To get an order dispensing with service under CPR, r 6.16. This will only be granted in exceptional circumstances, and only it seems if an attempt has been made by the claimant to serve;[16]

(iii) To remedy, under CPR, r 3.10, what is in effect a 'de minimus' or technical error in service.[17]

Each of these is a possible circumvention, but the circumstances need to be truly exceptional. The long and the short of it is: the rule is strict, and is strictly enforced. Too many exceptions would dilute the message: serve the claim form in time!

An application for renewal is made to an interim judge under Part 23, using an application notice supported by written evidence , setting out relevant time periods (for example, date of issue) and reasons why renewal has become necessary. Because

---

12 Albeit that the period of validity has already passed. See CPR, r 7.6(3). It is the steps taken to serve the claim form during its validity which matter: *Drury v BBC & Carnegie* [2007] EWCA Civ 497

13 E.g. *Kaur v CTP Coil Ltd* (2000) LTL 10/7/2000;

Vinos v Marks & Spencer plc [2001] 3 All ER 784; *Godwin v Swindon Borough Council* [2002] 1 WLR 997.

14 E.g. the general power to grant extensions of time, to grant relief from sanctions or remedy procedures in error, all found in Part 3. See

generally, discussion of case management at Ch. 13.

15 Under CPR, r 6.15(2). The ability to apply retrospectively for this order is a relatively recent development, brought about by the 2008 changes.

at this point there is no defendant on record, the application is made without giving notice to the other side.[18] If renewal is granted, the first the defendant may know about it, therefore, is when the (extended) claim form is served. A defendant who wishes to dispute the extension should first acknowledge service in the normal way, stating an intention to defend, and *then* apply on notice within seven days of service to have the order extending the validity of the claim form discharged. The same would apply to a defendant who has simply been served with an invalid claim form, although in this case the claimant will likely cross-apply for an appropriate court order.[19] In either case, it is important for defendants to act promptly in these circumstances, since delay could be taken as acceptance of valid service.

The rules on renewal essentially reflect the fact that, at the very least, the court must be satisfied that there was a compelling reason for a claimant not doing something as cheap and easy as 'popping' the claim form in the post (or letting the court serve it!). The ultimate no-no, of course, is to apply for renewal after *both* the limitation period and the claim form have expired, when the action will effectively be lost. Not only is r 7.6(3) very strict in its own terms, but the courts will be more reluctant to deprive a defendant of a limitation defence when the claimant issues proceedings at the very last minute. *Do not forget*, however, that so long as the limitation period in the action has *not* expired, it always remains the case that (unless the court has barred a claimant from re-litigating, and admittedly at some cost) a *fresh* action can be commenced.

continues/...

---

16 *Anderton v Clwyd County Council (No 2)* [2002] 1 WLR 3174.

17 See e.g. *Steele v Mooney* [2005] 1 WLR 2819; *Phillips v Symes (No 3)* [2008] 1 WLR 180.

18 See generally Ch. 4

19 Unless it is simply easier and no more expensive (assuming limitation has not expired as well) to issue another claim form and start again.

revision tips

- Be clear about the interrelationship, but also the difference between the limitation period in an action and the period during which the claim form issued in the case is valid for service. Do not confuse the two.

- Be clear about how very strict the rule is if the application to renew is made *after* expiry of the claim form. Even the overriding objective does not help here!

- If the claim form has become invalid for service, but the limitation period in the action has not yet expired, starting again is a possibility which should always be considered. It might even be the cheaper option!

It is worth reading ...

The judgments of Dyson LJ (who was then the Court of Appeal's resident expert on renewal, until he went up to the Supreme Court) in:

Hoddinott v Persimmon Homes (Wessex) Ltd [2007] EWCA Civ 1203, [2008] 1 WLR 806. This is partly a case about when and how a defendant disputes the court's jurisdiction, but also discusses the approach which the court should take when an application to renew the claim form is made while the claim form is still valid.

Drury v BBC & Carnegie [2007] EWCA Civ 96. An interesting defamation case. Eady J, whose decision was appealed against, is one of the foremost experts in the world on this complex subject. But even he was wrong-footed by the constraints of the court when faced with an application to renew after the claim form had expired!

CHAPTER 13

Case management: powers & sanctions

Once a case has been provisionally allocated to a case management track and the directions questionnaires have been returned, the procedural judge will essentially need to consider three things:

- Whether the claim or defence (or part of it) should be *curtailed at this stage*, for example by means of striking out[1] or summary judgment.[2] If appropriate, the court will fix an early appointment to hear argument from both sides;
- Formal allocation to the appropriate track, either by confirming the provisional allocation or transferring the case to another track. We saw in Chapter 8 that several factors will be relevant to this, including complexity, evidential needs and predicted length of trial, but normally the value of the claim will dictate which track it goes on;
- Case management. Directions upon allocation are generally given by reference to standard forms, adapted to the individual needs of the case at hand, although parties can ask the court to make agreed directions. Multi-track cases will tend to need more proactive management than fast track cases. Typically, initial directions on allocation include disclosure of documents,[3] exchange of witness statements, and expert evidence.[4]

---

1 Read on.

2 See discussion in Ch. 5

3 See generally Ch. 9

4 See generally Ch. 17

Once allocated, a case then proceeds on its given track through its interim stages to trial or settlement. Effective (indeed now, cost-effective) management of this progress by the courts is a crucial part of the ethos and effect of the CPR - without it, the overriding objective cannot be achieved. It had long been recognised that the system which the CPR replaced resulted in delay and expense which was often disproportionate to the issues or amount at stake in a case. The Woolf reforms' answer was to put the court firmly in the driving seat, giving it an array of powers and sanctions to control the conduct of litigation. But a decade on, it was still felt that some judges were too tolerant and forgiving of litigants (or often their legal representatives) who failed (for no good reason) to comply with directions and orders of the court. As Lewison LJ put it in 2012: '...courts at all levels ... have lost sight of the damage which the culture of delay and non-compliance is inflicting on the civil justice system'.[5] Jackson LJ's solution was to put a whip in the court's hand.

CPR, r 1.4(1) thus places a *duty* on the court to further the overriding objective by *actively managing cases*, which includes: encouraging a co-operative approach to the (procedural) conduct of litigation; identifying the real issues at an early stage and disposing summarily of others; encouraging the parties to use ADR where appropriate; controlling the pace and progress of cases, considering whether the 'likely benefits' of taking a particular step will 'justify the cost' of taking it; dealing efficiently with cases (for example by using technology or dealing with cases without a hearing); giving directions which ensure that if the case goes to trial, it proceeds 'quickly and efficiently,' and so on.[6]

The *ammunition* given to the court for this purpose is found in CPR, Part 3, which gives the court an exceedingly wide range of powers and punishments. These include making orders on its own initiative (without being asked, and with or without a hearing)[7]; making orders with conditions (for example, paying money into court)

---

5 *Perry v Brands Plaza Trading* [2012] EWCA Civ 224

6 CPR, r 1.4(2). It is worth reading and digesting this rule in its entirety.

7 Any party who is unhappy with such an order can apply to have it varied or set aside. See generally CPR, r 3.3.

and built-in punishments (so-called 'unless orders'[8]); contacting the parties in order to monitor compliance (which requires a 'prompt response')[9] ; imposing (and, less often now, giving relief from) sanctions for non-compliance with court directions and orders; extending or refusing to extend time; controlling the nature and extent of evidence to be adduced at trial and so on. In a nutshell, the court can do nearly anything it likes. Part carrot, but a lot of stick! Let's look at some of these powers and sanctions in turn.

1. STRIKING OUT

This is an attack on a party's statement of case or conduct of that case. Strictly speaking, causes of action are not struck out as such, but the term is used rather loosely. Of course if, say, a claimant's particulars of claim are struck out in their entirety, it follows that the action will be stayed or dismissed.[10] If a whole defence is struck out, the inevitable result will be judgment for the claimant. If only part of a statement of case is struck out,[11] then the rest of a viable claim or defence can continue. Striking out is the *most severe* sanction the court can impose. The court may strike out all or part of a statement of case if it appears:

(i)   that it discloses *no reasonable grounds* for bringing or defending the claim;

(ii) that it is an *abuse* of the court's process or is otherwise likely to obstruct the just disposal of the proceedings;

(iii) that there has been a *failure to comply* with a rule, practice direction or court order.[12]

---

8   As in, *"Unless you do what I say, you will be in trouble."* A typical 'unless' order might sound like this: *"Unless by (date/time) the defendant do file and serve a list of documents giving standard disclosure, the Defence will be struck out and judgment entered."*

9   As Master McCloud did in the case of *Mitchell v News Group Newspapers Ltd* [2013] EWCA Civ 1537

10 As to 'stays', see below

11 See wording of CPR, r 3.4(1)

12 CPR, r 3.4(2)

Ground (i) and (ii) cover statements of case which do not amount to a legally recognisable claim or defence[13] or which are unreasonably vague, incoherent, vexatious, scandalous, obviously ill-founded or otherwise amount to an abuse of process.[14] It is important to note that, where relevant, the court can and should exercise this power at an early stage (for example, when a claim is issued or a defence is filed), thus saving a party the expense of applying to strike out. A court official, for example, who receives a claim form that fails to meet the standards required, will issue it, but may then consult the judge who in turn may, on his or her own initiative, make an appropriate order in the circumstances. Possibilities include staying proceedings pending the filing of a 'proper' statement of case, requesting the filing of relevant further information, or, in the worst cases, striking out the offending statement of case (and entering such judgment as the other party may be entitled to).[15] The court may order a hearing to canvass the options.

Ground (iii) covers cases where the problem lies not in the statement of case itself, but in the way the claim or defence has been conducted. Sanctions for non-compliance are discussed below, but striking out on this basis (which is a little like a procedural death penalty) should normally be a last, not a first resort. Note the following.

(i) Built-in strike out sanction

Sometimes the strike out sanction is *built into* the rules themselves (for example, where there has been non-payment of fees payable at the track allocation and listing stages, the court will send a notice stating the date by which these must be paid, failing which, according to the rules, the claim will be struck out[16]) or is built into a court order (an 'unless order'). In both such cases, the sanction follows *automatically* if default occurs (unless an extension of time had been, or reprieve is given[17]). To obtain judgment (with costs) after

---

13 See examples in PD 3A

14 See, e.g., *Pickthall v Hill Dickinson LLP* [2009] EWCA Civ 543 (commencing proceedings knowing that the cause of action is vested in someone else is an abuse of process. Only the person with the vested right of action can bring the claim).

15 PD 3A, paras 2-4
16 CPR, r 3.7(2)-(4)
17 Under CPR, r 3.9, see below

an automatic strike out of this kind, the innocent party need only file a request.[18]

(ii) Strike out versus summary judgment

Striking out and summary judgment may be viewed as something of a twin-set, in the sense that many cases falling within CPR, r 3.4(2) may also fall within Part 24, which provides for summary disposal of claims or defences which have no reasonable prospect of success.[19] The overlap is not complete (summary judgment is not about non-compliance, and various procedural requirements relevant to Part 24 do not apply to CPR, r 3.4) but both possibilities should be considered in relevant cases.[20]

iii) Deadly weapon

Striking out is the court's *most draconian sanction*, and should be reserved for the most obvious and serious cases. In *Biguzzi v Rank Leisure plc*,[21] the Court of Appeal drew attention to the fact that there are several alternatives[22] to a strike out to be considered in any given situation before deploying the weapon of last resort. A court considering striking out should also consider the effect such an order would have on a party's right of access to the courts, which has particular importance under Art 6 of the European Convention on Human Rights. But each case must be decided on its merits. In the case of *Raja v van Hoogstraten*,[23] the defendant had arranged for the claimant to be killed in order to prevent him giving evidence - it does not get much more serious than that!

---

18 CPR, r 3.5 (this is rather like entering judgment in default in a money claim under Part 12, as to which see Ch. 5).

19 See generally Ch. 5
20 PD 3, para 1.7

21 [1999] 1 WLR 1926
22 As to which, read on
23 [2006] EWHC 1315 (Ch)

2. STRIKING OUT IS NOT THE ONLY FRUIT!: RANGE OF SANCTIONS FOR NON-COMPLIANCE

The court has various weapons which it can use to actively manage cases and give effect to the overriding objective. The power to impose sanctions for non-compliance is critically important for maintaining control of the conduct of litigation. Generally speaking, the philosophy behind the CPR will not work if the court's bark is always worse than its bite. The recent Jackson reforms were particularly predicated on the notion that if the court's bite were fiercer, this will prove a better deterrent, thus reducing the need for it to bark. The court now has a much greater range of sanctions at its disposal than before the CPR,[24] which should assist in ensuring that in any given case the punishment 'fits the crime'. Again, note the following:

(i) Timetable directions

Not *all* acts of non-compliance are of the most serious kind. An example of a minor default might be a failure to comply with timetable directions.[25] So long as the key case management events in a case remain unaffected,[26] the parties should seek to resolve such problems between themselves by agreeing a new date for compliance or some other solution. Furthermore, an 'innocent' party faced with an opponent who has not complied with a timetable direction should neither let sleeping dogs lie (by sitting back and letting the default get worse by the passage of time) nor immediately rush to the court. Instead, the middle ground of a written warning should first be given.[27] This should warn the defaulting party of the intention to make an application to the court if the direction is not complied with by a reasonable (stated) time. If this does not do the trick, an application to the court may be made for an order to enforce compliance or for a sanction to be imposed, or both. Sanctions may

---

24 Under the old rules, 'dismissal' of a claim or defence (not a statement of case, as such) was a sanction which took two forms, only one of which survived the advent of the CPR. This involved allegations of deliberate abuse of court procedures.

This is now more than adequately covered by CPR, Part 3, which can deal with the contemptuous litigant, as well as the merely lazy and disorganised. The other, known as 'dismissal for want of prosecution' has been rendered virtually extinct.

25 Directions tend to be more impersonal than orders. It is a bit like the difference between *"I want you children to play quietly in there"* (a direction) and *"Tommy! Put down that vase!"* (an order). Breach of the latter is often considered (other things being equal)

range from a costs sanction (minor) to the more draconian 'unless' order, but should be proportionate and effective.

(ii) Pre-action default

Another type of default is non-compliance with pre-action protocols or the pre-action conduct PD. Minor breaches will not cause much concern and certainly should not be viewed as an excuse itself for non-compliance by the other party, but where a failure to comply with appropriate pre-action conduct results in unnecessary litigation and/or costs, sanctions can follow. These would focus on punitive costs and/or interest orders as a punishment for not trying hard enough to avoid litigation (ignoring an offer of ADR, for example, could be construed as not giving it any serious consideration). It is now a requirement that the parties plead in their statements of case whether or not a relevant pre-action protocol has been complied with,[28] so lack of compliance should come as no surprise at the end of a trial (and may even be punished earlier).

(iii) Built-in sanctions other than strike out

We saw that the strike out sanction is contained within certain provisions of the CPR, or can be built into a court order (an 'unless order') in case of non-compliance. This applies to other sorts of sanctions as well. So, for example, CPR, r 35.1 says that if a party fails to disclose expert evidence as required,[29] that party will not be allowed to rely on that expert evidence, unless the court gives permission.[30] This is a common sense, tailor-made sanction which is intended, and usually does, encourage compliance! Similar sorts of rule-based sanctions tripped up defaulters in the recent cases of *Mitchell v News Group Newspapers Ltd* ('*Mitchell*')[31] (failure to file/serve costs budget in time) and *Durrant v Chief Constable of Avon and Somerset*[32] (failure to file/serve

---

more serious than breach of the former.

26 See Ch. 8

27 PD 28, para 5 (fast track) and PD 29, para 7 (multi-track)

28 PD Pre-action conduct, para 9.7

29 See generally below at Ch. 17

30 Some rule-based sanctions are more discretionary, allowing the court to make some other order if appropriate.

31 [2013] EWCA Civ 1537

witness statements in time) cases. In *Summit Navigation Ltd v Generali Ramania Asigurare Reasigurare SA ('Summit Navigation')*[33] the sanction (a stay) automatically followed upon non-compliance with a court order. Some such sanctions ultimately impact more upon a litigant's legal advisors (to keep them on their toes), than on the litigant directly, which can affect how forgiving (or not) a court will be of a party's default.

3. RELIEF FROM SANCTIONS

When a sanction is built into an order (an 'unless order') or mandated by a rule or practice direction, it will *automatically* take effect unless the defaulting party applies for (and is granted) 'relief from the sanction' under CPR, r 3.9.[34] The text of this rule has recently been amended, in keeping with the new policy of low, or no, tolerance to non-compliance. The old rule (which required the court to consider 'all of the circumstances' and then set out a list of obvious factors which might be of particular relevance) was thought to give judges too much scope for lenience. The new version now simply requires the court to consider all the circumstances of the case, so as to enable it to deal *justly* with the application, including the need for litigation to be conducted efficiently and at proportionate costs; and to enforce compliance with rules, practice directions and orders.

The application must be supported by written evidence, and the reason for the default had better be good! In *Mitchell*[35] , the Court of Appeal made clear that the courts are on a mission. In this case, they said that the court, in applying r 3.9, must apply the overriding objective and perform a balancing exercise, taking into account all relevant factors. But it stressed that the two most important factors were

---

32 [2013] EWCA Civ 1624

33 [2014] EWHC 398 (Comm)

34 If judgment is entered following striking out, then the application to set aside that judgment is determined by reference to r 3.9

35 *Op. cit.*

those listed in the rule, namely the need for litigation to be conducted efficiently and at proportionate costs, and the need to enforce compliance with rules, practice directions and orders. It also made clear that in exercising its discretion, the courts should take a holistic approach to justice. There was to be a 'shift away', as it was put, 'from exclusively focusing on doing justice in an individual case ... a tougher, more robust approach to non-compliance and relief from sanctions is intended to ensure that justice can be done in the majority of cases'.[36]

The court will, of course, look at the nature of the default - if it is trivial or insignificant (more of form than substance, or a narrowly missed deadline with no case management repercussions), then the court will usually grant relief from the sanction. Where the non-compliance is significant, then the court will look at why it occurred. In this context, inefficiency or incompetence of a party's solicitors (for example, overlooking a deadline, pressures of work) is unlikely be a good reason; circumstances outside the control of the defaulting party/solicitors might be.[37] The court's tolerance to non-compliance will thus now be very low, but its response to an application for relief will be rational as well as proportionate. It is not the aim of the Jackson reforms to 'turn rules and rule compliance into 'trip wires', nor into 'the mistress rather than the handmaiden of justice' - the point is to enable the cost-effective progress of litigation (and the administration of justice) by means of compliance with rules and court order, not to 'render compliance an end in itself'.[38]

Two other points were made in the Mitchell case. One is that an application for relief from sanctions presupposes that the sanction was in principle properly imposed. If a party wishes to contend that it was not appropriate to make the order, the appropriate procedural route is to appeal the order (or exceptionally, by asking the court which imposed it to vary or revoke it).[39] Secondly, if a party feels it needs more time to comply with a court order, then an application for an extension of time should be made. Applications made before time has expired will (as you might

---

36 Per Jackson LJ, quoted in *ibid*, [38]
37 See encapsulation of principles established in *Mitchell in Summit Navigation, op. cit.* [39].

38 See citation in *Summit Navigation, ibid*, at [49]. In that case the one who was wasting money and delaying the progress of the case was not the defaulter- but rather the defendants who thought they would could get a 'fortuitous' dismissal of the case against them

because of a 24 hour delay in the claimants giving security for costs!
39 *Mitchell, op cit*, [44]

expect) be looked upon more favourably than applications for relief from sanctions after the event.[40] So that the courts are not flooded with such applications, a new provision is proposed which will allow parties to *agree* such extensions of time for up to 28 days. If a longer extension is required, an email should first be sent to the court, including a brief reason for the extension, confirmation that the delay will not prejudice any hearing date, and a draft consent order. The court will consider the request and either endorse it or require a formal hearing.[41]

Worst case scenarios

Only in exceptional circumstances will the court let a failure to comply with a direction or 'unless order' lead to the postponement of the trial.[42] Where (in the worst case scenario) an action has been struck out following a failure to comply with an 'unless order' (or other contemptuous behaviour), a second claim brought on the same basis (even if not statute-barred) would normally also be struck out (as an abuse of process).[43]

Punishment to fit the crime

The cases on sanctions since the inception of the CPR show that each case must be decided on its own merits, and pre-CPR cases will be irrelevant and unappreciated in court unless they speak to the (new look) overriding objective. Cases before the Jackson reforms may not fare much better. A noticeable theme of these cases is that the courts should be fair and flexible in exercising their wide and varied powers, ensuring that any penalty is commensurate with the nature of the default. The post-Jackson era heralds a more robust approach, in the interest of serving the wider public interest in efficient and proportionate civil justice.[44] Even so, there are many procedural penalties available to the court to deter and punish delay and

40 *Ibid*, [41]
41 This will be an amendment to CPR, r 3.8(4)
42 See, e.g., *Woodward v Finch* [1999] CPLR 699
43 *Johnson v Gore Wood and Co* [2002] 2 AC 1
44 Mitchell, op. cit.

inefficiency (including the latest addition, costs 'capping' orders, which limits the amount of future costs which a party may recover). Some are more final than others! A sanction which deprives a party of fair access to the courts (for example, striking out) should still be seen as a sanction of last resort.[45]

4. OTHER CASE MANAGEMENT POWERS

Extension of time and correcting irregularities

The court has general power to extend or abridge time (or to refuse to extend or abridge time), to allow (or refuse to allow) the parties to overlook procedural errors and/or take steps itself to remedy procedural errors.[46] This power will be used in keeping with the new-look overriding objective: applications made in good time will fare best. Remember, however, that (as we have seen) this power may not be used in respect of applications to renew invalid claim forms which have expired.[47]

Applications to revoke or vary

The court's powers to make case management orders includes the power to revoke or vary an order. It will do so sparingly, to ensure that applicants do not get 'two bites at the cherry', and so as not to undermine the appeal process. The discretion to revoke or vary will normally be limited to cases where (i) there has been a 'material change in circumstances' or (ii) where the facts on which the original order was based were misstated, or (iii) where there was a manifest mistake on the part of the judge who made the order. In addition, the application must be made promptly.[48]

---

45 It was noted in *ibid* that the sanction imposed in that case caused no prejudice to the claimant himself. For costs capping, see CPR, r 3.19-21

46 Most procedural errors are 'irregularities', which means they do not invalidate the proceedings and are capable of correction by the court. CPR, r 3.10

47 See Ch. 12

48 *Tibbles v SIG plc* [2012] 1WLR 2591, cited in Mitchell, *op. cit.* [44]

Stays

This is a bit like the dog command. A 'stay' is an order producing a temporary halt to proceedings which can effectively become a permanent state of affairs.[49] While a stay is in effect, no other steps may be taken in the case (except an application to remove the stay).[50] The power arises and is applicable in all sorts of situations. Some examples are:

(a) A stay of proceedings in a personal injuries case so long as the claimant unreasonably refuses to undergo a medical exam.

(b) A stay of proceedings while a preliminary point is argued which may have the result that the action will proceed no further.

(c) If a claimant accepts an offer of settlement,[51] the proceedings will be stayed, effectively ending the case.

(d) The *Tomlin* order, which is a special form of consent order, stays any further proceedings in the claim which have been compromised, except for the purpose of putting into effect the terms set out in the schedule to the order.[52]

(e) A stay of execution pending an appeal.

(f) A stay in proceedings for a month to attempt a settlement. This is requested in the directions questionnaire (and so occurs after the defence has been filed).

Discontinuance

This is something a claimant (or a person in position of a claimant) does if he or she, having commenced proceedings, decides that the wiser course is to abandon the whole or part of a claim against the defendant. The claimant merely serves a notice of discontinuance on the defendant (agreeing, of course, to pay the defendant's costs).

---

49 It is not, however, the same thing as discontinuing an action or getting judgment.

50 But it does not stop time running for other purposes.

51 See Ch. 15

52 See Ch. 19

53 See CPR, r 38.2(2). If the claimant is acting under a disability (e.g. a child), then the court's approval must be sought. See Ch 3.

54 *Fox v Star Newspaper* [1900] AC 19, HL. Similarly, and for the same sorts of reasons, a defendant can apply to set aside a notice of discontinuance: CPR, r 38.4

55 CPR, r 38.7

The claimant does not require the permission of the court unless an interim order has been made (for example, an interim payment has been made) or there is some aspect of the case which might need 'unraveling' (for example, an undertaking has been given to the court or there is another claimant involved, who might be left in the lurch).[53]

If permission is required, the claimant will usually be given it, subject to appropriate orders as to costs and any corrective orders which might be needed (for example, to repay an interim payment). The court is usually only too delighted to be relieved of cases, although very occasionally it may feel that a case has progressed so far that the claimant ought to lose openly and publicly.[54]

If discontinuance follows the filing of a defence, then a second claim brought on the same (or substantially the same) facts would not be allowed, unless the court gave permission.[55]

revision tip

- Read all of CPR 3.1-3.11 and PD 3A carefully. The rules themselves are clearly set out. You need little else to remind you of the court's powers!

It is worth reading ...

The judgment of the Master of the Rolls in *Mitchell v News Group Newspapers Ltd* [2013] EWCA Civ 1537. Lots of procedural goodies here, including appeals leapfrogging from the master to the Court of Appeal on a point of public importance and lots about the Jackson reforms. It is readable and makes its 'clear message' clear. Notice though that the claimant himself suffered no prejudice to his claim or his wallet (his solicitors paid the price), so it was not that hard to be intolerant.

Compare *Mitchell* with *Summit Navigation Ltd v Gernerali Romania Asigurare Reasiguare SA* [2014] EWHC 398 (Comm), in which the party seeking to evoke (and indeed benefit in a big way from) the no-tolerance policy was said by Leggatt J to have 'turned *Mitchell* on its head'.

Lightman J's judgment in *Raja v van Hoogstraten* [2006] EWHC 1315 (CH) is still interesting on all sorts of levels. It is not all that often that such murder and mayhem goes on in the Chancery division!

PART FOUR

typical defendant's initiatives

CHAPTER 14

Security for costs

In the past, claimants made much of the running in litigation; the claimant, after all, is the party who sets the ball rolling and, generally speaking, it was historically the claimant who set the pace of the proceedings. With the introduction of the CPR, of course, all that changed - it is the court which now controls and sets the agenda.

Even so, defendants (if all they are doing is defending) will still of necessity spend much of the time reacting either to something the claimant has done (not least of all bringing the action) or to the court's management of the case. Defendants may respond with deadly effect, of course, but nevertheless they are often prodded into action by something or someone else. It is also worth remembering that a claimant with a weak case does not have to bring proceedings (and would be well advised not to do so). Unless and until a claimant sees reason, however, a defendant with a meritorious defence[1] really has little choice but to defend.

That being the case, and despite the fact that there are obviously many requests or applications which either party to litigation can make if necessary,[2] there are three very important procedural initiatives *typically (sometimes only) taken by defendants.* One of these is bringing in third parties. We looked at this in the context of parties and additional claims in Chapter 3. The other two are applications for security for costs, discussed in this chapter and offers of settlement, discussed in the next.

---

1 Not one so strong as to succeed in striking out the claim, perhaps, but still good enough to win at the end of the day.

2 For example, a request for further information, an order for disclosure of a particular document, an order to strike out, and so on.

Occasionally a claimant brings an action against the defendant simply for its nuisance value. The case may have a limited prospect of success,[3] but it has every ability to cost the defendant time, inconvenience, and expense. More mundanely, and much more commonly, a defendant may feel confident that there is a good chance of defeating a claim brought against him, but at the same time be concerned that the claimant, as loser, will be unable to meet any order for costs made against him.[4] In this context an impecunious claimant can be as much of a problem as an impecunious defendant.

Some, *but by no means all*, defendants are able to get protection in this kind of situation, in the form of an order for security for costs. If granted, the order must specify how and when security must be given. The usual order in the Queen's Bench division requires the claimant to pay a specific amount of money into court as security for the payment of any costs order which may eventually be made in favour of the defendant, and staying the claim until security is given.[5] The money is held as a fund out of which the successful defendant's costs can be paid.[6] Thus, the court has a *discretion* to order *a claimant (or person in the position of claimant[7])* to give security for his opponent's *costs* where the defendant can establish that the claimant is one of those sorts of claimants against whom it is *possible* to get such an order.

There are essentially *two hurdles* to be surmounted. The defendant must *first* establish that the claimant is one of those kinds of claimants against whom an order for security is *possible*. This is a *very narrow class* of what might be thought of as qualifying *claimants*[8] who are described by reference to situations which might make payment under, or enforcement of, a costs order difficult. In a nutshell, the possibilities[9] are where:

---

3 If it is completely and obviously without merit, of course, the claim could be struck out or the defendant might get summary judgment.
4 As to costs, see generally Ch. 18.
5 In the Commercial Court, claimants are usually given a reasonable time to comply (during which the case progresses), failing which the action is stayed or struck out. See the clear explanation cited in *Summit Navigation Ltd v Generali Romania Asiguare Reasiguare SA* [2014] EWHC 398 Comm, at paras 32-33
6 If the defendant loses, of course, the money will go back to the claimant.
7 Note that this would also include, for example, a counterclaiming defendant, who for the purposes of the counterclaim is a claimant

(i) The claimant is ordinarily resident outside the (domestic or European[10]) jurisdiction;

(ii) The claimant is an 'impecunious company'[11] ;

(iii) The claimant has changed his address so as to evade service;

(iv) The claimant failed to give a correct address in the claim form;

(v) The claimant is an 'impecunious', nominal[12] claimant;

(vi) The claimant has taken steps in relation to his assets which would make it difficult to enforce an order for costs against him.[13]

If a defendant cannot *surmount this first hurdle*, that is the end of the story - there would be *no scope* for an order for security for costs. Note, too, that impecuniosity is *not, by itself*, a ground for ordering security. It is part of the equation for conditions (ii) and (v), above, and may be relevant if the court is in a position to exercise its discretion, but impecuniosity alone is not enough to get the defendant over this first hurdle.

Even if the first hurdle is surmounted, however, it does not necessarily follow that the defendant will get security. There is a second. Such orders are *discretionary* and to make the order the court must be satisfied that having regard to 'all the circumstances' it is 'just' to do so. This is all the rule says.

Older cases[14] attempted to list the sorts of factors which the court might look at in order to do this. For example: are there any special difficulties in enforcing a costs order? Is it obvious (without conducting a mini-trial) that the merits clearly favour one side over the other? How clear is it that the defendant will win and not get his costs? Could the defendant recover costs from someone other than the claimant? What impact would the order have on the claimant? These are really just common sense considerations focused on the purpose behind the application - the risk that the defendant, if successful, will not recover his costs.

(unless the same is a purely defensive set-off). See CPR, r 25, 12(1) which refers to the order being made in favour of 'a defendant in any claim'. Claimants who try to avoid being claimants for these purposes can also be subject to an order: CPR,

8 This is my expression, not the CPR's.

9 See wording of CPR, r 25, 13 and WB commentary

r25.14. For the purposes of this discussion I will just use the descriptions 'claimant' and 'defendant', as this is the usual scenario.

for more detail.

10 As discussed in Ch. 4 (Service outside the jurisdiction).

11 'Impecunious' is used as shorthand. The actual wording in the rule is 'the claimant is a company or other body ... and there is reason to believe

In the post CPR case of *Nasser v United Bank of Kuwait*,[15] the court said that its discretion was to be exercised by applying the overriding objective (no surprises there) so as to afford *'proportionate protection'* against the 'difficulty identified' by the condition relied upon in making the application for security for costs. So, for example, if the claimant is resident outside the jurisdiction, how easy or hard it would be to enforce a costs order will be especially relevant. Are there capital assets in the jurisdiction? If the claimant is an impecunious company, the court might be more focused on how to protect the defendant without stifling a genuine claim. Is the defendant being a bully? Did the defendant contribute to the company's financial difficulties? Should the need to protect the defendant yield to the claimant's right of access to the courts?

Delay in making the application might also be relevant. Every case, and every application, will be determined on the basis of its individual facts.

An application for security for costs is made on notice to a master or District Judge (as the case may be), using the normal Part 23 procedure. The application notice must be served on the claimant at least three clear days before the hearing and be supported by written evidence, setting out the basis for the application and factors relevant to the exercise of the court's discretion. It should also include an estimate of the likely costs of defending the claim. Such applications will normally be made at the first case management conference - orders for security for costs are not appropriate in small claims track cases because of the restrictions on recovering costs in such claims, but they can be made in respect of the costs of an appeal[16].

If the court is minded to make an order for security, the next question is: for how much? The first point to make is that the amount of security to be ordered is *entirely within court's discretion*. Having said that, the amount chosen should 'be neither illusory nor oppressive.'[17] A conventional approach has been to fix the

---

it will be unable to pay the defendant's costs if so ordered'. Inability to pay requires credible evidence, not speculation. See WB, 25.13.12

12 'Nominal' essentially means that the claimant is just a frontman. Claimants suing in a representative capacity are specifically excluded from the description.

13 It is not necessary to establish any particular motivation here, simply that whatever has happened to the assets has made them less accessible to a debtor.

14 See, especially, *Lindsay Parkinson and Co Ltd v Triplan Ltd* [1973] QB 609

15 [2002] 1 WLR 1868

16 CPR, r 25.15. There is an example of an application notice in Sime, fig 26.1

amount of security at about two-thirds of the estimated costs up to the stage of proceedings for which security is ordered (so past as well as future costs can be included in the figure). It is common to order security in convenient stages, rather than one huge amount right up to end of trial (the case might settle, after all), but there is no hard and fast rule.[18] Orders should be case-specific, and geared to the specific risks revealed by the evidence.

Do not lose sight of the fact that this is an order about security for *costs*. It is nothing to do with damages. Winning defendants do not, of course, get damages; they *avoid* paying them. But (other things being equal) they would normally be entitled to their costs from the losing claimant.[19]

Joint claimants can complicate matters, especially if one, say, is resident outside the jurisdiction, but the other is not. Assuming no other ground is relevant, it is clear that an order cannot be made against the claimant who lives in this country, since that person is not what we are calling a qualifying claimant. But would the court make an order against the other claimant who does come within CPR, r 25.13(2)(a)? The courts get edgy about claimants who reside beyond the reach of the English (and European) courts, concerned that it is too easy for them to scurry away without meeting their litigation obligations, including payment of costs if they have lost or abandoned the case.

This may be why they are head of the list of qualifying claimants! But does the fact that there is another claimant within the jurisdiction make it more or less likely that the order will be made against the one who is not? As you might expect the answer is that it depends on the circumstances, and in particular how confident the court is that the defendant will be able recover his costs from the resident claimant.

Thus, it may be possible to get an order against the foreign claimant if the two

---

17 *Hart Investments Ltd v Larchpark Ltd* [2008] 1 BCLC 589
18 The claimant may apply to discharge or vary an order for security. This would be appropriate if the order was wrongly granted in the first place or there has been a significant change in circumstances since the order was made. See, e.g., *Gordano Building Contractors v Burgess* [1988] 1 WLR 890.
19 See generally discussion in Ch. 18
20 See discussion in *Slazengers Ltd v Seaspeed Ferries International Ltd* [1987] 1 WLR 1197

claimants are not relying on the same cause of action or each claimant will be solely responsible for his own share of the defendant's costs (or it is impossible to predict the liability on costs). Conversely, it may not be appropriate to grant the order against the foreign claimant where both claimants are relying on identical causes of action and will be jointly responsible for costs, and there are sufficient funds to enforce against - if, in effect, the defendant could recover all of his costs from the claimant who is inside the jurisdiction.[20] In essence, the court has to balance the protection afforded the defendant by the claimant within the jurisdiction against concerns about allowing foreign claimants to bring actions here without giving security.

revision tips

- Remember that it is *defendants to claims* who apply for orders for security for costs. Watch out especially for counterclaims, when roles are reversed! When dealing with any problem question in an assessment, make a quick note of who is doing what to whom. It is easy to get confused in the heat of the moment.

- Focus on claimants who are extra-jurisdictional or 'impecunious' companies - these are the most common types of qualifying claimant against whom such orders are sought, both in practice and in assessments. In 2013-14, the BPTC syllabus specifically referred only to these two grounds. Note the exact wording of r 25.13(2)(a) and (c). Remember that 'impecunious' is just shorthand.

- Remember the two hurdles! Focus any additional points in a SAQ on the grounds and issues raised by the facts of the problem.

It is worth reading ...

The judgment of the Court of Appeal in *Spy Academy Limited v Sakar International Inc* [2009] EWCA Civ 985. Not the thriller its name implies, but still a good read. And a fine example of some of the issues that arise in the exercise of the court's discretion whether or not to make an order for security. And there is an order for specific disclosure in the story too, so it's two for the price of one!

CHAPTER 15

Part 36 and offers of settlement

A formal offer of settlement is something defendants have been more apt to do than claimants, but claimants can and increasingly do make such offers as well. Part 36 of the CPR now deals with a whole range of situations where a formal offer to settle a case might be made[1]: by a claimant or by a defendant; before or after a claim has been commenced; where the relief sought is money and where it is not. These are known globally as 'Part 36 offers'.

As we have seen, much of the CPR is focused on getting parties to avoid unnecessarily resorting to, or prolonging litigation to resolve their differences. They are, for example, asked to consider alternative solutions, to focus on the real issues in dispute, to be open and cooperative in the conduct of litigation. Part 36 offers perform a vital part of this process by encouraging parties to settle their dispute at the earliest possible stage, rather than fighting it out to the bitter end. A party who receives a realistic offer of settlement should always give serious thought to accepting it because the risk is that the person making the offer ('offeror') will be awarded the costs incurred of continuing the litigation, if the person to whom the offer was made ('offeree') fails to achieve a better outcome at trial. This can be a very heavy price indeed.

Advising on the terms of an offer of settlement, and whether to accept or

---

1   Offers made in the context
of the RTA protocol are
covered in specially adapted
rules set out in sections II/III
of Part 36.

reject such offers, requires considerable professional skill and experience. At this point, what is important is to understand how the Part 36 scheme works in practical terms, which is what this chapter aims to help you do.

It is useful to distinguish between offers made by defendants and offers made by claimants.

1. PART 36 OFFERS BY *DEFENDANTS*

The principle behind the Part 36 procedure in this context is that a claimant should accept an 'acceptable' offer by the defendant to settle the case rather than proceed to trial regardless, thereby increasing the costs the defendant would have to pay when the claimant only wins at the end of the day what was earlier on offer. If a claimant fails to accept an offer which it turns out should have been accepted, the consequence is (almost invariably) that he pays the costs of unnecessarily continuing.

For many years, in money claims,[2] defendants actually parted with their money when putting formal offers on the table. These were known as 'payments into court' and were abolished in 2007.[3] Now *only the offer* goes on the table, whatever the nature of the claim. Defendants thus make formal Part 36 offers to settle, in proper written (usually standard) form,[4] which must normally remain on the table for a stated period of *at least* 21 days (or up to the end of trial if the offer is made less than 21 days before the trial starts)[5] - for the claimant to accept or not. This initial period is known in the rules as the 'relevant period.' For the discussion which follows I will assume this to be the *minimum* 21 days (which is typical), although it can be longer.[6]

In a nutshell this is how it works: if the claimant accepts the offer during

---

2   Non-money claims were never susceptible to payments of money into court, so these always involved a formal written offer.

3   Special cases still requiring a payment into court are now covered by CPR, Part 37 (not 36)

4   CPR, r 36.2 and PD 36A para 1 and example in Sime, fig 36.1
5   CPR, r 36.3(1)(c)(ii)
6   CPR, r 36.3(1)(c)(i)

this initial 21 day period, then all proceedings are stayed. The defendant will be required to pay the claimant's costs up to that point. If the claimant never accepts the offer, and the case goes to trial, the trial judge will not normally know anything about the offer. If at the end of the trial, the outcome for the claimant is 'more advantageous' than what was on offer,[7] then costs would be apt to 'follow the event' in the normal way,[8] which means that the losing defendant pays the winning claimant's costs. If, however, the outcome for the claimant is no *better or is worse* than what was on offer, the costs incurred *after* the offer was made (plus the initial 21 days) will be awarded against the otherwise successful claimant. From that point, the claimant will (almost always) have to pay the defendant's costs - and, of course, bear his own.

Strategically, the amount of a defendant's Part 36 offer should tempt the claimant into compromising the case, without offering too much!

Here are a couple of points to note generally:

(i) A defendant can make a Part 36 offer at *any stage* of proceedings (even during the pre-action phase and even during trial) and can *increase* the amount at *any* time. An offer is made when it is served on the other party; if the latter is legally represented, then service *must* be on the legal representative.[9]

(ii) A Part 36 offer is *treated as including all interest* (up to the end of the 21 day/relevant period).[10]

(iii) The claimant should be able to determine to what the offer relates and can seek clarification where required - in the first instance from the offeror, but by application to the court if necessary.[11] It is a formal requirement that it be made clear whether the offer is in full and final

---

7   Where the claim is for money, this can usually be determined by comparing the amount on offer with the amount awarded (comparing like with like so far as interest on the sum is concerned). Comparing offer with outcome can be a lot more tricky with non-

8   money claims.
    See Ch. 18 on costs generally.

9   CPR, PD 36A, para 1.2
10 CPR, r 36.3(3)
11 CPR, r 36.8(1)

settlement of all claims, or just some of the claims, and whether it takes into account any counterclaim or interim payment which has been made. The offer must also state that it is intended to have the consequences of Part 36. It does not have to (but often does) state that the offer is 'without prejudice except as to costs', since this goes without saying.[12]

(iv) A defendant's offer should normally be an offer to pay a single sum of money (payable within 14 days of acceptance), although there are special rules in personal injuries actions about how to deal with claims for future pecuniary loss, provisional damages and recovery of State benefits.[13]

(v) Usually, a defendant wants to offer the whole amount appropriate before the heaviest costs are incurred so as to take advantage of the costs protection. The earlier the realistic offer is made, the fuller the protection for the defendant. Having said that, it would be silly to make an offer without a fair degree of evidential information.

(vi) Normally offers are made and accepted under Part 36 *without the intervention of the court*. It is the *exception, not the rule* for the claimant to need permission to accept a Part 36 offer. Examples of when, exceptionally, permission is required include where the claimant is a child or otherwise acting under a legal disability[14] and where the trial has already started.[15]

(vii) A claimant who does not want to accept a Part 36 offer need not express this in any formal way - such offers are *not rejected, as such*, but simply not accepted. Even a counter-offer does not operate to extinguish an earlier offer.[16] The only way a Part 36 offer (which has not been accepted) is taken off the table is by the *offeror formally withdrawing it*. It is therefore possible to have several offers on the table at once!

---

12 CPR, r 36.2(2)

13 CPR, r 36.4-6. See also BCP 66.10

14 So the court can ensure that the interest of the vulnerable claimant are being served: CPR, r 21.10

15 CPR, r 36.9(3)(d). Because some great revelation may have occurred at the trial which puts the claim (and hence the offer) in a new light.

16 See *Gibbon v Manchester City Council* [2010] EWCA 726

(viii) The fact of a Part 36 offer should not normally be revealed to the trial judge until issues of both liability and quantum have been finally determined. The risk of prejudice is obvious, so this is an important principle. The exceptions are very limited.[17]

Both the White Book (Vol I, Guide D6) and BCP (Checklist 29) include a useful resumé of the procedural detail. What follows is an overview, looking at four different possible scenarios. Let's assume the defendant makes a Part 36 offer in a *money* claim, well before the trial date and complies with all necessary formalities. The relevant period is the usual 21 days:

A.   THE FIRST 21 DAYS

During this initial period, the claimant may accept the offer *and be assured of getting costs.* The claimant must notify the defendant in writing[18] that the offer is being accepted. It will follow that the claimant is entitled to 100% of his standard basis costs[19] up to the date of serving the notice of acceptance - these would include, typically, the cost of getting counsel's opinion on whether to accept or not. *During this period, the defendant may not withdraw* the offer (or change its terms to be less advantageous), unless the court gives permission.[20] Nor does the court have power to order payment of only a proportion of the claimant's costs.[21]

B.   AFTER THE 21 DAYS (BUT BEFORE TRIAL)

After the initial 21 days has expired, assuming the offer has not been formally withdrawn, the claimant may still accept it, subject to the parties agreeing liability for costs. The claimant will not necessarily get costs incurred after the end of the initial 21 day period; quite the reverse in fact. The usual outcome would be that the

---

17 One is where the defence is one of 'tender before action', which essentially means that the defendant says the liability has already been met.
18 There is no particular format- a letter will do: CPR, r 36.9(1). Notice must also be filed with the court: PD 26, para 3.1. There is no equivalent procedure for rejecting an offer. Even a counter-offer does not in itself extinguish an earlier offer, which remains capable of acceptance until formally withdrawn.
19 See discussion of costs below at Ch. 18
20 CPR, r 36.3(5). An application for such permission would be made in accordance with Part 23 (PD 36, para 2.2(1)).

claimant gets his costs up to that point, but the defendant would normally be entitled to costs from the end of the initial 21 day period until the date of acceptance. Where the parties cannot agree, the court will make an order as to costs (including the costs of having to ask the court to make the order as to costs!)

Where a defendant's Part 36 offer has not been accepted by the end of the initial 21 day period, the defendant may formally withdraw it and/or make a new offer. This is done by serving written notice; no permission of the court is required at this stage.[22] Note that a withdrawn offer (or one which does not comply with the formalities sufficiently to be considered a proper Part 36 offer) cannot give rise to an 'official' costs sanction under Part 36, *but it can* (and will) still be 'put into the mix' and taken *into account* by the court (as can any informal offer) in deciding final costs orders. What importance it might have on the order as to costs is entirely up to the wide discretion of the court. In a suitable case, the court can even treat a withdrawn Part 36 offer as having the same consequences as if it had not been withdrawn.[23]

C.   DURING TRIAL

If a claimant wants to accept a Part 36 offer once the trial of the action has started, this brings into play two conflicting propositions. The first is that the claimant requires the court's *permission* to accept the offer *once the trial* has started. Maybe the claimant's case is not going so well, and it would be unjust to let him take advantage of an offer which he has spurned for so long. But the rules also require that in the normal course of events the *trial* judge must not know about any Part 36 offers which have been made, until the case is over. So how does a claimant ask for permission from the court without the court finding out that the offer has been made?

Ask another judge, is the short answer. Of course, if (as is commonly the case) the defendant does not object to the claimant accepting the Part 36 offer even

---

21   There is a deeming provision to this effect. See WB discussion at 36.10.1 and *Lahey v Pirelli Tyres Ltd* [2007] 1 WLR 998.

22   CPR, r 36.3(6). The new offer (whether better or worse than the previous one) will take effect once the claimant has been notified.

23   CPR, r 44.2(4) and see BCP, para 66.19, WB, para 36.3.4

at this late stage, then it is unlikely to cause a problem because the only remaining issue will be the question of costs. The defendant might object, however, if the trial has revealed unanticipated weaknesses in the claimant's case. This happened in the old case of *Gaskins v British Aluminium Co.*[24] After failing in his application to the trial judge for permission to accept a payment-in (as it was then called), the claimant then made a second application to the judge for a re-trial because he (the judge) now knew about the fact of the payment-in. The Court of Appeal was not enamoured with this argument, especially as the only reason the trial judge found out about the payment into court was because the claimant had told him. They also pointed out that it would be strange if a claimant whose case is going badly at trial could get a new trial simply by seeking permission to accept the amount on offer, and when this is refused, necessarily getting an order for a re-trial. It was up to the judge to decide whether, all things considered, carrying on with the trial in such circumstances created an injustice.

This essentially remains the case, especially for an inadvertent disclosure of the fact of a Part 36 offer.[25] Even after an inappropriate disclosure at trial, the judge should think long and hard before ordering a new trial, and in particular about the expense and proportionality of such a course.[26] But where a claimant seeks permission to accept the defendant's offer after the trial has begun, the rules now suggest a simple solution - unless the parties are happy for the trial judge to deal with the matter, the claimant should simply apply to another judge.[27]

In the majority of cases, acceptance even at this late stage will be granted, although the court's discretion is unfettered and if the circumstances (and in particular a *change* in circumstances) warrant it, as in the *Gaskins* case, then permission will be denied.[28] If acceptance is allowed, either by consent or with the court's permission, the usual rule is that the claimant recovers costs up to the end

---

24   [1976] 1 All ER 208
25   *Garratt v Saxby* [2004] EWCA Civ 341

26   If the disclosure was intentional or clearly the fault of one party, and a new trial ordered, no doubt that party (or possibly his legal advisors) would be asked to pay (a considerable amount) for the wasted costs. Junior Counsel beware!

27   The same would apply to an application to withdraw the offer: PD 36A, para 2.2 and 3.2

of the initial 21 day period, and the defendant recovers costs thereafter - a claimant who has left it this long to accept the offer will end up paying a lot of money in costs!

D   THE CLAIMANT NEVER ACCEPTS THE OFFER

A claimant must obtain a judgment which is 'more advantageous' than the defendant's Part 36 offer in order to avoid the cost penalties of failing to accept it. For *money claims*, all that is required is that the claimant recovers more in money terms than the amount on offer, *however small the difference*.[29] So even if the claimant recovers only one penny more than the amount on offer, he will normally be entitled to his costs in the usual way.[30] But if the claimant falls short of this mark, the sanction kicks in: the usual order will be that the claimant will get his costs up to the end of the initial 21 day period, but *thereafter* he will have to pay the defendant's costs (*and of course bear his own*), unless such an order is unjust. This is sometimes referred to as a 'split order', since the defendant pays the claimant's costs up to a certain point, after which the roles are reversed. It is easy to see how serious this consequence can be - it can take a very large bite out of a damage award, or consume it altogether. And there can be some very hard cases, given the difference a penny can make.[31]

The costs consequences of 'not beating' (as the saying used to be) a Part 36 offer in respect of a money claim should be predictable, and so should not be departed from lightly. Having said that, there are circumstances when the specific sanctions *set out in Part 36* will not apply, namely:

(i)   where the court considers it would be unjust.[32]

(ii) where the offer had been formally withdrawn (or made less advantageous and the less advantageous offer has been beaten).

(iii) where the offer was not a properly formulated Part 36 offer.

28 For a current case on this, see *Capital Bank plc v Stickland* [2004] EWCA Civ 1677

29 CPR, r 36.14(1A), which was added to make a clear dividing line between success and failure in this context. It mimics the old rules when defendants made payments into court.

30 Assuming there was no other reason to deviate from the general rule that the winner gets his costs. See e.g. *Allison v Brighton & Hove City Council* [2005] EW CA Civ 548 (where the claimant exaggerated the claim and so got only 25% of costs in the pre-offer period). And see Ch. 18

31 As in *Carver v BAA plc* [2008] EWCA Civ 412, (see previous edition of this book) where the court took a logical, but worryingly (and unpredictably) holistic view of the meaning of

(iv) where the offer was made less than 21 days before trial (unless the court overlooks this fact), or

(v) where *qualified one way costs shifting* (QOCS) applies.[33]

Finally, remember that defendants can also make Part 36 offers in *non*-money claims. The process is just the same as for money claims, but when one is not dealing with hard cash, it can be more challenging to determine, in any given case, whether a judgment at the end of a trial is more 'advantageous' than an offer which was made, but never accepted. In such cases, the court simply has to look at the case in the round. As Ward LJ noted in *Carver v BAA plc,* '... in non-money claims, where there is no yardstick of pounds and pence by which to make the comparison, all of the circumstances of the case have to be taken into account.' [34]

2. PART 36 OFFERS BY *CLAIMANTS*

Claimants can, and are encouraged to, make Part 36 offers themselves. In other words they can offer to settle the action on stated terms in exchange for not pursuing the case to trial. Indeed, a defendant's Part 36 offer which is not accepted may well be met with a claimant's own Part 36 offer (a formal counter-offer in effect).[35] A claimant's Part 36 offer will be made and accepted just as one made by a defendant. So most of the matters and formalities applicable to the latter apply equally to the former, with appropriate adaptation. The main difference is the nature of the consequence to a defendant of not accepting an acceptable offer by the claimant. If the claimant's offer is made and never accepted, and the outcome at trial is *as or more* advantageous to the claimant than his own offer, various cost

'advantageous', thus prompting the definition added by r 36.14(1A).

32 By CPR, r 36.14(4), in deciding this question, the court will take all the circumstances into account, including the nature of the Part 36 offer, when it was made, what

the parties knew at the time the offer was made, and any other relevant conduct of the parties. Possibly Mrs Carver's costs order (see *ibid*) could better have been dealt with on this basis.

33 See BCP 66.37. Legal aid can also affect the

situation. See Ch. 1

34 *Op. cit.* at fn 31

35 But, curiously you might think, such a counter offer does not operate as a rejection of the first offer: CPR, r 36.9(2). And see *Gibbon* case, op.cit.

or interest 'penalties' will likely ensue - in effect because the defendant forced the claimant to litigate to the bitter end to get justice. *Unless it thinks it unjust*, the court *will* order that the defendant pay:

(i) a punitive rate of interest on the damage award (not to exceed 10% above base rate) for some period starting with the date on which the 21 day/relevant period expired;

(ii) costs at the indemnity (rather than standard) rate for the period after the 21 day/relevant period expired; and

(iii)interest on those costs (not exceeding 10% above base rate).[36]

In addition, a further 'reward' for claimants making successful Part 36 offers was introduced on 1 April 2013, as part of the Jackson reforms. This effectively amounts to a bonus to the damage award (or other remedy), and is described as an *'additional amount'* (not exceeding £75,000) calculated on a sliding scale depending on the size of the judgment. Thus:

(i) In *money* claims, the additional amount is 10% of the first £500,000 of *damages* (or other money), plus 5% of any amount above £500,000, up to £1,000,000 (using these figures, this is where the £75,000 maximum figure comes from).

(ii) In *non*-money claims, one works off of the costs figures, so the additional amount is calculated at 10% of the first £500,000, plus 5% of the next £500,000 of costs awarded to the successful claimant.[37]

This additional reward both encourages claimants to make sensible Part 36 offers and builds more pain into the process of punishing defendants who do not accept them.

---

36 CPR, r 36.14(3) and generally Ch. 18

37 CPR, r 36.14(3)(d)

As always, fairness and proportionality (as well as consistency) should determine what order the court makes. There are somewhat more permutations here, and every case is different. In one of the earliest cases, *Garfoot v Walker*, a chemist sued a former colleague at Boots (the chemists) for libel after she had accused him of rape. He was never charged, but following an investigation his employers moved him to another branch. The claimant said the allegation was completely false and had caused severe damage to his reputation. He made a Part 36 offer to settle for £25,000 in damages. The defendant did not accept the offer and at trial the claimant was awarded £400,000.[38] The defendant was ordered to pay considerable costs (it was a jury trial) at a punitive (indemnity) rate, and nowadays Mr Garfoot would also have got an additional £40,000 in damages.

Bear in mind, however, that a claimant only needs to win a case on the balance of probabilities. *Garfoot v Walker* was a very dramatic loss - there may be times when a defendant comes close to winning, and so may have been more justified in not accepting a claimant's offer [39].

---

38 *Garfoot v Walker,* The
    Independent, 8 February
    2000

39 See, e.g., *Daniels v
    Commissioner of Police
    for the Metropolis* [2005]
    EWCA Civ 312

revision tips

- Have a look at Form N242A used for making Part 36 offers to settle. Note the formalities.

- Revisit Part 36 when revising costs orders. Be clear about the different sanctions when considering offers by defendants and offers by claimants. Don't forget the 'additional amount' to reward claimants for making successful Part 36 offers!

- Be confident about the implications of making and accepting (or not) Part 36 offers. This is fertile examination territory,

It is worth reading …

In the conjoined appeals of *Gibbon v Manchester City Council; LG Blower Specialist Bricklayer Ltd v Reeves and another* [2010] EWCA Civ 726 the Court of Appeal considered the case of *Carver v BAA* plc, (especially in the context of the second case, which suffered from an abundance of Part 36 offers!), and shows why it was reversed by r 36.14(1A).

The judgments in *SG v Hewitt* [2012] EWCA Civ 1053, about acceptance of a Part 36 offer well after the relevant period, and when the court might depart from the usual order in such circumstances. The facts are easy to grasp and as the claimant was a child, you can revise that aspect of procedure too!

PART FIVE

trial matters

CHAPTER 16

Preparations for trial

Civil cases do not often go all the way to trial. Some are put down early by the court; most are compromised by the parties. Trials vary in their complexity, but one thing they all have in common is that they are very expensive. The cost of many trials will far exceed the expense of all the interim proceedings in the case put together!

If, however, the parties cannot agree a settlement, the dispute will have to be determined by the court. In such cases, there may be a number of pre-trial matters or preparations to bear in mind. These can include:

A. NOTICES

'Notices to admit' and 'notices to prove' further the overriding objective by helping to narrow the issues in a case in a cost-effective way. This shorthand is not very descriptive. To make it clearer, I will supply the missing element (in brackets).

(i) Notice to admit (facts)

One party can serve on another a notice to admit such facts or part of his case as is set out in the notice. These tend to focus on what are *essentially uncontroversial matters*.

No application to the court is required. A party just serves the notice on his opponent (no later than 21 days before trial), setting out the facts to be admitted.[1]

---

1   CPR, r 32.18

To the extent that the facts are admitted, they cease to be an issue at trial.[2] To the extent they are not admitted, there is no sanction built into this specific provision, but the CPR cost rules are wide enough to produce the result (as existed under the previous rules) that the party refusing to admit the facts in the notice may have to pay the costs of proving those facts at trial, regardless of the ultimate outcome of the case.

The cost rules require the court to have regard to the *conduct* of the parties when making an order for costs, including whether it was 'reasonable for a party to … contest a particular issue'.[3] Much will depend, therefore, on how silly or sensible it was not to admit the fact or facts in question. The procedure must not be used oppressively, or indeed unreasonably. In other words, parties should not ask their opponents to admit what is clearly a real issue in dispute. No costs consequences would follow when an opponent predictably refuses to make such an admission.

Suppose, for example, a claim in negligence following a car accident, the outcome of which will depend on how well those in control of the cars were driving at the time. To ask the defendant to admit his negligence would be ridiculous - that is the main issue in dispute. But if the defendant had failed to admit the fact of the accident itself, then (assuming it clearly happened as alleged), then serving on him a notice to admit this fact would be appropriate. If he does not admit it, the claimant will still have to prove it, but the defendant will be ordered to pay the costs of doing so, unless he can come up with a good reason for putting the claimant to proof of the fact.

(ii) Notices to prove (the authenticity of documents)

The gist of this is that it is assumed, and a party is *deemed* to admit, that documents *inspected by him on disclosure* have not been tampered with or otherwise fabricated. This is because, generally speaking, it is not the authenticity of a document which

---

2 The admissions can only be used against the party in the proceedings in which the notice was served and only by the party serving the notice: CPR, r 3.18(3)

3 CPR, r 44.5(3). And see generally Ch. 18

is at issue in any given case, but rather the document's evidential or legal effect. If, however, authenticity *is disputed*, a 'notice to prove' its authenticity must be sent to the disclosing party. This puts the disclosing party on notice that authenticity of those documents is in issue.[4]

B. REFERENCES TO THE EUROPEAN COURT AND HUMAN RIGHTS QUESTIONS

These are two *different* considerations, and they must not be confused!

(i) References to the European Court

Sometimes cases tried before our national courts raise issues about the application or interpretation of the laws of the European Union, by which (as members) we are bound. The intention is that these should be applied consistently throughout the member states. If the domestic court in question cannot answer the question without doing so, a reference to the Court of Justice of the European Union in Luxembourg ('CJEU') may be necessary. The court would usually do this before the trial starts, as a preliminary issue, but in any event, if a reference is made, the domestic trial will be stayed until a ruling by the CJEU is given. Only a judge (Circuit or High Court), the Court of Appeal or the Supreme Court can refer a question.

If the issue has already got to the highest court in the land[5] (usually the Supreme Court), then that court *must* make the reference unless the point has already been decided (and there is no need to re-refer, as it were) or it is obvious how the EU law is to be applied. Lower courts *may* make a reference if it 'is necessary to enable it to give judgment'.[6] This discretion is quite wide.

A good example is the pub landlady in Portsmouth, Karen Murphy,[7] who was taken to court by the English Premier League for screening football matches via a Greek

---

4 CPR, r 32.19

5 The court from whom there is no further judicial remedy: Art 234(3) of the EC Treaty

6 Art 234(1) and (2).

7 See, e.g., 'Pub Landlady 1-0 up over cheaper TV football', *The Guardian*, 4 February 2011

satellite instead of paying Sky, which holds the rights to broadcast in the UK. Sky's fees are considerably higher than those charged Ms. Murphy by the right's holder in Greece. The case began in the criminal (magistrate's) court, but the High Court became seized of the matter on appeal on a point of law. Because the case turns on laws governing 'freedom of movement of services' within Europe, the judge made a reference to the CJEU. Until the latter gave its judgment on the question referred to it, the action against her remained on hold.[8] For more detail on CJEU references, see generally CPR, Part 68 and accompanying Practice Direction.[9]

(ii) Human Rights Issues[10]

The effect of the Human Rights Act 1998 ('HRA 1998') is to make rights under the European Convention for the Protection of Human Rights and Freedoms ('Human Rights Convention') 'directly enforceable' against 'public authorities', thus obviating the need for individuals to apply to the European Court of Human Rights.[11] 'Public authorities' include, but are by no means limited to, the courts, which under s 3 must minimise interference with the Human Rights Convention, and interpret legislation so as to be compatible with it. Where a court is satisfied that a provision in primary legislation is not compatible with a Convention right, it may make a 'declaration of incompatibility.'

Lay clients are apt to find breaches of their human rights around every corner. But parties must be cautious to raise points only when appropriate.[12] The rights which are most likely to figure in civil litigation are Art 6 (right to fair trial), Art 8 (right to respect for private life), and Art 10 (freedom of expression).

Procedurally, note the following:

---

8 To find out what happened, see http://www.bbc.co.uk/news/business-17150054 (but note that 'she' did not go to the CJEU, except possibly as a spectator - the question did, having been referred there by a High Court Judge).

9 Plus practitioner commentary in WB or BCP (Ch. 75)

10 BCP devotes an entire chapter to this subject (Ch. 88)

11 This is a very different jurisdiction to the CJEU

12 See, e.g., *Williams v Cowell* [2000] 1 WLR 187

- Details of any human rights point raised must be set out in the statement of case (or appeal notice).[13]
- Claims for declarations of incompatibility may not be heard by a judge below the status of High Court Judge.[14]
- If there is a real prospect of a declaration of incompatibility being made, this is obviously a factor in deciding whether to transfer a case from the County Court to the High Court.[15]
- Declarations of incompatibility strike at Acts of Parliament, so the government has an interest which is protected by allowing the relevant minister to 'intervene'.[16] Appropriate notice must be given.[17]

It is very important *not to confuse* the rules designed to ensure that sufficient safeguards are in place when arguing a human rights point in the domestic courts, with the procedure required on those occasions when it is necessary to refer a point of EU law for adjudication by the CJEU. The latter is more akin to appealing a particular point to a higher authority; the former merely ensures that all interested parties are before the English court, where the human rights point will be argued before a judge of sufficient standing.

C.   TRIAL ARRANGEMENTS AND TIMETABLE

When a case is listed for, or is approaching trial, the court may have to make decisions (in consultation with the parties) about any number of things, such as whether there are any preliminary issues to be dealt with (for example, if a disputed point of law is particularly relevant to the outcome or there is a reference to the CJEU); whether there is any reason why the trial (or some aspect of it) should not be conducted in public, as is the general rule;[18] and how the trial itself should 'play out'. This latter

---

13 PD 16, para 15.1
14 PD 2B, para 7A(2)

15 CPR, r 30.3(2)(g)
16 Another means by which parties are sometimes added to proceedings. CPR, r 19.4A(2)

17 CPR, r 19.4A(1)

is called the trial 'timetable' and involves considerations of how long should be spent conducting various aspects of the trial, including speeches, reception of expert evidence and allocating time limits on questioning (especially cross-examination). Decisions may need to be made about the reception of certain evidence.[19] The parties can express views on these in the pre-trial checklist; in multi-track cases, such decisions will usually be made on a pre-trial review. Remember the rules give the courts a great deal of flexibility regarding how they will deal with trials. Have a quick look at BCP 's procedural checklist 28.

D.   TRIAL BUNDLES

All documents likely to be referred to in a fast or multi-track trial must be put into a paginated file known as a 'trial bundle'. The claimant is responsible for preparing this, and so it is the claimant who should file the bundle not more than seven days and not less than three days before the start of the trial (not too early, not too late!).[20] The parties should agree the contents, so far as this is possible. Identical bundles should be made available for each party, the judge and a further set for use by the witnesses while giving evidence. Rival bundles are never lodged (although disagreements between the parties can be noted in the bundle itself). Unless there is some ruling or order to the contrary, all the documents in the bundle are admissible as evidence of their contents.[21] Have a look at PD 39A, para 3 which sets out the requirements for trial bundles, including what should be included in them and their presentation. The idea is that all participants have easy access to the relevant documents in the case (statements of case, witness statements, expert's report and so on). In High Court cases (in the QBD and ChD), reading lists must also be lodged with the trial bundle, so that during what is often referred to as a 'reading day' the judge can easily get up to speed with the case. An agreed case summary often helps with that process.

---

18 CPR, r 39.2. See Ch. 17 for exceptions

19 For example, evidence by deposition. See generally Ch. 17

20 CPR, r 39.5(2)

21 Where possible, originals of all relevant documents should be in the bundle: PD 39A, para 3.3

E.   SKELETON ARGUMENTS

We have seen that these are used for the more complex interim applications. They are also compulsory for High Court trials[22] and are often a good idea for (or required by direction in) the County Court. These should concisely summarise the submissions to be made in relation to any issues raised, and cite authorities to be relied upon (which should be in the reading list!). They should be filed two days before trial (QBD) or with the trial bundle (ChD). It is often a good idea to provide a short chronology of the important events.

Skeleton arguments allow the judge to do effective pre-reading and focus the mind of the advocate who prepares it. They are not, however, a substitute for effective questioning and oral advocacy.

F.   TRIAL RUNNING ORDER

The trial will follow the timetable previously laid down (or that laid down by the trial judge at the beginning of the trial) - or it will follow the traditional sequence of events:

Opening speech (if required)

It is usually the claimant who begins, as it is his case. An opening speech should put the case into context, but it can be dispensed with. A judge, having read the papers in the trial bundle, may feel it is unnecessary.

Claimant's case

The claimant presents his case. This includes real and documentary evidence, and of course the evidence-in-chief, cross examination (and, if necessary re-examination) of witnesses. This is discussed in more detail in Chapter 17.

---

22 Practice Direction
    (Civil Litigation: Case
    Management) [1995]1
    WLR 26

Submission of no case to answer

If the defendant is going to make a submission of *no case to answer*, then this is the time to do it, although the defendant should first be asked whether he wants to call any evidence (you might think he would not, if the claimant's case is weak enough to give rise to a submission of no case), because it is considered rather compromising to ask a single judge sitting alone (as is usual) to rule on the merits of the claim if the evidence is incomplete. If the defendant, having been put to his election, decides to call no evidence, then the submission of no case will be determined on the balance of probabilities (this is really rather like hastening the end of the trial, and judgment will be entered for whichever party succeeds on the submission).

If (unusually) the defendant were not given the choice, the submission should be determined by reference to whether the claimant has no real prospect of success. In this situation, were the submission to fail, then the defendant would be allowed to carry on and call his evidence in the usual way[23].

Defence case

It is now the turn of the defence to call evidence. If the defence is to call evidence, it may (but usually does not) make an opening speech. It then calls its evidence in the same way as the claimant. Where there is more than one defendant, they present their evidence in the order in which they appear on the record (for example, on the statements of case).

Closing speeches

Where the defendant has called evidence, the defence closing speech goes before that given by the claimant. Closing speeches should be focused on inferences to be drawn from the evidence and any legal points that have arisen. They should be focused and persuasive. Remember, most civil trials are in front of a single, professional judge -

---

23 See generally BCP, para
   61.46

24 See generally *It's Criminal!*
   (by the author)

this is a very different audience than most criminal trials, where speeches are more commonly directed at lay people (magistrates or juries).

Judgment

After the trial, the judge must decide the case and give judgment. This often happens immediately, but in complex cases can be reserved. Once all the evidence has been heard (for example, after speeches), the parties are not usually allowed to adduce more evidence, but a judge may accede to a request to reopen if judgment has not yet been given, if to do so would be in keeping with the overriding objective. Once judgment is given (but before it has been recorded), the test is much more as it would be if the case went on appeal (and if the Court of Appeal would give permission to hear new evidence, then it would probably be sensible for the judge to do so at this point).

On the rare occasions where a civil trial is heard by judge and jury (for example, defamation) then the procedure and conduct of the trial will much more mimic that in Crown Court cases[24].

revision tips

- Be careful not to confuse references to the Court of Justice of the European Union with the raising of human rights arguments in domestic trials.
- Have a look at what is on a pre-trial checklist. This is Form N 170 and can be found on the WB online service via Westlaw.
- Review BCP's procedural checklist 28.

It is worth reading …

The judgments in *Williams v Cowell* [2000] 1 WLR 187, an interesting case about a bi-lingual Welshman who refused to speak English in court (even though it was his second language). He claimed that being forced to do so violated his human rights. There is a heartfelt plea from the judges (one of whose surnames is Judge!) about not turning trials into 'human rights seminars'.

CHAPTER 17

Evidential matters in civil cases

By and large whether a case succeeds or fails at trial will depend on the facts of the case. What view the court takes on these will, in turn, depend on the quality of the evidence before it. It is therefore very important to have a firm grasp of the rules and principles about the admissibility and reception of evidence in civil cases, not only for any examination you will be required to pass (that goes without saying) but also as a foundation for embarking on practice with confidence.

Of necessity this is an overview of a vast subject. Because the strict rules of evidence do not apply to small claims track cases,[1] the focus here will be on fast and multi-track cases. For more depth and detail, consult the text of your choice.[2] If the truth be told, criminal evidence is the more entertaining branch of the family, and most evidence textbooks will concentrate on it. It is also the focus of the evidence chapters in the companion to this book, *It's Criminal! A Guide to Learning Criminal Litigation, Evidence and Sentencing* ('*It's Criminal!*')[3]. BCP usefully has an entire chapter devoted to civil evidence,[4] written by Adrian Keane, co-author now with Paul McKeown of the excellent *Modern Law of Evidence* ('*Modern Law*').[5]

Before reading on, you should ensure you have a grasp of the basic concepts of

---

1   CPR r 27.8/PD 27, para 4.3
2   If you have a choice. Textbooks differ in their approach, and you may find that one works better for you than another. It is like cars – take a test drive before committing yourself to a major purchase!

3   *It's Criminal!*, Worth Publishing 2013
4   Ch. 49

5   (2013) 10th Ed, Oxford University Press. For an older, but still enlightening introduction to essential evidential concepts, see Christopher Allen's *Practical Guide to Evidence* Routledge- Cavendish, ('Practial Guide').

the law of evidence (especially relevance, admissibility and weight, and the difference between these) and terminology (for example how different 'types' of evidence are described) of the law of evidence. It is especially important to understand the *distinction between facts in issue and collateral facts*. The latter are those which relate to a subsidiary matter which, while not among the facts in issue in a case, can nevertheless affect whether a fact in issue has been proved or not. Examples are matters going to the *competence* of a witness to testify, and facts relevant to some other *pre-condition to the admissibility* of an item of evidence (since these are matters which need to be determined before the evidence is admitted, they are also known as 'preliminary' facts or issues). The most common example of collateral facts, however, are those which affect the *credibility* of the evidence, although it is important to note that there are times when evidence relevant to credibility merges with evidence directly relevant to a fact in issue, and indeed an item of evidence can be relevant to *both* of these.

In addition, there are two important principles to bear in mind when considering the evidential issues in this chapter.

(i) Whether an item of evidence is admissible will depend in the first instance on the law of evidence. Evidence must be *relevant*, but it will only be admissible if, in addition, it is *not excluded* by any of the rules of evidence[6]. These are considered below.

(ii) The CPR gives the court an *overarching discretion to exclude* otherwise admissible evidence, if this is in keeping with the overriding objective. The rules specifically provide that the court may control the evidence in a case by giving directions as to *what evidence it wants to hear, on what issues and in what form*.[7]

---

6 Historically, the common law rules of evidence tended to focus on what could not be admitted at trial, not what could. Modern statutes are often more positively expressed.

7 CPR, r 32.1, and r 32.2(3). See precise wording.

This chapter covers a lot of territory. For the sake of convenience, I have divided it into three sections: (1) pre-trial evidential considerations; (2) admissibility and reception of special categories of evidence; and (3) witnesses and the course of testimony.

1. PRE-TRIAL EVIDENTIAL CONSIDERATIONS

A. BURDEN AND STANDARD OF PROOF IN CIVIL CASES

Burden of proof

The burden of proof is the obligation imposed on a party to prove a fact in issue. A party who fails to discharge this burden will lose on the issue in question. This is often referred to as the 'legal burden' and should be *clearly distinguished* from the so-called 'evidential burden', which is not a burden of proof at all.

In civil cases, the pleadings will tell us what facts are in issue - they will consist of all of the matters (not admitted by the defendant) which a claimant must prove in order to succeed in his case, plus any matters raised by the defendant (not admitted by the claimant) which must be proved in order to succeed in the defence and/or any counterclaim. The facts in issue are thus partly determined by the *substantive law* (for example, the constituent elements of a breach of contract claim), and partly by the *statements of case*.[8]

It is important to understand that only *one* party bears a burden of *proof* on any given fact in issue.

In civil cases the incidence of the legal burden of proof may sometimes be pre-determined by agreement between the parties concerned, as in some standard form contracts of insurance.[9] Sometimes, it is allotted by statute.[10] But generally speaking the legal burden of proof is determined by reference to various, sometimes competing,

---

8 If you put the statements of case side by side, and contrast and compare, it should be clear what the issues in dispute are.

9 See BCP, para 49.38

10 See *ibid*, para 49.39

common law principles. The first general principle is: 'he who asserts must prove (not he who denies)'. So if, for example, the claimant sues in negligence, it will be for him to assert in the particulars of claim, and thus prove (except as admitted by the defendant) the nature of the duty of care owed to him by the defendant; breach of that duty by the defendant; and the recoverable damage suffered as a result. And, if, for example, the defendant alleges contributory negligence, the burden is on him to prove this. In 99% of cases, the principle 'he who asserts must prove'[11] tells us in a civil case where the burden of proof lies.

But sometimes, especially when dealing with contractual clauses which limit or exclude liability, it can be difficult to know who is asserting what. There may also be a particular outcome which the court, in the circumstances, thinks is fair. In such cases, other principles come into play, including: 'it is more difficult to prove a negative than a positive' and 'when in doubt place the burden on the party who can more easily discharge it'.

In the case of *Constantine (Joseph) SS Line Ltd v Imperial Smelting Corp Ltd* [12] a ship, which had been hired out on charter, was destroyed by an explosion. The charterers claimed damages from the ship owners for breach of contract (because the ship was no longer able to carry its contracted load). The ship owners' defence was frustration. The charterers argued that the owners could not rely on frustration unless they proved that the explosion was not their fault (or the fault of their on-board crew). Because the cause of the explosion was unknown, the allocation of the burden of proof on this issue (was it caused by negligence or not?) became decisive, as is the way with these cases.[13] The House of Lords, concerned to arrive at a just result, held that, once the owners had proved the frustrating event (the explosion), the charterers bore the burden of proving fault on the part of the ship owners because it was difficult, if not impossible, for the latter to prove a negative, in other words, that they were not negligent.

---

11 Or should have asserted in the case of a poorly drafted statement of case: see BHB *Billiton Petroleum Ltd v Dalmone SpA* [2003] EWCA Civ 170 which said that the pleadings are a guide to what is being asserted, but not necessarily definitive.

12 [1945] AC 154

13 Although courts should resolve cases in this way only as a last resort and not as an excuse for indecision: *Stephens v Cannon* [2005] EWCA Civ 222.

As Viscount Simon LC put it:[14]

> Does the application of the doctrine require that the owners should affirmatively prove that those on board were keeping a good lookout, were obscuring lights, were steering as directed and so forth?

Ease of proof is the principle which unites the *Constantine* case with that of *Levison v Patent Steam Carpet Cleaning Co.*,[15] but the result was different. The difference is sometimes explained by the fact that the latter is a bailment case, but in reality this was a device to achieve justice in the case. The claimants had sent an expensive Chinese carpet to the defendants for cleaning. The defendants failed to return it and concluded that it had been stolen. They relied on a clause in their contract with the claimants limiting their liability for loss, the effect of which was to make them liable for £44 rather than the £900 the carpet was worth. Lord Denning MR hated exclusion clauses on the best of days, and they were only operative if the party relying on them had not been in 'fundamental breach' of contract. The question then arose: was it for the Levisons to prove the defendant's breach or for the defendants to disprove it? The Court of Appeal held that it was for the defendants to prove that they had not been guilty of a fundamental breach, because they could more easily discharge the burden. The Levisons did not know what went on at the cleaner's premises; the defendants were the ones who knew what had happened to the carpet once they took possession of it and so were better placed to show that they had handled the carpet properly (or not, as it turned out).

In civil cases, then, the approach to such quandaries is largely pragmatic and guided by fairness in different circumstances. Thus, on those rare occasions (and they are rare) when 'he who asserts must prove' does not provide the answer to the question (or seems to answer it in the wrong way, perhaps), the court will be apt to

---

14 Op.cit. at pp.161-2   15 [1978] 1 QB 69

find it by asking which party would find it easier to discharge the burden of proof on the issue in question, even if that involves proving a negative.

Standard of proof

Unless in a special category of case[16], the standard of proof in civil cases is the 'balance of probabilities'.[17] This is so even where the allegation is so serious as to amount to the commission of a criminal offence (for example, fraud or assault). The courts have wrestled over the years with how to deal with such allegations in a civil context, but it now seems clear (if it was not before) that the *standard stays the same*, however serious the allegation. Previous attempts, including that of Lord Nichols in *Re H and others*[18] to distinguish between the standard of proof (which is immutable) and the strength of evidence which might be required to meet that standard, were frowned upon (perhaps a bit unfairly) in *Re B (Children) FC*,[19] another child abuse case where nobody's evidence could be believed on some key issues of fact. The court was at pains to say, in slightly exasperated tones,[20] that:

> Once and for all, there is only one civil standard and that is proof that a fact in issue more probably occurred than not … Inherent probabilities are simply something to be taken into account, where relevant, in deciding where the truth lies … [and] neither the seriousness of the allegation nor the seriousness of the consequences should make any difference to the standard of proof to be applied in determining the facts.

'Evidential burden'

The evidential burden is *not* a burden of *proof.* It is an obligation to put forward enough evidence on a particular issue to allow the question to go before the fact finder for a decision; the burden is discharged when there is sufficient evidence to justify, as a possibility,

---

16 Committal proceedings, for example (see Ch 19) or where required by statute, such as applications for Sexual Offender Orders under the Crime and Disorder Act 1998, s 2. See BCP, para 49.41

17 This translates into proving that it is 'more probable' or 'more likely' than not that something happened.

18 [1996] AC 563 (a gruesome child abuse case).

19 [2008] 2 FLR 141 (UKHL 35), [2009] 1 AC 11

20 Lord Hoffmann quoted here, at ibid. [13]. In an earlier case he had given a useful example by saying that as a matter of common sense it would take more compelling evidence to satisfy the court that "the creature walking in Regent's park was, more likely than not, to be a lioness, than to be satisfied to the same

a favourable finding. The evidential burden is a low threshold - certainly discharging it does not by any stretch mean the legal burden of proof will be discharged. A party bearing a legal burden of proof on an issue, who cannot even discharge the evidential burden on that same issue, will lose, without the other side having to say anything.[21]

By and large the party with the legal burden on an issue also bears the evidential burden, so they tend to go together as a twin-set. There are several exceptions in criminal cases where a defendant has an obligation, when raising certain defences,[22] to put forward sufficient evidence to make the issue a live one; but the burden of proof remains squarely on the prosecution to disprove that defence beyond reasonable doubt. The only situation in a *civil case* where the legal burden of proof and an evidential burden might be 'split' between parties in a similar way is by virtue of the operation of a rebuttable presumption 'of the evidential variety',[23] where adducing some evidence to the contrary is all it takes to rebut the presumption operating in favour of the person with the legal burden of proof. This is discussed in the next section.

Presumptions[24]

So-called 'presumptions' can have an effect on the burden and standard of proof. They operate, to a greater or lesser degree, by allowing fact finders to draw certain conclusions ('the presumed fact') for other facts ('the primary facts'). One tends to refer to three 'types' of presumption, although only one is a 'real' presumption.

(a) 'Presumption of fact'

This is not a presumption so much as an inference to be drawn, as a matter of common sense, from certain facts. Such presumptions are really just examples of commonly recurring circumstantial evidence. The way these operate is that if the primary fact is proved, the presumed fact *may* be presumed. There is *no compulsion*.

---

standard that it was an Alsatian." *Secretary of State for the Home Department v Rehman* [2001] 1 AC 153, at [55].

21 Except "*I win!*" Submissions of no case to answer are much more prevalent in criminal cases than in civil, where such actions would likely be struck out or summarily determined well before trial.

22 For example, self-defence, duress. See generally *It's Criminal!*, Ch. 15.

23 See below

24 This is a short section, but even so check your syllabus. Not all include presumptions, as such, for examination purposes.

Examples from the criminal law include notions like the 'doctrine of recent possession', which is an inference to be drawn from the fact that a person is in possession of recently stolen goods. An example more germane to civil cases is the so-called 'continuance of life' which allows a fact-finder to conclude that if a person was alive on a certain date then, unless there is evidence to suggest otherwise, that person was still alive on a later date. This depends, of course, on how long the period is and how well the person was in the first place.

This presumption can also work in individual cases. Remember the case of the missing canoeist who 'came back from the grave'?[25] He was presumed dead on the basis of the alleged circumstances of his disappearance (parts of a broken canoe, clothes found washed up on the beach and so forth) and the fact that he had seemingly not reappeared, which made it a logical inference.[26] The coroner had been under no compulsion to agree, however, because less than seven years had passed.[27]

(b) Irrebuttable (or conclusive) presumption of law

This is not a presumption so much as a rule of substantive law. It works like this: if the primary fact is proved, the presumed fact must be presumed. It is compulsory. This kind of presumption is incapable of being rebutted.

One good example of this in civil cases is the deeming provision regarding service of the claim form[28], which effectively creates an irrebuttable presumption of due service. Another is s 13 Civil Evidence Act 1968, which says that in the context of defamation proceedings, a person convicted of an offence shall be *conclusively* taken to have committed that offence. This is a rule to avoid re-running criminal cases in the context of the civil claim.[29]

(c) Rebuttable presumptions of law

These are true presumptions, of which there are many examples.[30] Their purpose is

---

25 See, e.g., Telegraph online for 4 December 2007, which includes a video of him looking very much alive!

26 As it happened he hid in the house next door while his wife waited to claim the life insurance money, then they both fled to Panama

27 At which point the 'presumption of death' could have been relied upon. See below.

28 See generally Ch. 4

two-fold: firstly, to *save time and effort* when in 99 cases out of 100 the presumed fact follows from the primary fact (for example, the 'presumption of legitimacy') or, to *resolve a dilemma* (for example, the 'presumption of death'). As to the latter, these are only applicable when there really is a dilemma. If the court will make the inference you want from the facts at hand, you do not need to resort to a dilemma-resolving presumption!

Rebuttable presumptions operate as follows: if the primary fact is proved, the presumed fact *must* be presumed, *unless* there is evidence to the contrary.

A rebuttable presumption thus casts a burden on the party against whom it operates. How onerous this burden is (that is to say, how much evidence is needed to rebut the presumption) varies from presumption to presumption. In some cases, the presumption can be displaced if *some evidence* to the contrary is produced (a so-called 'evidential presumption'); in others, it can only be displaced on the balance of probabilities (a so-called 'persuasive presumption'). As a broad generality, the greater the social interest in the state of affairs to which the presumption is directed, the harder it is to rebut. For example the presumptions of legitimacy and marriage are harder to rebut than the presumption of proper working order, since the law is reluctant to brand people harlots and bastards!

As one example, the presumption of death works like this: if there is no acceptable evidence that a person was alive at some time during a continuous period of seven years or more, that person will be presumed to have died at some time during that period if it can be proved that:

- people exist who would be likely to have heard from him/her during that period;

and

- they have not heard of him/her during that period;

and

- all appropriate enquiries have been made[31]

---

29 Civil Evidence Act 1968, s   30 See generally discussion
    13(1)   at BCP para 49.11 to 49.20

Note that the presumption is merely that death occurred at the latest by the end of the seven years. It says *nothing about the date of death.* It would seem that, in civil cases anyway, this is an 'evidential presumption',[32] which would be consistent with the law being reluctant to declare dead, people who may be alive! But there is no clear authority, perhaps because any substantial evidence that the person was alive would stop the presumption from operating in the first place.

Presumptions of this kind may conflict. If they are of equal strength (for example both 'evidential presumptions'), they are thought to cancel each other out, so that the case is determined on the basis of the ordinary rules regarding the burden of proof, although again the court will have regard to policy considerations.

B.   PRIVILEGE AND RELATED CONCEPTS

Many of the exclusionary rules of evidence developed out of a desire to ensure a fair trial. For the same reason, openness underpins much of the conduct of civil litigation. The justification for the principles relating to privilege and public interest immunity, however, has less to do with these motivations, important though they are, and more with another competing idea which is given priority, namely that there are occasions when the benefit in withholding evidence from inspection by the court or an opponent should prevail over the public interest in openness and putting all of one's 'cards on the table'. For this reason, it particularly impinges on the rules about disclosure of evidence.[33] Occasionally secrecy will trump transparency.

It is important to distinguish between the various forms of privilege and between privilege and public interest immunity claims. There are essentially two

---

31 *Chard v Chard* [1956] P 259

32 See *Prudential Assurance Co v Edmunds* (1877) 2 APP Cas 487

33 See generally Ch 9

types of privilege: the privilege against self-incrimination, and legal professional privilege (which itself takes two forms). These privileges are personal - they must be claimed or waived by *the* person they protect. There is also the protection of 'without prejudice' communications (often referred to as a privilege, but perhaps more accurately described as a protection), which (if applicable) must be waived by *all* parties whom it protects.[34]

Public interest immunity ('PII') is not a privilege as such - it imposes a *duty*, not a right to withhold disclosure and obliges the court to exclude evidence on the grounds that its disclosure would damage the public interest. Such an obligation cannot be waived by anyone. PII can and should be distinguished from legal professional privilege.

The litigation context in which these issues usually arise in the first instance is during disclosure of documents and other evidence. The basic principles are as follows:

(i)   Privilege against self-incrimination

The privilege against self-incrimination is as old as the rule of law. It is designed to protect a person from being compelled by the State to give incriminating evidence against himself. The classic formulation was given by Lord Goddard LJ when he said that 'the rule is that no-one is bound to answer questions if the answer would, in the opinion of the judge, have a *tendency to expose* [him] to any *criminal* charge, penalty or forfeiture which the judge regards as reasonably likely to be preferred or sued for'.[35] The privilege is of particular importance, of course, in criminal cases; less so in civil cases, where some judges have considered its invocation archaic and unjustified.[36] Indeed, over time statute has whittled away at the privilege in some specialist civil contexts where the public interest in obtaining the information is thought to outweigh

---

34 For special rules about the protection (or not as the case may be) of journalist's sources, see Contempt of Court Act 1981, s 10.

35 *Blunt v Park Lane Hotel* [1942] 2 KB 253, at 257, CA

36 See, e.g., *Lord Templeman in AT&T Istel v Tully,* as cited in Keane & McKeown, *Modern Law*, p 593

the 'right to silence.' There are now various legislative provisions which require specified persons in specific circumstances to answer questions or produce documents or information, notwithstanding that to do so may tend to incriminate them.

A prime example in civil cases relates to Search Orders,[37] where the right to rely on the privilege to avoid compliance has been removed by s 72 Senior Courts Act 1981 in cases involving *intellectual property and passing off*. Although the privilege against self-incrimination may not be relied upon in such cases to avoid complying with the order, there is a protective *quid pro quo*: namely that the answer and information supplied as a result of complying with the order may *not be used in evidence* in any resulting *prosecution*. The latter charge would have to be made out using other evidence.

In other cases, the threat or risk of self-incrimination may be removed by the promise that the disclosed evidence or information will not be used in any criminal proceedings. Such safeguards and trade-offs keep these specific inroads into the privilege against self-incrimination from interfering with the Art 6 right to a fair trial.[38]

(ii) Legal professional privilege

There are two 'heads' of legal professional privilege. It is important to distinguish between them:

Head 1: 'Legal advice privilege'

Confidential communications between professional *legal advisor and client* (or any person representing that client) made in connection with the giving or receiving of legal advice to that client are protected by legal professional privilege. *This is so whether or not litigation is contemplated or underway at the time.*[39] Here the communication is a two-

---

37 See Ch 7

38 See generally Keane & McKeown, *Modern Law*, p.597ff. WB 31.3.32

39 Compare this with Head 2.

way street and can be thought of in the form of a straight line, with the client at one end and the legal advisor at the other.

Legal advice is not confined simply to telling a client about the law; conversely, not all advice (and certainly not every communication) is privileged.[40] Communications in furtherance of a crime or fraud are a well-recognised (and sensible) exception to the principle - it is no business of lawyers to be hatching criminal plots! In complex cases, issues can arise about who is a client (if not an individual) and what is legal (as opposed, say, to financial[41]) advice. But the essential idea is straightforward enough. The reason for this privilege, of course, is that it is in the public interest that people should be able to get legal advice in complete confidence. Other parties are therefore not entitled to know of the content of such communications, unless the privilege is waived (by the client).

Head 2: 'Litigation privilege'

This brings a third person into the equation. *Confidential communications* between a professional legal advisor and/or his client *and a third party*[42] are privileged where the *dominant* purpose in creating the document (or making the communication) is to use it or its contents to obtain legal advice or help in the conduct of *litigation* which at that time was at least reasonably in prospect.[43] The typical example is an expert's report. So long as the right person (that is, the person commissioning the document) has the right motivation (litigation), then it is immaterial whether the litigation actually takes place. Here the lines of communication form a triangle, involving three parties instead of two.

The rationale here is that parties should be free to *conduct* litigation confidentially. A party thus need not produce such documents for inspection at the disclosure stage. This can be useful when, for example, litigants receive an unfavourable report from their own expert. As we shall see, however, such evidence as one proposes to *rely* on

---

40 See the interesting list in BCP, para 48.47

41 See, e.g., *Three Rivers District Council v Bank of England* (No 6) [2004] UKHL 48, [2005] 1 AC 610

42 Not in the Part 20 sense, of course.

43 *Waugh v British Railway Board* [1080] AC 521

must be disclosed pre-trial[44] in the interests of openness.[45] In effect, the party seeking to adduce the evidence must waive his privilege in the information before (not merely as) the evidence is adduced. This is so no-one is taken by surprise, and everyone can respond sensibly to the evidence at trial. But a party who does not want to rely on such a privileged document, can bin it.[46]

Waiver of legal professional privilege

Legal professional privilege belongs to, and can be waived by, the client. Waiver can be express or implied, but usually the purpose and degree of the waiver is clear - a typical example was referred to in the previous paragraph when discussing the exchange of expert evidence pre-trial. Sometimes the content of certain legal advice may be important to explain relevant behaviour on the part of the client, and the question may arise as to the extent to which the privilege has been waived. The answer is usually determined objectively, bearing in mind the importance of the role of legal professional privilege in assuring fair trial.

In *Re D (a child)*[47], for example, the mother of the child in question needed to explain away two diametrically opposed accounts of the father's involvement (or not) in the child's injuries. In one witness statement she said the father was blameless; in a second, she said it was the father who had injured the child. She explained the change of heart by reference to various meetings with her solicitor and barrister and set out parts of what was discussed in those meetings. It was held that she had waived legal professional privilege in all the meetings with her legal advisors over the five week period leading up to the change of story which was set out in a second witness statement. This was so despite the fact that (1) her witness statements had been drafted by her solicitor and (2) the waiver was unintentional (neither she nor her solicitor realised that the material in her second witness statement would amount to a waiver of privilege).

---

44 But usually post-disclosure of documents

45 In effect, a party must waive his privilege in such documents if he wants to rely on the evidence at trial.

46 Although it might well provoke a re-evaluation of the case!

47 [2011] 4 All ER 434

(iii) 'Without Prejudice' communications

In a sense this can be viewed as something of a 'mirror image' of litigation privilege, because it also involves the solicitor or client and another person - specifically the other party to the litigation. *Without prejudice communications (oral or written) made in a genuine attempt to seek a settlement of a dispute*[48], are protected from disclosure to the court at trial (the other side, of course, knows all about it). The purpose of this rule, which protects both sides jointly and can only be waived if both sides consent, is to encourage open and effective negotiation by removing the fear that any admissions apparently made during the discussions will be used at trial against the party who made them, the attempts to settle having (rather obviously) failed. There is thus a focus on protection from the revelation of *concessions or admissions*, although most attempts to by-pass the rule by cutting and pasting around such admissions in otherwise protected correspondence have failed.[49]

The court will look at the substance, rather than the form of the communication, so that the over-enthusiastic use the words 'without prejudice' (usually written in bold letters by amateurs) does not necessarily afford protection to the document (and vice versa - a document may be protected even if those words are not used). It is the *purpose* behind the communication which matters. Note that, in effect, the protection extends to negotiations which *fail*. If or to the extent that they *succeed and the case settles*, the protection has served its purpose, and so the without prejudice communications leading up to that settlement would now become admissible to prove, where relevant, *the terms of the compromise agreement*.[50] Otherwise, the longstanding principle of 'once privileged, always privileged'[51] would seem to apply; the protection is only to be lost in exceptional circumstances (for example, where the rule is being unequivocally abused).[52]

---

48 Including where the parties contemplate or might reasonably contemplate litigation if they cannot reach agreement: *Framlington Group Ltd v Barnetson* [2007] IRLR 598, CA

49 See, e.g., *Re New Gadget Shop Ltd* [2005] EWHC 1606 (CH)

50 As in 'the claimant promises to discontinue the action in consideration of the defendant agreeing to pay £X and pay the claimant's costs'.

51 *Calcraft v Guest* [1898] 1QB 759

52 *Unilever plc v Proctor and Gamble Co* [2000] 1 WLR 2436. For admissions revealing criminal behaviour, see also discussion of *R v K(A)* [2010] 2 WLR 905, in *It's Criminal!*, p. 283

(iv) Public Interest Immunity ('PII')

This is a very different concept to those discussed above. Certain documents must be withheld from disclosure and/or inspection if it is found that revealing their existence or contents (or both) would be injurious to the public interest. Typical examples in a civil litigation context might be Cabinet minutes, social work records, and the design of military or police equipment. Public interest immunity is thus a *duty, not a privilege* and such claims can fall into two types: class claims (a claim that all documents of a certain class, for example diplomatic dispatches relating to national security, need to be protected) and individual claims (a claim that a specific document needs protection because of its contents). The former are regarded more sceptically than once was the case.

Typically, a relevant minister provides a certificate stating the grounds for objecting to disclosure and/or inspection. The certificate is not conclusive and it is for the *court* in each instance to determine where the public interest lies.[53] To this end the court must *balance* the public interest in concealment against the public interest in the fair and open administration of justice.

It is for the party seeking inspection to show why the public interest lies in openness. This can be made difficult by CPR, r 31.19(1), which says a PII claim may be made *without notice*, and any order made on such application must *not*, unless the court orders otherwise, be served on any other person. Thus it strikes both at disclosure *and* inspection, unlike legal professional privilege which prevents inspection but not disclosure as such.[54] With a PII claim, the other side may have no idea what is going on, which can have obvious human rights implications.[55]

---

53 *Conway v Rimmer* [1968] Ac 910
54 Since its existence appears, however obliquely described, on the disclosure list. See generally Ch. 9
55 See BCP, para 50.80ff. More controversially still (but very different) is the so-called 'closed material procedure', recently extended to civil cases by the Justice and Security Act 2013, whereby a *party* (and legal team) can, exceptionally, be *excluded* from the proceedings, during which time that party's interests are represented by a 'special advocate.' See CPR, Part 82 (newly added).

2. ADMISSIBILITY AND RECEPTION OF DIFFERENT CATEGORIES OF EVIDENCE

A. OPINION EVIDENCE

As a *general rule*, opinion evidence is not admissible at trial. Witnesses must normally confine themselves to telling the court about the facts, and not express opinions about those facts. To do so would either be considered an irrelevance (unless the state of mind of the holder of the opinion is pertinent) or an intrusion on the role of the judge[56] deciding the case, whose opinion is really the only one that matters. There are, however, some *important exceptions* to this general rule. The main ones are: (i) the opinions of other courts, (ii) the perceptions of witnesses of fact, and most importantly (iii) the opinions of experts.

(i) Previous judgments

Judgments of a court are a form of opinion evidence, since a finding of guilt or a finding of negligence, for example, is really nothing more than the opinion of the tribunal trying the case. Before statutory intervention, there was a rule that decisions in previous criminal or civil trials were not admissible in subsequent cases as evidence of the facts on which they were based. This is known as the rule in *Hollington v Hewthorn*.[57] The logic of that decision is that the opinion of a previous court on facts which were not rehearsed in front of the present tribunal are irrelevant. It is the latter's opinion that counts.

This decision had its obvious drawbacks and so was reversed for civil cases (at least in part[58]) by the Civil Evidence Act 1968, s 11-13. Section 11 creates a rebuttable presumption that a convicted person (whether convicted on a guilty plea

---

56 Most civil cases are decided by a single judge, but there are juries in some cases, most notably libel actions: see CCA 1984, s 66/SCA 1981, s 69

57 *Hollington v Hewthorn and Co Ltd* [1943] KB 587

or not) *committed the offence(s)* in question, 'unless the contrary is proved'. A very typical example of the use of s 11 would be in a personal injuries action arising out of a car accident. If the defendant driver had, in respect of the same accident, been convicted of dangerous driving, this would be cogent evidence of his negligence, since the criminal standard of proof is higher than the civil standard.[59]

For precisely this reason, it is very difficult, but not impossible, to discharge the burden of rebutting this presumption. According to Lord Diplock in *Hunter v Chief Constable of West Midlands Police*, although the standard to be met in proving the contrary was the 'balance of probabilities', in the face of a conviction after a full hearing this is "likely to be an uphill task".[60]

The conviction must be pleaded *in the particulars of claim*. Details of the date and type of conviction, and a statement of its effect, including the issue in the case to which it relates, must be included.[61]

Previous acquittals do not say nearly as much about a person's innocence as a conviction says about guilt. For that reason, evidence of an acquittal is generally not admissible in a subsequent trial, unless there are exceptional features.[62]

(ii) Non-experts: perception evidence of witnesses of fact

To an extent, we see the things we think we see, and so there is always some element of opinion in statements like *"It was dark"* or *"I saw her"*. But it would be very time-consuming (and tedious) to over-analyse such observations. Therefore, an ordinary witness will be allowed to express an opinion as a 'shorthand' way of describing things personally perceived, where attempting to differentiate between fact and inference would be difficult, if not impossible. It is useful to think of this as *'perception' evidence*. Examples include: *"He was drunk"*, *"The car was very old"*, *"The weather was stormy"*. How much easier to let a witness estimate a person's age, than to have to

---

58 See BCP, 49.100

59 S 12 performs a similar function insofar as previous findings of adultery and paternity are concerned and s 13 creates an irrebuttable presumption insofar as the evidential value of convictions in defamation cases. See BCP, 49.97/98

60 [1982] AC 529, at 544
61 CPR, PD 16, para 8.1
62 See BCP, 49.99

delineate all the various features of his or her demeanour. Where the 'opinion' best conveys the facts perceived, it will be admissible (and of course can be challenged).[63] This is a common sense exception, which is about ordinary witnesses describing ordinary things. It is very different from the next exception.

(iii) Expert witnesses
Admissibility

Often aspects of civil cases require a level of knowledge which ordinary people (including judges) do not possess, unless they have special training. For example, if the claim were against a surgeon for carrying out an operation negligently, it would be difficult for the judge to know what a specialist, carrying out such an operation, would (or should) have done in the circumstances, which will be important in deciding liability. The judge is a judge, not a doctor. This is where the important role of the expert witness comes into play.

As an exception to the general rule, therefore, *relevant expert opinion* evidence is admissible where needed to help the judge decide the case. It is important to appreciate the necessary requirements for admissibility and to note the following:

> *Expert's opinion must be necessary*
>
> The first requirement for admissibility is that the court *needs* the assistance of the expert to do its job properly, because the matter at issue is beyond normal human behaviour and experience. Typical examples in civil cases include medical evidence on the cause and extent of personal injuries, surveyor's evidence on the state of allegedly defective buildings, handwriting experts where authorship of signed documents is disputed. If the matter is within the experience of most

---

63 Civil Evidence Act 1972, s 3(2).

64 [1993] ICR 66

people, then an expert's opinion is inadmissible. A good example is found in *Larby v Thurgood*,[64] where it was held that the claimant's *motivation* to find higher paid work was a matter within ordinary experience, but the *likelihood* of his finding such work (given the job market, the claimant's qualifications and so on) was not. Thus the opinion evidence of an employment consultant was admissible on this latter issue, but not on the former.[65]

Expert must be qualified

The second requirement is that, if such evidence is needed, it should come from a *suitably qualified expert* competent in a *relevant and recognised area of expertise*. How experts gain their expertise is not usually important, so long as it has been acquired, although these days most experts will be 'professionally' qualified. Usually the more letters the better after the expert's name.

Experts must keep to their subject.

It is important to remember that an expert may only give expert opinion evidence on matters within his expertise. So in our example, a doctor is a good start, but not good enough. The appropriate expert would be a surgeon (usually a consultant) with recognised expertise in the specific type of operation carried out on the claimant - in effect, the sort of person the claimant may, with hindsight, have wished operated on him.

The quirky expert

Some areas of expertise are more experimental or quirky than others,

---

65 See also *Liddell v Middleton* [1996] PIQR p36 (CA) on when accident reconstruction experts would and would not be necessary.

and the question can arise as to whether, and if so when, the court should refuse to entertain opinions of doubtful reliability. A witness's area of expertise must be one the court is prepared to recognise. But science is constantly evolving and creating new areas of expertise. The English Courts have tended to be rather open-minded about these things, so that by and large unorthodox approaches are more likely to affect the weight than the admissibility of an expert's evidence. Even so, where the expert's opinion is pushing at scientific boundaries, or where medical knowledge is incomplete, courts should exercise caution.

Primary vs secondary facts

Remember that expert witnesses are expressing opinions on certain facts in the case at hand (such as, in our example, what actually happened during the operation in question). It is important to appreciate that those underlying facts must themselves be proved by admissible evidence. These are called the 'primary facts' and this is known as 'laying the proper groundwork'. Having said that, the research or reports or other materials ('secondary facts') which an expert uses or relies upon in forming and expressing his opinion need not themselves be admissible, but will be made available for the court and the other parties to examine.

Judge ultimately decides the issues

Cases often turn on the nature and quality of the expert evidence. Expert evidence tends to trump non-expert evidence (if the issues calls for expertise).[66] If each side has an expert, whose evidence conflicts, it is fairly obvious that a judge will have to choose whose is to be preferred.

---

66 This does not always follow. See. e.g., *Fuller v Strum* [2002] 1 WLR 1097, where the evidence of attesting witnesses to a (contested) Will was preferred over a handwriting expert.

But bear in mind that although an expert can express a view on an issue in dispute,[67] it is ultimately the judge, not the expert who must decide the case. The role of the expert is to *assist, not usurp* the role of the judge. Expert evidence can be rejected if there are sensible grounds for doing so. This is possible *even if* there is only one joint expert speaking to the issue. It will be rare for a judge to do this, but it can happen.[68]

Reception

One of the most significant procedural changes wrought by the CPR occurred in the area of expert evidence. In the old days, parties brought along their own experts (who may have had varying degrees of interest in the overall justice of the case) to slug it out in court against each other - the court exercised little control over the process. The situation is completely different today. As we have discussed, not only does the court manage the pace of litigation, but it also controls the evidence to be adduced at trial (which may involve excluding otherwise admissible evidence) by making directions about the amount of, and manner in which any evidence is received. This power is to be exercised in accordance with the overriding objective and is *particularly important when dealing with the evidence of experts*, which can be both time-consuming and expensive.

This dramatic reversal of the former freedom of litigants to conduct their cases as they wished was brought about by the very strong feeling that the 'bonfire of the vanities' arising from the widespread, adversarial use of experts had become a lengthy and costly exercise in bias.[69] So, for most straightforward, lower value claims, out goes the 'tame' expert witness for both sides; in comes the single expert, either jointly selected and instructed or court-appointed.[70]

Expert evidence is not usually allowed in small claims track cases, so the

---

67 There was a time when even this was not allowed, for fear of usurping the function of the tribunal of fact, but this rule (the so-called 'ultimate issue rule') was abolished in civil cases by the CEA 1972, s 3(3).

68 See, e.g., *Armstrong v First York Ltd* [2005] 1 WLR 2751

69 Experts have always owed a duty to the court in expressing their views, but one-sided instructions undermined their independence.

70 This concept was borrowed from family law cases dealing with care of children.

discussion below concentrates on fast track and multi-track cases. As we have seen,[71] directions concerning expert evidence will usually be made when allocating a case, or at a case management conference.[72]

The first point to make is that 'no party may call an expert or put in evidence an expert's report without the *permission* of the court'. If there is no direction, there can be no expert evidence. When seeking permission, a party should now provide an *estimate of the costs* of procuring such evidence (because experts can be very expensive), *identify* the proposed expert's *field of expertise* and the *issues* which the expert evidence will address, and (where practicable) give the court the expert's name.[73] This information allows the court to do a cost-benefit analysis and assess whether the expense of the expert is justified (and indeed whether the issue in question requires expert evidence).

Secondly, the court is under a duty to restrict evidence to 'that which is *reasonably required* to resolve the proceedings'.[74] The burden will lie on the party seeking to rely on expert evidence to justify doing so and the principle of *proportionality* will be an important consideration. The idea is to reduce the inappropriate use of experts to bolster a case, and the court will have to balance the desire to save time and costs against the requirement to do justice.[75]

In larger, more complex claims, *competing experts* on an issue will often be necessary and, if so, are still apt to be permitted. This is most likely to happen in multi-track cases.[76] But in smaller, more straightforward claims, the value of two opposing experts will not ordinarily justify the expense, particularly where they are merely being used to lend 'authority' to facts which can be proved in other, more straightforward ways - for example, by admitting certain readily understandable statistics. In many cases where the question, 'What is good practice?' is capable of being answered by one knowledgeable person in the relevant field, the court will not

---

71 See generally Ch. 8

72 Experts should be served with a copy of any direction or order which affects them: PD 35, para 6A

73 CPR, r 35.4 (as recently amended)

74 CPR, r 35.1

75 This is an in-built tension in the overriding objective

need or want to sample from a buffet of experts' opinions - the fixed price menu will do.

Joint instruction of a mutually acceptable expert - the so-called single joint expert[77]- is thus the norm whenever expert evidence is needed in *fast track* cases. In such cases, the court essentially asks itself, 'Is expert evidence really necessary?', and if so, 'Is there any reason why such evidence should not come from a single joint expert?', [78] looking at all the circumstances of the case.

The single joint(ly instructed) expert

Pre-trial

A single joint expert is what is *usually ordered in a fast track case*.[79] The parties may already have agreed to this, which the court can sanction, or the court can make a direction on its own initiative, even if the parties do not want it!

Such a direction requires that the parties participate both in the *selection and the instruction* of the expert. Instructions should be clear, setting out the expert's role, relevant background information and purpose of his or her evidence.[80] If possible, the parties should try and agree a single set of instructions for the expert, but if this is not possible, they should disclose to each other the (different) instructions they have given the expert.[81]

Experts expresses their opinions in the form of a *report*, which must comply with certain requirements, to include details of the expert's qualifications, the substance of the instructions the expert was given, an indication as to whether opinions *other* than that expressed by the expert are possible, give reasons for the expert's own opinion (or inability to express an opinion, if that is the case), and so on. Such reports should be written as clearly and concisely as the nature of the case allows, be addressed to the court, and make clear that the expert understands that his or her overriding duty is to the court (and not to any party who may be paying their fees). The report should be verified by a statement of truth.[82]

---

76 If the court is considering a single joint expert in a multi-track case, a case management conference must be called, unless the parties agree.

77 See discussion of nomenclature in Ch. 2

78 CPR, r 35.4 (3A) and see especially common sense

factors sets out in PD 35, para 6

79 Or small claims track if, exceptionally, such evidence is allowed at all. It is possible, if not common, for the court to order that the expert evidence be limited to that already gathered by the

claimant in investigating the strength of his case. It does save time and money, but can carry the risk of bias.

80 See discussion in Ch. 2 about selection process. And see PD 35, Annex: Expert's Protocol, para 8(1) for detailed guidance

Where both parties instruct (and share the cost of) an expert, then of course both are entitled to a copy of that expert's report.[83] If necessary, written questions can be put to the expert by one or other party, but only by mutual agreement (or court order) if the query goes beyond simply *clarifying* what is in the report. Any answers given to such questions are treated as part of the expert's evidence.[84] In a sense, this sort of witness belongs to both parties, and to neither party, because there is only one and because an expert's principle allegiance is always to the court.[85]

At trial

The way in which expert evidence is received at trial is also controlled by the court. In fast track cases, the presumption is that the single joint expert's evidence will be given in the form of a report - and *not* orally. The expert will not attend in person to give evidence unless the court orders.[86] Remember that fast track cases only last one day and the trial costs are fixed. To be allowed to have the expert there at the trial, the court would have to be satisfied that oral evidence from him or her has probative value which would outweigh the attendance costs.

In any event, the report prepared by the single joint expert would 'represent' the evidence in the case on the issues to which it relates, and should not normally be amplified or tested in cross-examination[87] at trial, although as always the discretion remains with the court.

Expert evidence in complex and controversial cases

Pre-trial

In complex cases, or where the expert evidence is very technical or controversial, the court will more likely allow the parties to have their own expert (at least on the issues which are controversial[88]). This is more usual on the multi-track. In such cases,

---

about instructing experts.
81 CPR, r 35.8(2)
82 See CPR, PD 35, para 3
83 See CPR, r 35.10 and PD 35, para 3.2 as to the form of expert's reports.

84 CPR, r 35.6(3)
85 CPR, r 35.3
86 CPR, r 35.5
87 Remember that the single joint expert is the one expert – it is not a competition!

88 It is possible to direct a single joint expert on some issues and allowing the parties to call their own experts on others: See, e.g., *Peet v Mid-Kent Healthcare Trust* [2002] 1 WLR 210

the rules about how instructions should be given, and the form reports should take (discussed above), still apply. As does, with even greater purpose, the requirement that the expert's primary duty is to the court, and not to the party instructing him. In addition, the court may direct without prejudice discussions between the experts, if this would help to identify areas of agreement and narrow the issues in dispute.[89] In such cases, the experts must normally prepare a statement for the court setting out the issues on which they agree, and those on which they disagree (and, in summary, why).

At trial

Where there are experts on each side, not only will they (unlike most witnesses) sit in court throughout proceedings to assist the party instructing them, but they will also normally give their evidence *orally*, where they may be asked to explain aspects or technicalities in their report (which will be put into evidence before evidence-in-chief) or to respond to other evidence which has been heard, and then be tendered to have their views tested and cross-examined in the usual way. If there are a lot of experts in a complex case, this can take some considerable time as each expert goes into the witness box individually and sequentially. To make this part of the process more efficient and effective, a recent innovation is the court having the ability to direct (typically at the first case management conference) that contested expert evidence ('of like disciplines') be heard 'concurrently'. This has become known colloquially as 'hot tubbing'. The idea is that, an agenda having been set (focused on areas of disagreement), the experts gather together (round a table, perhaps, rather than in a tub!), and give their evidence at the same time. The judge will usually initiate the process by asking each expert for his or her views on the relevant matters, asking follow up questions as necessary. At appropriate moments, one expert may be asked to comment on the evidence of another. Thereafter, the parties' representatives may then question the experts. Such

---

89 CPR, r 35.12

questioning may test or seek clarification of the evidence which has been given, but should not merely go over ground which has already been covered. After questioning, the judge may summarise the different positions.[90]

Disclosure of **opposing** *expert evidence pre-trial*

Where both sides are involved in instructing a single joint expert, both sides will naturally see the (one) report (so disclosure naturally happens from the outset). Otherwise, an expert's report, as we saw earlier, is the quintessential example of a privileged document, which protects it from inspection by an opponent at the disclosure of documents stage. However, a party who is given permission and seeks to *rely* on such evidence at trial must *disclose* it to the other side *before the trial*. In effect, the privilege must be waived if a party wants to *make use of* the evidence at trial. This rule ensures that the parties can know the nature and strength of the case against them, and so make informed decisions about compromising the action. It is very important, and sanctions for non-compliance are severe. A party who *fails* to disclose an expert's report, may *not* use the report at trial or call the expert to give evidence orally *unless* the court gives permission.[91]

Where the defendant has participated in the selection of the claimant's expert during the pre-action phase, but the claimant chooses not to rely on that expert but seeks to instruct another, then the court may well order the claimant to disclose (and thus waive the privilege in) the original report as the price of being allowed to rely on a new expert's evidence. This is intended to discourage 'expert shopping' and is known as an *Edwards-Tubb* order (you may be forgiven for thinking that tubs are featuring more prominently in expert evidence on the multi-track these days!).[92]

Where the parties both instruct a mutually agreed expert, then disclosure in effect occurs all along the way.

---

90 See CPR, PD 35, para 11   91 CPR, r 35.13   92 Named for *Edwards-Tubb v JD Wetherspoon plc* [2011] 1 WLR 1373

Where directions allow the parties to instruct their own expert, then they will be directed to exchange the expert evidence they propose to call. Usually such disclosure is ordered to be mutual (or simultaneous, so one has not seen the other's beforehand), but in some cases it may be appropriate to allow sequential disclosure (for example, where there is a prospect that a claimant's report might be agreed by the defendant, which would save costs). It is important to remember that it is only evidence which a party proposes to rely on at trial which needs to be disclosed (subject to conditions like that in the *Edward-Tubbs* case); if it is not part of the case, it need not be disclosed, and this can include draft reports.[93]

Sometimes (as in *Edward-Tubbs*) an expert's report is disclosed to the other side, but not ultimately relied upon at trial. This does not happen often, but in such circumstances, any party to whom the report was disclosed may *put the report in evidence himself*, although not for the purpose of impugning it.[94]

B.   WITNESSES OF FACT

Just as with expert's reports, the rules[95] also provide for the *early exchange* of the evidence of the *witnesses of fact to be adduced* at trial. This is done by exchanging witness statements. We saw that these are used as the means of putting evidence before the court when making interim applications.[96] They are also the format in which the evidence to be given by a witness at trial is disclosed to the other side, although the court may, exceptionally,[97] give permission for such evidence to be disclosed by exchange of a witness summary (which are never used in interim applications).

Witness statements, like experts' reports, must comply with certain requirements, including the formal title of the proceedings, information in the top-right hand corner about when, by whom and on whose behalf the statement was made, identifying any exhibits (and whether it is a first, or subsequent statement

---

93 *Jackson v Marley Davenport Ltd* [2004] 1 WLR 2926

94 There is a general rule that parties may not impugn their own evidence. The main exception to this is the so-called 'hostile witness', as to which see below

95 The main rules are found at CPR, r 32.4 and 32.10

96 See generally Ch. 4

97 For example, when some practical problem arises in completing the formalities of the witness statement. See CPR, r 32.9(1) and WB, para 32.4.3

in the case). It should be made clear in the opening paragraphs of the statement, who the witness is, why they are making the statement. The statement should be expressed in the first person, make clear what information is not within the witness's own knowledge, and be verified by a statement of truth. Documents referred to in the statement must be *formally exhibited*. Witness statements should be only as long as necessary to cover effectively and efficiently, the issues in dispute.[98]

The point of the pre-trial exchange of the evidence of the witnesses of fact is to promote openness and efficiency in the conduct of litigation, and encourage early settlement of cases. The Jackson reforms have made amendments geared to ensuring that such witnesses give evidence only as required and in a cost-effective manner. Note the other procedural similarities with expert evidence:

(i)   Directions for the exchange of witness statements are usually made upon allocation to the fast or multi-track, or at a case management conference. They may be made on other occasions, as necessary. Witness statements are not usually exchanged in small claims track cases.
      The evidence of witnesses of fact is as capable of control by the court as is expert evidence. The court can give directions limiting the amount and extent of such evidence, whether by identifying who can be called and whose evidence may be read and/or limiting the length and format of witness statements and/or limiting the issues to which factual evidence may be directed.[99] Again, the idea is to ensure that time and costs are not wasted on marginal issues and the production of wordy and irrelevant witness statements.

(ii) Normally *mutual* exchange between the parties is ordered so that one side's evidence is not tainted by having read the other side's version of events,

---

98 See CPR, PD 32, WB at 32.4.5 and example in Sime at figure 32.1

99 This is explicitly stated in the newly added r 32.2(3) so as to discourage the production of unnecessarily lengthy and unwieldy witness statements.

although occasionally there may be some benefit in sequential exchange.

(iii)　Normally, this mutual exchange of witness statements is directed to take place some weeks *after* disclosure of documents. This allows witnesses time to consider and comment on some of the documentation, if relevant to do so.

(iv)　Privilege in the witness statements is *waived on disclosure.*

(v)　If the evidence is *not exchanged as directed*, the witness may not be called to give oral evidence, *unless* the court gives permission. Whether the court gives permission will depend on the circumstances of the case and the nature of the default. Whatever decision the court makes should be proportionate.

(vi)　Statements that need to be exchanged are those of the witnesses a party *intends to call at trial.* There is no need to disclose a statement from someone who will not be called as a witness at trial.

(vii)　In addition (fairly obviously) witness statement should only include matters capable of being adduced at trial. They should not include inadmissible evidence.

Use of witness statements at trial
By the party calling the evidence:

A witness statement is not evidence in itself, unless it is admitted as a hearsay statement.[100] Rather it is a means of disclosing what the evidence of the witness will be. It is a longstanding principle that normally evidence is given at trial orally and on oath.[101]

Having said that, the rules invoke a useful time-saving device: where a witness is called to give evidence, his witness statement shall *stand* as his *evidence-in-chief,*[102]

---

100 CPR, r 32.5 (1) and see below

101 Or by affirming

102 In effect, the court treats the witness as having given the evidence in the witness statement

103 Which the court might do if the evidence is very complex or if there are doubts about the credibility of the witness or the court otherwise wants to hear the evidence-in-chief directly from the witness

104 Such witnesses would need to verify that the statement is theirs and true to the best of their knowledge

105 CPR, r 32.5(3)

106 New CPR, r 32.5(4)

unless the court orders otherwise.[103] However the evidence-in-chief is given, it will start off in the same way (the witness will be called, take the oath, identify himself, and so on) and end up in the same way, when the witness is tendered for cross-examination. To the extent that the statement stands as the witness's evidence-in-chief, the gap between those two will be very short.[104]

Where witnesses do give evidence orally, they may 'amplify' their witness statement and/or give evidence on new matters which have arisen since the statement is made, *only* if the court gives permission.[105] There needs to be a 'good reason', in keeping with the overriding objective, not to 'confine' witnesses to their statements,[106] since the other side may be taken by surprise by new material, which is precisely what the rules about disclosure are intended to avoid.

By the other side:

Where the witness is called to give evidence.

The other party or parties may *cross-examine* the witness on any aspect of the disclosed witness statement, regardless of how much of the evidence in the statement might have been referred to in any oral examination-in-chief.[107]

Where the evidence is not adduced at trial in any form[108]

In this situation, any other party may themselves put the *disclosed* statement in as hearsay evidence.[109] The rules now expressly provide that a witness statement can only be used for the purposes of the proceedings in which it was disclosed, unless the witness consents in writing or the court gives permission or the witness statement has been put in evidence at a hearing in public.[110]

---

107 If the witness statement stands as the evidence-in-chief, then it has effectively been covered in its entirety in any event.

108 Including as a hearsay statement – see below

109 CPR , r 35.5(5). It is not very common that evidence which is not going to be adduced at trial will be disclosed to the other side, but it can happen. And occasionally the party to whom it has been disclosed can make use of it.

110 CPR, r 32.12

C.   HEARSAY EVIDENCE IN CIVIL TRIALS

Admissibility

The rule against hearsay is a venerable, if not always venerated, rule of evidence. Hearsay evidence can be defined as an assertion which is *not made by a person while giving testimony* in court, but which is nevertheless relied upon (in those same proceedings) to establish the *truth* of what was asserted.   Very broadly, the rule excludes evidence of the *"Mary told me the car she saw was red"* variety, which cannot be easily tested under cross-examination.   If the colour of the car is pertinent, let's have Mary tell the court what she saw.

To understand whether an out-of-court statement is or is not hearsay, one must focus on the *purpose* to which the evidence is being put.   In relation to any such item of evidence one must ask: What job of proof is this statement being asked to do?   Is the tribunal of fact being asked to believe that what was said in the statement is true?[111] Or is it relevant for some other purpose - for example, to show that the statement was made at all, or the tone of voice in which it was made?[112]   If the former, the assertion is hearsay; if the latter, it is not.[113]

There are now many exceptions to the rule against hearsay.   The common law rule was abolished in civil cases many years ago,[114] principally because juries are rare in civil trials.   Evidence is thus not excluded in civil trials *solely* on the grounds of its being hearsay (it may be excluded on some other basis).   It is still important, however, to know whether or not an item of evidence is hearsay[115] because of the need to give advance notice to the other side of the intention to adduce such evidence.   If the evidence is not hearsay, these special rules do not apply.

Reception at trial

Thus, in civil proceedings, no hearsay - of whatever degree[116] - may be excluded

---

111 Often referred to as 'truth of contents'.

112 The person who heard the statement can give direct evidence of these facts.

113 See, e.g., *Subramanian v Public Prosecuter* [1956] 1 WLR 965

114 By the Civil Evidence Act 1995 ('CEA 1995')

115 Identifying hearsay evidence is covered in more detail in *It's Criminal!,* Ch. 20

116 CEA 1995, s 1(2)(b)

117 E.g., because of unsound mind

merely by virtue of its being hearsay, except where the live witness, as it were, would not have been competent to testify when the statement was made.[117] But there are requirements to tell the other side of the intention to adduce hearsay evidence, and other safeguards.[118]

The only issue for the judge, when considering hearsay evidence adduced at trial, is what *weight* to ascribe to it. This depends in part on common sense considerations, including how easy it would have been to call the witness to give direct oral evidence, how close in time the statement is to the event it describes, whether it involves multiple hearsay, whether there is any ulterior motive in keeping the witness away.[119] It can also depend on the extent to which the party relying on the hearsay evidence has complied with the notice rules.[120]

Hearsay comes in different shapes and sizes - oral, written, first and second-hand and so on. How proper notice is given of the intention to adduce hearsay evidence, depends in part on what form it takes. Thus:

(a) Where the hearsay evidence takes the form of the *witness statement* of a person who is *not* being called to give oral evidence, then the party intending to adduce that evidence must, when exchanging the statement, 'inform' the other parties of that intention and explain why the witness is not being called.[121] No formal notice as such is required. It is important to appreciate that in this situation, parties on the other side may, with the court's permission, require that the 'live' witness attend to be *cross-examined* on the statement[122] - if indeed he or she is alive (a dead witness is a particularly compelling reason for wanting to adduce a hearsay statement). The purpose of the general admissibility of hearsay evidence is not, after all, to keep witnesses who can give evidence away from a party's opponents.

---

118 Unless the evidence would have been admissible before the CEA 1995
119 CEA 1995, s 4(2)
120 Relating to adducing such evidence at trial. They do not apply to interim hearings: CPR, r 33.3/CEA 1995, s 2(4)(b)
121 CPR, r 33.2(2)
122 CEA 1995, s 3(2). In such cases, the witness statement stands as the witness's evidence-in-chief

(b) If the hearsay is merely contained *within* the evidence of a witness who *is* being called to give oral evidence, then beyond the exchange of the relevant witness statement nothing further need be done.[123] The other side, by reading the witness statement, can instantly see the nature and source of the hearsay contained within it, and can cross-examine the witness on it.

(c) But if the hearsay takes some *other form* (for example, an invoice from a shop or a diary entry, not exhibited in a witness statement), then the party wanting to adduce the evidence complies with the rules by serving *formal notice* to the other side, clearly identifying the hearsay evidence, stating the intention to adduce it and again giving reasons for not calling the maker of the statement (here the person who wrote up the invoice or made the diary entry).[124] Such a notice must be served no later than the time for exchanging witness statements.[125]

Remember that a failure to comply with the notice rules does not render the hearsay evidence inadmissible as such, but it can affect the *weight* attributed to it and/or result in an adverse costs order.[126] But always bear in mind that ultimately it is for the court to decide what evidence it wants to hear, on what issues and in what form.[127] *The bottom line is that the court has the power to exclude admissible evidence, if it would be in keeping with the overriding objective to do so.*

One reason for the relaxation of the hearsay rule is that sometimes such evidence is the best on offer or the most cogent (for example, business records). But this is not always the case, so remember that the more crucial the evidence, the less a party will choose (assuming there is a choice) to rely on a second-hand account of an event which will carry less weight than evidence which can be tested by, and stands up to, cross-examination. In other words, just because you can do something, does

---

123 CPR, r 33.2(1)   125 CPR, r 33.2(4)   127 CPR, r 32.1
124 CPR, r 33.2(3)   126 CEA 1995, s 2(4)

not necessarily mean you should. Other alternatives, such as taking the evidence by deposition pre-trial, may need to be considered.[128]

D. CHARACTER EVIDENCE IN CIVIL CASES

The law has always been more lenient about the reception of bad character evidence in civil cases without juries - that is to say most civil cases. The assumption is that judges sitting alone are able to make the necessary distinctions between evidence which is relevant to culpability and evidence which is relevant to credibility - an important distinction in principle, but one which in any case can be difficult to maintain.

Character evidence can be relevant in one of three ways:

(i)   It can be a fact in issue (as in defamation cases);
(ii) It can be relevant to a fact in issue if it demonstrates that it is more likely that the party is or is not capable of doing what is alleged. This is known as evidence of 'disposition' or 'propensity';
(iii) It can be relevant to the credibility (or 'credit') of a witness. If the witness is an habitual liar, perhaps their version of events is not to be believed.

It is useful to distinguish between good and bad character evidence.

Bad character relevant to credibility

People giving testimony in a civil case, including parties to proceedings, are open to attack on their credibility as witnesses by means of evidence of their bad character, subject to the restrictions set out in *Hobbs v CT Tinling and Co Ltd*[129] and the court's general discretion to control cross-examination.[130] According to the *Hobbs*

---

128 An alternative to admitting a hearsay statement if the evidence is important, but the witness may be unavailable for trial, is to apply for an order that the witness evidence be taken on oath before trial under CPR, r 34.8-34.12.

This is a costly alternative to a hearsay statement, but if the information is vital, this option allows the evidence in effect to be cross-examined and tested in a formal setting. Use of video-conferencing can defray the expense.

See BCP, para 58.2.
129 [1929] 2 KB 1
130 CPR, r 32.1(3)

case, such questions are only proper if the nature of the imputation would seriously affect the opinion of the court as to the credibility of the witness on a matter to which he had testified.[131] If the evidence of bad character is very remote in time or character, it will struggle to meet this test. Indeed an attempt to 'delve into a man's past ... to drag up such dirt as can be found'[132] might smack of desperation.

Bad character showing propensity

As regards evidence of *disposition or propensity* (to do something 'bad'), the test for admissibility in civil cases is essentially *one of relevance*. So long as the evidence is '*logically probative*' of the matter in issue, it will be admitted unless it would be oppressive or unfair to do so.[133]

The leading case is *O'Brien v Chief Constable of South Wales*,[134] involving an allegation of malicious prosecution following a miscarriage of justice review. The House of Lords (as it then was) held that the test in civil cases is different, and less strict, than in criminal cases. Lord Philips said that the test was that of relevance in that the evidence is admissible if it is 'potentially probative' of an issue in the claim. He went on to say that the policy considerations giving rise to the position in criminal cases (and in particular the Criminal Justice Act 2003) should be kept in mind by a civil court when giving effect to the overriding objective. Where the risk of prejudice was '*disproportionate' to its relevance*, the judge should 'manage' the case accordingly by excluding the evidence, but the civil courts are *not* bound to apply the criminal test to a civil suit.

Any arguments on whether evidence of bad character should be admitted, therefore, will turn on its probative value (which need not be huge) measured against its prejudicial effect, which should not be disproportionate to the persuasive value of the evidence. Criminal lawyers will recognise this balancing act - it is not very

---

131 *Op.cit.*, (per Sankey LJ)
132 See, e.g., *R v Sweet-Escott* (1971) 55 CR App R 316 (per Lawton J, at p 320). Criminal cases, of which this is one, are now governed by statute, as to which see *It's Criminal!*, Ch 19.

133 *Mood Music Publishing Co Ltd v D Wolfe* [1976] CH 119, CA.
134 [2005] 2 AC 532

135 In criminal cases the court is concerned to ensure that the probative value 'outweighs' the prejudicial effect. 'Disproportionality' is a somewhat wider notion.

different from the general discretion to exclude prosecution evidence in criminal cases.[135] Bear in mind, however, that the implications of losing most civil actions are not generally so severe as to make it particularly easy to convince a judge that it would be disproportionate to allow in relevant evidence of this kind. But again, every case is different and claims alleging the most serious allegations will be those where this balancing act is most difficult to execute.

Good character evidence

Some of the older cases suggest that evidence of good character is never admissible in civil cases, presumably because even very virtuous people can be careless once in a while. It must be doubted whether this could be so in a case involving very serious misconduct or allegations of a criminal nature. Perhaps a more modern approach is to say that admissibility depends on relevance and the probative value of the evidence, bearing in mind that none of us are perfect all of the time. See, for example, *Hatton v Cooper*,[136] a case arising out of a collision where there was little evidence of what had actually happened. The Court of Appeal held that the trial judge improperly relied on evidence from the claimant's employer to the effect that the claimant was an excellent driver. But in so doing, the court referred not to a blanket ban as such, but to its lack of probative value in the case - "completely worthless", was how Jonathan Parker LJ put it.

3. WITNESSES AND THE COURSE OF TESTIMONY

A. COMPETENCE AND COMPELLABILITY

As you prepare for trial, it is important to know whether the witnesses you want to

136 [2001] RTA 544

call are legally capable of giving evidence - and if so, whether they can be required to give evidence if they are unwilling to do so voluntarily. *Competence* refers to the first of these; *compellability*, to the second.

The *general rule* is that *all* persons are *both competent and compellable*. Exceptions in criminal cases involve spouses and civil partners of the accused and defendants themselves. There are *no such exceptions in civil cases*.[137] An important exception relating to children (and persons of unsound mind) applies in *both* criminal and civil cases. The tests differ, although they borrow from each other.

Children

Test for competence

The manner in which a child's[138] evidence is given is tied up with competence. The first question is whether the child is competent to give sworn evidence. The test is one which used to govern both the civil and criminal law, and is known as the test in the case of *R v Hayes*.[139] Does the child understand the *'solemnity of the occasion'* and the *special obligation* to tell the truth, over and above the ordinary social duty to do so? This is sometimes referred to as being *'Hayes* appreciative'. The idea behind the *Hayes* test was to move away from the need for belief in the divine sanction against lying, and so secularise the test for the giving of sworn evidence.

If the child does not satisfy the *Hayes* test, the court can look to s 96 of the Children Act 1989, which applies to a child who is called as a witness, but who does not, in the court's opinion, understand the nature of the oath (in the *Hayes* sense). Such a child's evidence can be heard *unsworn*, if, in the court's opinion, the child understands that it is his duty to tell the truth and he has *sufficient understanding* to justify his evidence being heard.[140] This in essence is not only about intelligibility, but also about being able to distinguish between the truth and a lie. It seems to be a

---

137 Spouses are both competent and compellable witnesses in civil cases. Statutory confirmation may be necessary to make it absolutely clear that the same is true of former spouses in respect of events occurring during the marriage. See BCP para 49.45

138 A person is a child in the legal sense if under the age of 18

139 [1977] 1 WLR 23
140 Children Act 1996, s 96(2)

somewhat stricter test than in criminal cases.[141]

If the child does not pass the requirement for the giving of unsworn evidence either, then that child is *not competent* to give evidence.

Procedure for assessing competence

It will be for the court to form an opinion on these matters before hearing the child's evidence (obviously). The judge, if necessary, will do this (possibly on an earlier occasion if the issue is controversial) simply by asking the child some questions, in part to determine intelligibility and in part to ensure the child understands the importance of telling the truth, especially in the context of a trial. Except in family law cases,[142] all such inquiries will be made in open court. Whether a child warrants such an examination is a matter for the judge - there is no fixed age for these things, but as a rule of thumb, inquiry would be made of a child under 14, although much would depend on the child in question. The 'watershed' which divides children who are normally thought to be able to give sworn evidence from those who are too young to do so tends to fall between about eight and ten years. Following *Hayes*, questions will be secular in nature. It will be for the person tendering the child as a witness to prove the child is competent.

A child who is judged competent to give evidence (whether sworn or unsworn) will also be *compellable* to give that evidence. If this seems a little harsh, remember that arrangements can be put in place to assist the child in giving his or her evidence.

Special arrangements

Special arrangements can be made for any vulnerable or frightened witnesses, including children. The general rule that evidence is to be given orally and in open court is qualified by the court's ability to control the way in which evidence is

---

141 In criminal cases, children who are 14+ years of age and *Hayes* appreciative can give sworn evidence (and there is a rebuttable presumption that a child of 14+ is *Hayes* appreciative). Children under 14 can give evidence unsworn if they can understand and give intelligible (not to say intelligent) answers to questions: Youth Justice and Criminal Evidence Act 1999, ss 53-57. See *It's Criminal!*, Ch. 17

142 These are not covered by the CPR and will usually be heard in private

received. For example, CPR, r 32.3 provides that a witness may provide evidence through a 'video link' or 'by other means'. In *Polanski v Conde Nast Publications Ltd*[143] it was said that videoconferencing orders are readily available to all litigants in civil proceedings. 'Special measures' as they are called in criminal cases,[144] include screens, videotaping examination-in-chief, giving evidence, by video link and so on. There does not seem to be any reason why these cannot equally be employed as appropriate[145] in civil cases: consideration and decisions about such measures can be made at a pre-trial review, if not earlier.

Note too that interpreters, signers and so on can be used to help witnesses with special needs to give their evidence.

Persons with mental incapacity

In civil cases, persons with mental incapacity must be able to satisfy the *Hayes* test to be competent to give sworn evidence. It is important to remember that not all mental impairment leads to an inability to give evidence on oath. But if this is not possible, note that there is *no provision* (as there is for children) enabling such a person's evidence to be heard unsworn. Examiners may well test you on this difference.

Just as with children, the court will assess the competence of the witness before the evidence is heard. It may be necessary to hear expert evidence about the mental condition in question, and in particular how it would impact (or not, as the case may be) on the ability to give sworn evidence.

Again, if the witness is found to be competent, that witness is also compellable to give evidence. Special measures may be put in place as appropriate.

Witness summons

As we have seen, in civil cases, where a witness is competent to give evidence, he

---

143 [2005] 1 WLR 637

144 See generally *It's Criminal!*, Ch. 17

145 If the witness statement stands as the evidence-in-chief, then it is really only the cross-examination which you need to worry about.

or she is also almost always compellable. Judges are one notable exception to this rule. They cannot be compelled to give evidence relating to their judicial function. They are competent to do so, however, and it has been said that if the evidence is really vital, judges should not invoke their non-compellability in order to avoid giving evidence.[146]

Most witnesses attend court voluntarily. A compellable witness who is reluctant to attend may be ordered to do so by the court. The mechanism by which a witness is ordered to attend is a witness summons (literally 'summonsing' that witness to court). This is a document, issued by the court, which requires one named witness to attend at a named court address at a named date and time, to give evidence *and/or* produce specific (relevant) documents in a named case.[147] To facilitate compliance, travelling expenses will be offered or paid. This is logical, given the compulsory nature of the summons. The figure on the notice is said to 'include an amount by way of compensation for loss of time'.[148]

Issuing a witness summons in civil cases is usually purely administrative, although the court can set aside or vary the summons if appropriate (like entering judgment in default in most money claims[149]). It should be served at least seven days before trial. Permission to issue a witness summons is only required where it is very close to trial (less than seven days) or where attendance is required to give evidence or produce documents at an interim hearing or some date other than the trial date.[150]

A witness summons is a court order and failure to comply (for example by not turning up at all or turning up and refusing to give evidence or answer legitimate questions as required) is a contempt of court, punishable by fine or imprisonment. The circumstances will dictate whether, and if so, what punishment should be given. In the County Court, if no travelling expenses were offered or paid at the time of serving the summons, then no fine can be imposed.[151]

---

146 See, e.g., *Warren v Warren* [1996] 4 All ER 664, CA. See also BCP para 49.48/9

147 CPR, r 34.2(1)

148 Form N20. See example in Sime, Fig 39.1

149 See Ch. 5

150 CPr, r 34.3(1)

151 See generally BCP, para 57.7

Witness summonses obviously have their place (and can be helpful where a witness wants to be seen to have been compelled), but it is as well to remember that no order of the court can make a person give favourable evidence. One should always think twice about calling reluctant witnesses. There may be no sensible alternative, but unless you are prepared (and have a game plan in mind), they can sometimes do more harm than good.

B.   WITNESS HANDLING/ADDUCING EVIDENCE AT TRIAL

There are some important evidential and procedural rules relating to the course giving oral evidence at trial. Some of these rules can be confusing for beginners, so by way of introduction, it may help you to bear in mind the following in order to make sense of what might seem a disparate set of rules.

The three stages of oral testimony are examination-in-chief, cross-examination and (if necessary) re-examination. Context is very important, and so you should be able to differentiate the rules which only pertain to evidence-in-chief, those which only pertain to cross-examination and those which apply across the board. This will help you to understand and remember them.

It is important to remember that a witness's credibility, or 'credit' as it is sometimes called, is a relevant fact in any given trial because it is something which makes that witness' version of events more or less likely to be true. Some of the witness handling rules require an appreciation of the difference between questions going *soley* to the credit of a witness and questions which are relevant (or also relevant) to a fact in issue in the case.

There is always a rationale which lies behind each of the witness handling rules, which (even if rather outdated) can help you remember them.

(i) Examination-in-Chief

First we begin with some rules about presenting one's own evidence and examining witnesses-in-chief. It is as well to remember that, although a judge may ask questions of a person giving evidence from time to time, it is essentially the advocate's job, not the judge's, to question witnesses. Moreover, the credibility of the witness is an important aspect of getting one's case across. There are, however, *limits* on what an advocate may do to *bolster* the quality of the evidence being presented. The prevalence of letting a witness's statement stand as his or her evidence-in-chief, renders some (but not all) of these rules a little redundant in civil cases. Indeed examination-in-chief is something of a dying art in civil trials, but you need to be aware of these rules for those occasions when you need to re-examine a witness following cross-examination or indeed when (or to the extent that you may be) called upon to examine a witness-in-chief in the old-fashioned way. It does happen from time to time. These rules also appear in assessments!

The rule against asking leading questions in examination-in-chief

Leading questions are those which include or suggest a particular answer, thus 'leading' the witness from the one to the other.[152] An obvious example might be: "*You were driving slowly as you approached the bend, weren't you*?" which (assuming the driver's speed is at issue and controversial) invites the curt response "*Yes*". The purpose of the general prohibition against asking leading questions in chief is obvious and really just a matter of common sense. The evidence is meant to come from the witness who directly perceived the event in question; not the advocate, who did not. The idea behind questioning your 'own' witness, who may well be inclined to want to give helpful evidence, is to *elicit* the evidence from them, not put words into their mouths. This is sometimes easier said than done. The rule, however, is not strictly applied

---

152 Or assume facts not in evidence. An example might be (assuming it is not established that the traffic light was green,) "*When the traffic light turned green, what did you do?*"

where introductory or formal matters are concerned or where the subject matter of the question is not in dispute.

The so-called 'hostile witness'

An advocate conducting an examination-in-chief should know what the evidence of that witness is! Sometimes, witnesses get muddled or say the wrong things or suddenly remember something differently. There is nothing an advocate can do about a witness who is 'unfavourable' in this sense, except soldier on as well as possible. This is because there is a general rule against impugning or contradicting your own witness. You cannot on the one hand put a person forward as a truthful witness for your own cause, and then turn around and suggest that the testimony is not to be believed when that witness does not say what you wanted or expected him to say.[153]

However, if a witness actively does not wish to tell the court, truthfully, what he knows, then that witness may, with the court's permission, be declared 'hostile'. This allows the advocate in effect to cross-examine the witness to the extent of asking leading questions and putting to him, and if necessary proving, that he made a previous statement which is 'inconsistent' with what he is (or is not) now telling the court.[154] Typically, this will be his witness statement. If the latter stands as the evidence-in-chief, then, of course, there is no real scope for the application of this rule.

If the hostile witness adopts the evidence in the previous statement under questioning, then it simply becomes his evidence on the day. If he does not, then the previous statement can be proved against him and is admissible as evidence of its truth.[155] In the latter case, it will be for the judge to decide which version he or she believes - the oral evidence, the previous statement, or (in view of the contradictions) neither.

---

153 Although other witnesses can be called to try and repair or counteract the damaging testimony.

154 Criminal Procedure Act 1865 (which applies in civil cases)

155 CEA 1995, s 6(3),(5)

Unless you are prepared, it is not generally a happy situation to have a 'hostile' witness on your hands (after all, the witness is supposed to be on your side!) and mercifully it does not happen very often. However, knowing what to do and making the best of it, is better than just sitting down with a baffled look on your face.

The rule against previous consistent statements

A 'previous consistent statement' is a statement made by a witness on an occasion *before* the trial which is *consistent* with that witness's testimony *at* trial. The general rule, in both civil and criminal cases, is that such statements (also called self-serving statements) are not admissible to bolster the *credibility* of the witness's evidence *in court*. The rationale for the rule is that the evidence does not improve with repetition, and there is a risk that a witness may be tempted to manufacture evidence and so artificially increase the credibility of his story by merely repeating it several times before the trial takes place. Do not confuse this rule with the hearsay rules, or indeed with the fact that usually the witness statement stands in for a witness's evidence-in-chief in a civil trial (in which case the witness statement is *not a previous* consistent statement) - these aspects of one's evidence can interact with one another, but they need to be distinguished conceptually.

As ever, there are exceptions to this rule against self-serving statements. The two common law exceptions which apply to civil (as well as criminal) cases are (a) statements rebutting an allegation of recent fabrication and (b) memory refreshing documents. In addition, (c) such statements are admissible in civil trials with the *permission* of the court.

(a) Statements rebutting allegation of recent fabrication
This is a common sense exception. If, under cross-examination, a

witness's version of events is challenged as being a 'recent' invention, it would be very unjust if the general rule prevented that witness rebutting that allegation by pointing to earlier statements which are consistent with his evidence-in-chief. Where applicable, this would be done in re-examination, but only to the extent relevant to, and necessary to rebut the allegation. Note, however, that if the allegation is that the story has been untrue from the outset, then the general rule would prevail.

(b) Refreshing memory

This rule is based on the assumption that evidence-in-chief is given orally, which does not often happen in civil trials anymore because usually the witness statement itself fulfills this function. But when the occasion arises (or if there is a question on the exam), in order to understand the rules, it is useful to distinguish between refreshing the memory *before* giving evidence ('out of the box') and *while* giving evidence ('in the box').

- In the box:

This is all about *facilitating* the giving of oral evidence by reference, while giving oral evidence, to a memory refreshing document - for example, a log book or diary entry. Thus a witness who experiences difficulty in recollecting events to which his oral evidence relates may refer, while giving that evidence, to a document or written statement in order to refresh his memory provided certain conditions are met. The first is that the document was made '*contemporaneously*'.[156] The document must be produced for inspection by the court and opposing parties.

---

156 This needn't be literally contemporaneously, but it should have been made as soon after the events as possible and in any case while they were still 'fresh in the mind'. *R v Richardson* [1971] 2 QB 484

Such documents can be used not only to refresh or 'jog' a memory (in which case a true copy will do if the original no longer exists), but also where the witness no longer has any independent recollection of the events in question, but can give evidence of the accuracy of the document (in which case the *original* must be produced). In either case, it is important to remember that it is the testimony of the witness, *not the memory refreshing document*, which constitutes the evidence in the case.[157]

• Out of the box:

It is a matter of common sense (and practice) for witnesses to refresh their memories from notes made by them, and in particular their own witness statements, *before* going into court to give their evidence. This is done routinely and is uncontroversial; the giving of evidence is a test of veracity, not a feat of memory. Opposing counsel would be entitled to see any document used in this way. Usually, this would be the witness statement, which should have been exchanged and will be in the trial bundles. If the witness statement is not to stand as the evidence-in-chief, the witness will not have access to it while the evidence is given (if, as is more usual, the witness statement does stand as the evidence-in-chief, then the witness will simply have access to his statement, verify it as being his and true to the best of his knowledge, and then be tendered for cross-examination).

It is open to the judge, as a matter of discretion and in the interests of justice, to permit a witness who has *started* giving oral evidence-

---

157 But see below about the possible effects of cross-examination

in-chief, to take a break and refresh his or her memory (out of the box) from a statement made by that witness closer to the time of the events in question - again, usually the witness statement. This is allowed if:

- the witness says he cannot now recall all of the details of the event because of lapse of time;
- the witness made a statement much nearer the time of the event, w hich records his recollection at that time;
- thewitnessdidnotreadthisstatementbeforegivingevidence; *and*
- the witness wishes to read the evidence before continuing.

If the judge gives permission, the witness can either withdraw or read the statement 'in the box' (during a sort of 'time out'), but in either case the document must again be removed from the witness before continuing to give oral evidence-in-chief.[158]

• Evidential status of memory refreshing documents
A document used to refresh the memory does not, as such, become evidence in the case. It merely *facilitates* the witness in giving his or her oral evidence. The cross-examining advocate is entitled to inspect any memory refreshing document, without making it evidence in the case. Equally, he or she is entitled to cross-examine on the contents of the document without making it evidence, provided the questioning does not go *beyond the parts* used by the witness to refresh his or her memory. However, where the advocate's cross-examination goes beyond the parts of

158*R v Da Silva* [1990] I WLR
  31. The witness can only
  do this once!

the *document* used in examination-in-chief, this entitles the party calling the witness to put the document in evidence and to let the tribunal of fact see it.[159] This principle is of greater significance in criminal cases, but the fact remains that, where relevant, an advocate will always have to weigh up the possible advantage of cross-examining beyond the memory-refreshing parts of such a document against the possible disadvantages of the entire document being put in evidence.

(c) *Permission of the Court*

The need and scope for refreshing the memory while giving oral evidence in chief has been much reduced as life and litigation has modernised. First, almost everyone who is called upon to give oral evidence will be sensible enough to re-read their witness statement so that they are well prepared for what can be a stressful occasion. Secondly, in most cases, the witness statement stands as the evidence-in-chief of the witness (so one can move swiftly on to cross-examination). If the evidence is not in fact given orally, then there is no scope for the rules to apply.

And there is a third reason, and that is the ability of the court to give a party *permission* to put into evidence a previous statement made by a witness, who has been, or was to be called to give to testify.[160] So if, for example, a witness were giving oral evidence-in-chief and ran into problems remembering things, it would probably be easier for the court to allow the party who called the witness to admit the previous consistent statement of that witness instead of getting bogged

---

159 *Senat v Senat* [1965] P 172

down in the memory refreshing rules. Having said that, a court, when exercising this discretion, would be attentive to the general policy behind the rule against previous consistent statements and want to ensure that in such a case a party was not getting two pieces of evidence in (on the stand and as a previous consistent statement) for the price of one.

Evidential status of admissible previous consistent statements
It is important to remember that the rule against previous consistent statements (and the exceptions to it) are all about earlier statements being admitted (or not) to show *consistency* with, and so bolster the *credibility* of the evidence given in court. *The rule makes no sense without evidence being given in court*, which is capable of being bolstered in this way. There has to be something with which to show consistency! The rule thus collides with, but should not be confused with, the admissibility of hearsay in civil cases, which covers a wider range of out-of-court statements (including many when the maker of the statement is not present in court). As discussed above, hearsay evidence is generally admissible in civil cases, and so if evidence of previous consistent statement is admissible as an exception to the general prohibition, then not only can it show *consistency* with the evidence of the testifying witness, it will also be admitted to show that the matters stated are *true*.

(ii) Cross-examination

Unlike examination-in-chief, cross-examination works on the assumption that the

160 CEA, s 6(2)(a)

witness does *not* favour the case of the party on whose behalf it is conducted. So some of the limitations imposed on the former do not apply to the latter. For example, there is no general ban on leading questions since it is not thought that the witness will be very motivated to follow the cross-examiner's lead. Similarly, because the witness has not been called in support of the case of the party conducting the cross-examination, the latter is free (by all proper means) to discredit the witness.

In this context, there are two particularly important rules applicable to cross-examination in civil cases.[161]

(a) The rule against rebuttal on collateral issues

If parties were allowed to call evidence to rebut a witness every time an unfavourable reply was given in cross-examination, trials might take a very long time indeed to complete. And if the time is not well spent, lengthy proceedings are not in the public interest. So, to keep trials efficient and focused, an important limitation is put on a party's ability to contradict a witness in this way. The rule, which is applicable at common law to both civil and criminal cases, is that answers given in cross-examination on *purely collateral* matters (for example, questions merely going to the credibility of the witness but which are *otherwise irrelevant* to any of the issues in the case) may *not* be contradicted by rebuttal evidence. This is sometimes called the rule of 'finality of answer', which is a confusing description, because the rule does not mean that the judge must accept the truth of the answer given, nor does it mean that the questioner should not be given every reasonable opportunity to extract the admission in cross-examination which he or she seeks. What it does mean is that evidence may not be *adduced* by the party asking the questions to rebut the answer given by the witness. Hence, it might be better described as the rule *against rebuttal*.

The purpose of the rule is to prevent advocates getting off the point and

---

161 See also *It's Criminal!*,
   where these rules are
   considered in more detail
   (they apply to criminal as
   well as civil cases).

proceedings getting bogged down on peripheral and essentially irrelevant issues.

There are two points to bear in mind when considering the rule against rebuttal. First, it can *only apply to matters which have been properly put* to a witness in cross-examination. If the question cannot be asked, then there will be no answer to rebut! It's worth remembering this: there are more restrictions on cross-examination in criminal trials, but the civil judge has a discretion to 'limit' cross-examination.[162]

Secondly, the difficulty with applying the rule is that it is not always easy to determine what matters are relevant to an issue in the case, and what are relevant only to credibility or some other purely collateral issue. It is important to appreciate (both in practice and for examination purposes) that the rule only precludes rebuttal evidence in respect of questions going solely to collateral matters. Even if a line of questioning speaks to a witness's credibility, if it also speaks to a fact in issue in the case, then the limitation does *not* apply.[163]

In addition, there are, as always, the inevitable *exceptions* to the rule. Thus, it is permissible to adduce evidence to rebut answers given in cross-examination by a witness on the following collateral issues:

- *To prove previous convictions of the witness*
  If a witness is properly cross-examined about a previous conviction (which is usually only relevant to credit), and denies it or refuses to answer, then the conviction may be proved against him.[164] Dishonesty offences are typically used in this way, but other offences may (depending on the circumstances) also speak to a witness's credibility. If the conviction is spent, the judge would have to think very carefully about whether it would be fair to allow questioning on or proof of a spent conviction.[165]

---

162 CPR, r 32.1(3) and see, e.g., *Watson v Chief Constable of Cleveland* [2001] EWCA Civ 1547

163 See generally BCP, para 49.66

164 Criminal Procedure Act 1865, s 6. The way to prove convictions is by providing a duly signed certificate and proof that the named person is the person whose conviction is to be proved.

- *To prove the witness's general reputation for untruthfulness*
  Whether or not a witness has a relevant previous conviction, a witness's credibility may be impugned by others speaking to his or her general reputation for telling lies.[166] This is a long-standing, common law exception, but is not often invoked.

- *To prove the witness is biased*
  Evidence is admissible to contradict a witness's denial of partiality for or against one of the parties to proceedings, in order to show that he is prejudiced as to the outcome of the case.[167] For example, in *R v Shaw*[168] it was held that the accused was permitted to call evidence to contradict a prosecution witness who, in cross-examination, denied having threatened to 'get even' with the accused after the two had argued. This is a common sense exception to the rule against rebuttal. If a witness has a vested interest in the outcome of a case, the fact finder ought to know about it. But there has to be some basis to the allegation of bias (which brings the exception into play) beyond a mere attack on the credibility of the evidence, and this can sometimes seem a fine distinction. For example, it has been said that a denial that a bribe was *offered* to a witness could not be contradicted, whereas a denial that a bribe had been *accepted* could, because it was only the latter fact which actually said something about the partiality of the witness.[169]

- *To prove a physical/mental disability affecting the reliability*
  If a witness has a mental or physical impairment affecting the

---

165 *Thomas v Commissioner of Police of the Metropolis* [1997] QB 813

166 *R v Richardson* (1968) 52 Cr App R 317

167 See, e.g., *R v Mendy* (1977) 64 Cr App R, 4.

168 (1888) 16 Cox CC 503, Assizes

169 See discussion in Keane & McKeown, *Modern Law* p. 215-216.

reliability of his evidence, then this is something which those whose job it is to assess that evidence (the judge, in most civil cases) should know. Thus if, for example, an identifying witness denies in cross-examination that he suffers from night blindness or is prone to hallucinate, then evidence may be called to prove that he does suffer from such disabilities. As Lord Pearce observed in the leading case of *Toohey v Metropolitan Police Commissioner:*[170]

> Human evidence ... is subject to many cross-currents such as partiality, prejudice, self-interest and above all, imagination and inaccuracy. Those are matters with which the jury, helped by cross-examination and common sense, must do their best. But when a witness through physical (in which I include mental) disease or abnormality is not capable of giving a true or reliable account to the jury, it must surely be allowable for medical science to reveal this vital hidden fact to them.

The evidence of disability can itself be rebutted, although only insofar as is necessary to meet a specific challenge to the witness's reliability and should not extend beyond this in an attempt merely to bolster the credibility of that witness.[171]

Previous inconsistent statements

Clearly, one of the most effective ways of undermining a witness in cross-examination is to put to that witness a statement made by him or her on an earlier occasion which contradicts the evidence given at the trial. Unsurprisingly, these are known as previous *in*consistent statements and so long as the statement is relevant 'to the subject matter of the ... proceedings', then the witness may be cross-examined on it and, if

170 [1965] AC 595

171 This used to be known as 'oath-helping'.

necessary, the statement may be adduced to rebut the witness's testimony in court. This is by virtue of ss 4 and 5 of the Criminal Procedure Act 1865, which applies to both civil and criminal cases and sets out the manner in which such statements are to be put to a witness. The point is to protect witnesses from being unfairly surprised during cross-examination and to give them a chance to deal with the inconsistency.

In a nutshell, the circumstances of the making of the previous statement are put to the witness, who is given a chance to accept the fact and truth of that statement, before being contradicted. Under s 5, which relates to documents only, the witness should be shown the statement, asked to read it and then asked if he stands by his evidence on oath. This may be enough for the witness to see the need to change his testimony. If not, the advocate may put the document into evidence to show, at the very least, inconsistency. In civil cases, the document will also go in for truth of contents because there is no rule against hearsay.[172] Again, the advocate will have to weigh up the advantages in doing this against any possible disadvantages (for example, other aspects of the document which support or confirm the other side's case, which may not be worth admitting merely to show up a minor inconsistency).

---

172 The same is true in criminal cases by virtue of the Criminal Justice Act 2003

revision tips

- Appreciate the differences between legal professional privilege (LPP) and public interest immunity (PII): the former confers a right to withhold from inspection; the latter, confers a duty to withhold from disclosure. LPP resides in the client, and can be waived; PII is a matter of public interest and it is for the court to determine where it lies, given that one starts from the proposition that in general the public interest is 'better served by candour than suppression.'

- Remember also to distinguish between legal advice privilege and litigation privilege, both heads of LPP. Be aware of when such privilege might or might not be waived.

- Regarding hearsay evidence, be aware of what *form* hearsay evidence takes, which can dictate how advance notice to the other side is given.

- Regarding expert evidence:

  - The norm in small claims track cases is no expert evidence

  - Use of the single joint expert on any given issue is the norm on the fast track, the evidence to be admitted in written form, unless court orders otherwise.

  - Separately instructed experts, giving oral evidence, will be more acceptable and common in multi-track cases.

  - The expert's duty is to the court, to express true and complete and independent professional opinion, even if this is adverse to the case of the party calling him/her.

- Do not confuse civil and criminal tests for competence of special witnesses, e.g. children.

- Do not confuse the rules governing evidence-in-chief with those governing cross-examination.

It is worth reading ...

CPR, r 32.1 (if you have not already).

The judgment in *Edward Tubbs v J.D.Wetherspoon plc* [2011] EWCA Civ 388. The facts are easy to follow and the judgment covers the interface between privilege and disclosure of expert evidence.

The judgment in *Warner v Penningtons (A Firm)* [2010] EWHC 1753 (Admin). This case is not long and it covers at least 5 aspects of litigation in addition to expert evidence, including summary judgment and third parties (of which there are several). A good one for a revision check!

PART SIX

last orders

CHAPTER 18

Paying the piper:
Costs, funding and legal aid

Costs are a highly significant aspect of civil procedure - they overshadow almost every aspect of the litigation process, from start to finish. At least four different parts of the CPR are devoted to the subject.[1] A related issue is how litigation is financed. Litigants are primarily responsible for paying their own legal fees, which will be incurred on their behalf from the moment they first engage solicitors, but there may be various funding options open to them, depending on the situation.[2] If someone is publicly funded, it will (since April 2013) be the Lord Chancellor, acting through the Legal Aid Agency ('LAA') who pays the lawyers, with or without contributions from the litigant himself. One way or another, costs can quickly add up.

There is, however, a generalised expectation that a losing litigant will usually be required to pay the winner's costs. This obviously helps the winner with his legal bills. But the extent to which this is what the court actually orders can depend on other factors, and in particular the conduct of the litigants. The courts have become very adept at case specific costs orders. Personal injuries actions now have special costs rules. The interplay between costs and public funding can, moreover, throw up a host of special considerations. The unifying theme is: who pays for the expense of litigation?

---

1   CPR, Parts 44-47 as recently overhauled

2   Funding options are considered in more detail below.

Much of this book, as indeed much of civil litigation, is devoted to what goes on before trial. There are a host of *interim* applications which might be made, at the end of which there will be an order for costs. Logically, these are known as interim costs orders. What order a judge makes on an interim application will depend on the situation. There may be a clear winner. Or success may be tempered by some aspect of failure or poor litigation behaviour, resulting in the court's 'docking' a percentage of that litigant's costs. Some applications are essentially managerial and/ or otherwise to be treated as part of the general 'costs of the claim'. If the application arises only because one of the litigants failed to follow the rules, that party may have to pay the costs thus 'thrown away,' whatever the outcome.[3]

You need to be aware of the various possible interim costs orders, what they mean and in what circumstances they might be ordered- some of the more common are conveniently set out in the rules themselves.[4] Most are self-explanatory, although there are some interim costs orders which can confuse beginners. One is understanding the difference between 'costs in the case' and 'claimant's (or defendant's) cost in the case'. 'Costs in the case' means that whoever wins the substantive case at trial will recover (from the loser) the costs of that interim application. 'Claimant's (or defendant's) costs in the case' is a little more favourable to the named party: it means that if the named party wins at trial, he will recover from the loser the costs of the interim application, but if he loses, he will not be asked to pay the other side's costs of that application (so the latter will have to bear his own costs of that interim application, no matter what happens at trial).

Where the court decides the parties should each bear their own costs, then the order can either be 'each party to pay its own cost' or 'no order as to costs.' In most cases, the result is effectively the same if the court really does make no order as to costs (that is to say, is silent on the matter).[5] Such an order may be appropriate when

---

3 *For* example, on a successful application to set aside default judgment which was properly entered, discussed in Ch. 5

4 PD 44, para 4.2. BCP, para 68.29 also has a useful list of the common costs orders, interim as well as final, and their meanings.

5 There are some exceptions (e.g., where the court has given leave to appeal, the default position is costs in the case): see CPR, r 44.10

there are no obvious winners and losers, or everyone is a winner and loser, or it just seems fair in the circumstances. Interim costs orders should be capable of meeting any kind of situation.

Although much of what follows also applies to interim costs orders, the focus of this chapter will be *final* costs orders, that is, costs orders made after final determination of the issues at trial. In particular it will review basic principles, and highlight some of the more complex issues that can arise in making such orders.

Let us start with *two important propositions*. The first is this: whether, when and in what amount costs are ordered to be paid by one party to another, are in the *discretion* of the court.[6] It is vital to remember this. Nevertheless, there are various principles, guidelines and indeed rules and statutes which inform, shape and sometimes constrain the exercise of this discretion, the most dominant of which is that the general rule (or starting point) is that *the loser should normally pay the winner's costs*.[7]

1. VARIOUS WAYS OF ASSESSING COSTS

Remember that it is the advocate's responsibility to seek the appropriate order for costs. This requires knowledge of what to expect regarding how (or how quickly and accurately) costs will or should be quantified in any given case, and what submissions may be necessary. There are basically four possibilities. Costs, or aspects of costs, might be:

(i) *Agreed*, for example, if the case settles. Parties often settle on terms which include payment of costs.

---

6   CPR, r 44.2(1)   7   CPR, r 44.2(2)(a)

(ii) *Fixed,* in which case set amounts will be used which are 'fixed', usually by reference to the *value* of the case (the greater the value, the greater the amount). In order to keep the expense of litigation down, fixed costs are becoming more and more prevalent. *They are especially aimed at reducing lawyer's fees.* Fixed costs are used for the following:

- *early disposal* of simple cases (for example, money claims exceeding £25 where default judgment was obtained or summary judgment given), unless the court orders otherwise (which it would do if there was any complexity involved)[8];
- *small claims track cases,* where no lawyer's fees are recoverable at all, and only certain fixed amounts for court costs (for example, costs of issuing proceedings) and expenses (for example, travel costs) can be recovered, unless warranted by a party's unreasonable behaviour.[9] Beware describing this (as some do) as the 'no costs' rule in small claims track cases - it is only lawyer's costs which are banned outright!
- *brief* fees (that is, advocates' fees) for *fast* track trials (these fixed rates essentially only cover the advocate's fees, plus an bit extra if the solicitor's attendance was necessary - other sorts of costs are not covered by fixed fees). Such fees are fixed by reference to the value of the claim: for a successful claimant, the relevant value is taken as the amount of the judgment, not including interest or costs, less any reduction for, say, contributory negligence. If it is the defendant who succeeds, the relevant value is determined by reference to the amount claimed on the claim form (or, if the claimant cannot add up properly, the maximum which could have been recovered on the pleaded case).

---

8   CPR, r 45.1(1),(2)   9   CPR, r 27.14 and see Ch. 8

The court can award a lower amount than the relevant fixed figure if the behaviour of a party warrants it.[10] These costs are relatively small (and for straightforward cases), and so if a case has been allocated to the fast track, but it begins to look as if the trial may be more complicated than at first supposed, this might be a good reason to move it up to the multi-track.

- *RTA or EL/PL low value personal injury claims.* We discussed the new pre-action protocols for these sorts of claims (£1,000-£25,000, where liability is admitted) in Chapter 2. Where such claims 'exit' off of this special protocol procedure and enter onto the fast track (because the parties cannot agree damages), then recoverable costs will continue to be fixed (the fees are fixed on the protocol as well). Effectively, therefore, almost all fast track personal injury actions (there are some exceptions) will be covered by a fixed costs regime from July 2013.

(iii) *Summarily assessed*, that is to say, quantified on the spot and on a somewhat rough-and-ready basis. On a summary assessment winners will typically ask for their costs to be assessed (where the amounts are not fixed) by reference to *the figures in their schedule of costs*, which will have been filed beforehand (24 hours before any interim hearing and two days before any fast track trial).[11] It will be for the other side to argue that certain figures should not be allowed, either at all or in a reduced sum.[12] Summary assessment is used for:

- interim hearings lasting no more than one day
- appeals lasting no more than one day
- 'unreasonable behaviour' assessments in small claims track cases

---

10 CPR, r 45.38/39

11 If a winning litigant failed to file a schedule of costs as required, he may well be penalised by being required to pay for a detailed assessment of costs which the court ordered as a result: *Wheeler v Chief Constable of Gloucestershire* [2013]

EWCA Civ 1791

12 Applying the same sorts of principles, discussed below, about what is a reasonable amount, reasonably incurred.

- most fast track final costs orders (brief fees being fixed)

This is *not*, however, an appropriate method of calculation for publicly funded litigants.

(iv) The subject of a *detailed assessment*. This is a complex procedure used for long interim applications, and multi-track cases, and is appropriate for cases of any complexity and where the receiving party is publicly funded.[13]

So, subject to the above, there are essentially two issues to think about regarding *final* orders as to costs: firstly, who pays, and scondly, how much?[14]

2. WHO PAYS?

The *guiding principle*[15] is that, as a general rule, costs should (as it is sometimes quaintly put) 'follow the event'. Officially, this is described as meaning that an 'unsuccessful' party will be ordered to pay the costs of a 'successful' party.[16] It is sometimes also (less quaintly) referred to as 'costs shifting' (since the winner's burden of paying his own legal costs 'shifts' to the loser). The basic idea is to make litigation an unattractive alternative of last resort.

Nevertheless, the court can (and often does) make other orders. In deciding what order to make, *the court must have regard to all of the circumstances*,[17] including the complexity of the case, the amount of money involved, and so on. CPR, r 44.2(4) particularly requires the court to have regard to the following:

(i) the *conduct* of the parties (both pre-action and the manner in which the

---

13 CPR, PD 44, para 9.8. As to costs payable by a publicly funded party see discussion below.

14 As to *when* costs are payable, the general rule is that a party must comply with a costs order within 14 days of a summary assessment, of the issue of a certificate after a detailed assessment, or such other date as the court orders: CPR, r 44.7

15 This principle, which is hardwired into the civil costs system, seems to have survived most of the Jackson reforms.

16 CPR, r 44.2(2)

17 CPR, r 44.2(4)

case was pursued or defended),

(ii) whether a party has been *partially, even if not totally* successful, and

(iii) *any offer* of settlement made (even if it is not one to which Part 36 strictly applies).

So, for example, was the appropriate pre-action protocol complied with? Did the claimant exaggerate his claim? Was it reasonable to pursue a particular allegation? Did a party flout the rules? Did the claimant unreasonably (in the circumstances) reject a proposal to engage in ADR or an informal offer to settle?[18] The idea was to move away from 'all or nothing' costs awards, and towards those which are more case sensitive. The court was given wide powers to achieve this, even if it means awarding different costs on different aspects of a case to different parties. The possibilities include court's ordering (either by themselves or in combination):[19]

(i) a proportion of another party's costs (also called 'percentage orders');

(ii) a stated amount in respect of another party's costs;

(iii) costs from or until a certain date only (sometimes called 'time specific' orders);

(iv) costs incurred before proceedings have begun;

(v) costs relating to particular steps taken in the proceedings;

(vi) interests on costs from or until a certain date, including a date before judgment.

Issue based costs alone can get complicated, and not a little messy, which is why using some (or a carefully chosen selection) of these other alternatives, and in particular 'percentage awards' has become increasingly popular. Nowadays, when a party is 'partially successful', the trial judge will be apt to award that party only a *percentage* of

18 See CPR, r 44.2(5)

19 See range of possibilities in CPR, r 44.2(6)

his generalised costs (to reflect the extent to which the party was in fact 'successful'), rather than awarding actual costs on a more piecemeal basis. It can sometimes be simpler and save a lot of hassle.[20] There are also, it should be said, some special variations for special situations, as discussed below.

In any event the courts are very sophisticated these days about fine tuning costs orders to be case specific. In *Straker v Tudor Rose*[21] it was said that the judge should first identify the successful party and then consider whether there were reasons for departing from the general rule and, if so, to make clear the factors justifying this. In *Midland Packaging Ltd v HW Chartered Accountants*[22], for example, the claimant had clearly won in money terms, having been awarded substantial damages, and beaten a Part 36 offer made by the defendants. But the judge decided that in other respects the success had only been partial. In particular the claimant had grossly exaggerated the amount of the claim and had been unsuccessful on points which occupied a significant amount of court time. The judge concluded that the defendant had in fact been successful on six out of eight issues which the court had been required to determine and that there had been no real attempt to narrow the issues on the part of the claimant, who had overplayed its hand and fought the case to the bitter end. He therefore awarded the defendant 75% of its costs from the date of its Part 36 offer (plus the relevant 21 day period), to be offset against the costs otherwise due to the claimant.

3.   HOW MUCH?

A.   AS BETWEEN THE PARTIES

When the figures are not fixed and the court determines how much one party may have to pay to another in costs (orders 'inter partes'), there are two 'bases of

---

20 See, e.g., *English v Emery Reimbold and Strick Ltd* [2002] 1 WLR 2409. But see below discussion about multiple parties.

21 [2007] EWCA Civ 368

22 [2010] EWHC B16 (Mercantile)

assessment': the *standard* basis and the *indemnity* basis. Both of these only allow such costs as were 'reasonable in amount' and 'reasonably incurred', but the standard basis (and only the standard basis) has a *further* requirement of *proportionality*, which now means that costs which are *disproportionate in amount may be disallowed or reduced, even if reasonably incurred and even if necessarily incurred*[23]. In short, proportionality trumps both necessity and reasonableness: in other words, did the value/complexity of the case justify the expense? Furthermore, any doubts on any of these matters are resolved in favour of the payer on the *standard* basis and in favour of the payee on the *indemnity* basis. The indemnity basis of payment is therefore the *more expensive* for the payer and is only used in exceptional circumstances or to be punitive. As the name implies, *the normal basis of assessment is the standard basis.* Unless specific reference to the indemnity basis is made, the presumption is that costs should be assessed on the standard basis.[24]

B.   AS BETWEEN SOLICITOR AND OWN CLIENT

There are several ways in which litigants might be able to fund litigation.[25] If money is no object, then there is always the traditional retainer. But private funding is expensive - a solicitor's bill typically includes the solicitor's remuneration for work done on a case (at an hourly 'charge-out' rate, plus a 'unit' costs for letters and phone calls), together with counsel's fees (briefs and paperwork), plus 'disbursements' (court fees, travel costs, expert's fees). Often the client will be asked to make a payment on account, and could be paying out for some time before being awarded any costs from the other side at the end of the day (if successful).

There was a time when the main alternative to private funding was legal aid, but as the availability of the latter has disappeared, other forms of funding arrangements have attempted to fill the void. Other possibilities are:

---

23 This enhancement of the proportionality test was added as part of the Jackson reforms: CPR, r 44.3(2)(a), and 44.3(5) on the commom sense meaning of proportionalty.

24 CPR, r 44.3(4)

25 For more detail see BCP, Ch. 5

(i) Trades union or other third party funding. Some trades unions pay for legal costs of claims made by their members arising from accidents at work. This of course would depend on union policy and the claimant being a member of the trades union. Other third party funding would normally take the form of big players effectively investing in the outcome of a high value case.

(ii) *Before* the event legal expenses insurance ('BTE' insurance). This is commonly allied to a person's home or motor insurance, and covers a person against the risk of having to pay legal costs in litigation (sometime just one's own, sometimes also the risk of having to pay the other side's costs). It is called 'before the event' insurance, because it is taken out *before* the need to pay for lawyers arises.

(iii) *After* the event litigation expenses insurance ('ATE' insurance). This is an insurance policy taken out *after* the need arises. It can cover one's own legal expense, but is commonly taken out, about the time a claim is made, to cover the *risk of an adverse* costs order. Not surprisingly, such insurance can be very expensive. ATE insurance is/was often taken out in conjunction with CFA agreements, discussed below.

(iv) Conditional Fee Agreement ('CFA'). A CFA is a form of 'no win, no fee' agreement with solicitors, which was originally intended to help fund personal injuries actions when legal aid was withdrawn from such cases.[26] The lawyers work (and charge) as normal, but agree that if the client loses the case, he will not have to pay anything to the lawyers acting *for him*; but if he wins the case, his solicitors will be entitled to charge him at the usual rate for the usual things('base costs'), plus a pre-arranged 'uplift' by way of a 'success fee'. ATE insurance is needed

---

26 CFAs do not apply to family cases.

to protect against the risk of having to pay the other side's costs if the case is lost. The extent of the success fee is intended to reflect the risks involved in taking on the action, so that if the case is a sure winner, the success fee should reflect this, although sometimes if types of cases are viewed in the round, the success in one case can be viewed (by the solicitors, anyway) as financing failure in another.[27]

Over time, both the success fee and the costs of ATE insurance began to be recoverable from the unsuccessful party, but it soon became apparent that these were the 'principal drivers' of the high cost of litigation.[28] As a result, from 1 April 2013, *neither* the success fee *nor* the costs of ATE insurance (except ATE premiums for expert reports on liability and causation in clinical disputes[29]) *is any longer recoverable from the loser.* This, of course, would leave a successful litigant distinctly out of pocket, and so (as from the same date) it is now possible to enter a new variant of the no-win, no-fee agreement: the 'DBA' (discussed below).

(v) Damages-Based Agreement ('DBA').[30] These are available in *all* civil claims and are really a form of contingency fee agreement (which used to be banned for most purposes). They are a form of 'no win, no fee' because the client pays nothing (except disbursements) while the litigation is running, and if the claim is lost, nothing more will be payable to his legal team (and so one still needs to guard or be protected against having to pay the other side's costs). But if the claim is successful, the client agrees to make a 'payment' (to include counsel's fees) out of the damages recovered. This typically is a percentage, which in non-personal injury claims *must not exceed 50%* of the sums

---

27 The more sophisticated CFAs reflect varying degrees of effort and risk (e.g. lower success fees for cases that settle early and higher success fees for cases which go to trial or settle at the court door). CFA's were removed from the BPTC syllabus in 2013-14.

28 See Jackson LJ's preface to WB

29 Legal Aid and Punishment of Offenders Act 2012 (LASPO 2012), s46

30 LASPO 2012, s 45

ultimately recovered, and in *personal injuries* claims *must not exceed* 25% of the damages comprising PSLA and past pecuniary loss (not counting the sums recovered by the CRU, since these go not to the client, but to the State). So a DBA agreement may *not take bites out of damages payavle on a personal injury claim for future* pecuniary loss. The DBA must be in proper form, in writing and with the terms and conditions carefully set out (to include the claim or action to which the DBA relates, what the payment includes and why it was set at the chosen rate and so forth).[31]

DBAs are part of a *triumvirate* package intended to protect claimants and quell the market in *personal injuries claims*. They help a claimant fund their claim. In addition, and to help compensate successful personal injury claimants for no longer being able to recover their CFA 'success fee' and ATE insurance premium, a second part of the package is that PSLA damages have been given a 10% uplift by virtue of the decision in *Simmons v Castle.*[32] Last (but not least), personal injury claimants also now benefit from costs protection in the form of QOCS, which are discussed below.

Note, however, that DBAs have had a few growing pangs, so keep an eye out for changes and refinements in this aspect of funding.

In general, a party's funding arrangements do not affect the order for costs which the court might make (although as you might expect, subject to special rules regarding pro bono representation, costs actually need to have been incurred to be the subject of a costs order). Moreover, it is rare for the courts to be asked to interfere with (or make any determination in respect of) the fees owed by parties to their own legal team, but it can and will if there is a dispute. As regards the traditional retainer,

31 See BCP, para 5.20   32 [2013] 1AER 334.

as well as certain aspects of CFAs or DBAs, when there is such an assessment, *the indemnity basis applies, modified* by various presumptions regarding client approval and so on - a basis, clearly, which is *more* 'expensive' than the standard basis, which is the usual basis of assessment of costs between parties to litigation.

It is easy to see, therefore, that even if the case is won, what a party has to pay his own legal team (whether the solicitors' bill is disputed or not) will usually be more than what will be recovered from the unsuccessful opponent in litigation - and so there will usually be some gap between outlay and what one, as winner, recovers in costs from the loser. This is now particularly true of CFA funded litigation. This discrepancy, which may vary in its size, is one of the risks of litigation. Even if relatively small it represents 'nuisance value' and is relevant to any decision to litigate or settle. Lay clients are much better informed these days, than they used to be, about how much of a bill they are running up with their solicitors, and so should have a clear idea both before and throughout the litigation of what the costs-benefit risks are all along the way.[33]

4. PUBLIC FUNDING AND COSTS

The availability of civil legal aid has been much reduced over the last decade. It has very strict eligibility requirements and many types of claims are *specifically barred* from its ambit, most notably *personal injury actions* (including now most clinical negligence actions), defamation, conveyancing and matters relating to company or partnership law. One way or another many civil claims are simply ineligible - full stop (whatever the applicant's means). If available at all, legal aid is also now only available to individuals.[34]

---

33 Solicitors are under a professional duty to provide this information to clients.

The means testing is also very strict[35] - so that only the very poorest can qualify. There is something of a sliding income scale under which litigants receiving public funding will be required to contribute some money of their own towards the cost of litigating.

In addition there are nine criteria for full representation,[36] which include considerations of alternatives to litigation, whether the small claims track can deal with the claim, whether alternative funding is a viable option. An important factor in money cases[37] is the cost-benefit ratio, which is a crude way of assessing value for money. In the general run of such cases, funding will only be granted if:

(i)   The prospects of success are very good (80%+),
      and the value of the claim *exceeds* the likely level of costs.
(ii) The prospects of success are good (60% - 80%),
      and the value of the claim is *twice* the level of likely costs.

or

(iii) The prospects of success are moderate (50% - 60%), and the value of
      the claim is at least *four times* the level of likely costs.

If the case is 'borderline' (that is, difficult to call but not hopeless), the merits criterion will only be met if the matter is of public importance.

The LAA pays civil legal aid lawyers in accordance with relevant provider contracts and rates of pay either negotiated or set by the relevant regulations,[38] and to an extent, such costs should be recoverable from a losing litigant (assuming that party is not also publicly funded). But as with private funding, there is always apt to be a short fall between what has been paid out and what is recoverable in costs

---

34 LASPO 2012, s 9(1)
35 Based on gross and disposable income and disposable capital.
36 There are lower levels of service, including 'legal help' or 'help at court'.
37 In non-money claims the test is whether the likely benefit outweighs the costs, such that a person paying privately would be prepared to risk the litigation.
38 This work is now contracted out to whole firms and organisations

from the other side. In particular, the LAA may have costs or have authorised expenditure that is not recoverable as litigation costs; these might include various administrative costs, the cost of extending funding and so on. Thus there may well be a gap between what the LAA expends in the litigation and what it recovers in costs from the losing litigant (and any contribution from the funded litigant). *This shortfall is not written off by the state!* A winning publicly funded claimant will be required to make up the difference out of his damage, or other award. That is to say, the LAA has a *first charge* on any '*property recovered or preserved*' by a publicly funded litigant to *recoup their costs of financing that person's litigation*.[39] This is known as the '*statutory charge*' and it arises whenever the LAA has to pay more to finance a funded party's litigation than it recovers from that person's own agreed contribution to his representation, plus any costs paid by the other side. The underlying principle is that the publicly funded litigant should be in a similar position to a successful privately paying litigant.

The statutory charge is of critical importance and is of particular relevance where the publicly funded *winning claimant* does *not* get an order for costs against the loser. It can mean that a huge proportion of any damage award would just go to the LAA, pursuant to the statutory charge, to pay for the litigation costs incurred by them.[40]

Let's look at two typical situations where public funding affects costs orders.

A. WHERE THE LOSER IS PUBLICLY FUNDED

If the loser is publicly funded, s 26(1) of LASPO 2012 comes into play. This provision gives some protection against an adverse costs order by limiting a publicly funded loser's liability to pay costs to that amount, if any, which it is 'reasonable' for him to pay, having regard to all the circumstances, including the *resources*[41] of the parties and their *conduct*. Certain items are excluded from consideration as a resource in this

---

39 See BCP, para 7.19

40 This often arises in family law cases where the property which was 'recovered or preserved' is the family home. Typically the LAA would take a charge, but not execute it in such a case.

41 An order can sometimes be made, but not enforced without the court's permission, in case the legally aided party 'comes into money'.

context, including the first £100,000 of the publicly funded person's 'dwelling house'.[42]

Obviously there is a correlation between a litigant's ability to qualify for public funding and his lack of resources, so it is not uncommon to find that due to the operation of this statutory 'costs protection', a publicly funded loser will be ordered to pay little if anything in costs to the winner. A privately paying claimant will thus want to think twice before suing an impecunious defendant who will be publicly funded, since that claimant (unless insured) will likely have to pay for the pleasure of winning, to say nothing of the fact that the defendant may well not be able to pay any damages either!

But at least claimants can choose whether to litigate. This is not true of defendants. What about the privately paying defendant who has no choice but to fight or settle, while the claimant is publicly funded? In this situation, help may be available from LASPO, s 26(6)(d) which allows the court to order that the state pay the costs of the successful defendant if *certain strict conditions* are met. In summary (for first instance cases) an order for costs against the LSC can be made if the following criteria are met:

(i) The party in whose favour the order is made is:
- *successful* (the matter was 'finally decided in that party's favour'),
- *unassisted* (not publicly funded),
- *a defendant* (did not start action at first instance[43]);

(ii) The *loser's own liability to pay has been considered* (under LASPO 2012, s 26);

(iii) It is *just and equitable* to make the order;

and

(iv) The defendant would *suffer financial hardship* if an order were not made. This last requirement is meant to exclude insurance companies and 'wealthy folk' who would not really miss the money.[44]

---

42 LASPO 2012, s 25

43 Beware the defendant bringing a counterclaim. He becomes a claimant in respect of that action.

44 *Per Denning MR in Hanning v Maitland* (No 2) [1970] 1 QB 580

B.   PART 36 OFFER SCENARIO

We saw how Part 36 offers work in Chapter 15. Let us assume a publicly funded claimant is suing a defendant, who has made a Part 36 offer. The claim is a money claim and the offer is not accepted and the case goes to trial. If at trial the claimant's damage award is 'more advantageous' than the defendant's Part 36 offer, then costs may well 'follow the event' as usual.[45] If, however, the award is not more advantageous, then the costs situation is effectively reversed after the initial period for acceptance (usually 21 days) had expired. But this claimant is legally aided and is given costs protection by s 26 LASPO 2012, thus precluding the court ordering such a person to pay more than a reasonable amount (if any) in costs.

Costs orders can, of course, be set off against each other - that is just common sense. Moreover, the claimant in this scenario has just been awarded some damages and the defendant might well say that the claimant should pay costs out of the money which has been recovered in the action. The LAA, however, may say that because of the statutory charge, they have a first claim against that fund for financing the claimant's litigation. *Cook v Swinfen*[46] considered this and decided that the *defendant takes priority over the State.* That is to say, the defendant is entitled to set off some or all of the damages he is obliged to pay the claimant against the costs he would normally be entitled to recover from the claimant who failed to better his Part 36 offer of settlement.[47] Anything left could be subject to the statutory charge - overall, a devastating result for the claimant.[48]

5.   SPECIAL COSTS SITUATIONS

Finally, there are several situations to look out for which require a variation on the usual costs theme.

---

45 Assuming no other reason to deviate from the general rule.

46 [1967] 1 AER 299

47 A variant of this is the so-called 'Lockley Order' which allows interim costs payable by a publicly funded litigant to be set-off against any eventual award of damages. *Lockley v National Blood Transfusion Service* [1992] 1 WLR 492

48 Furthermore, to the extent that an unassisted defendant does not recover all of his costs from the legally aided claimant, there may be scope for getting an order from the LAA, as discussed above. See the interesting case of, *Kelly v London Transport* [1982] 1 WLR 1055 which considered the meaning of 'successful' in the context of the old system of payments into court.

A. COST PROTECTION IN *PERSONAL INJURY/FATAL ACCIDENT CASES*: 'QOCS'

This is a form of costs protection, given *only* to claimants in personal injuries and fatal accident actions from 1 April 2013, in part to compensate them for losing the ability to claim the costs of CFA success fees and ATE premiums from an unsuccessful defendant. It works very much like s 26 of LASP0 2012.[49] It is just a pity it has such an unglamorous official title: qualified one-way costs shifting - or QOCS, for short.[50]

This is basically how they work: claimants will recover their costs from the defendant if they win, but will not be required to pay the defendant's costs if they lose (thus obviating the need for ATE insurance). So the shifting only works one way, but it is 'qualified' by exceptions intended to weed out those who do not deserve such protection, for example where the proceedings have been struck out as an abuse of process or the claimant (or his representative) has otherwise conducted themselves in such a way as to obstruct the just disposal of the proceedings, or where the court finds, on the balance of probabilities, the claim to be fundamentally dishonest.[51]

What actually happens is that, when QOCS applies, the court will make the normal costs order, but it will not be *enforceable* without the court's permission unless the amount of costs is less than or equal to the amount of any damages (plus interest) awarded to the claimant. This is important when defendants make Part 36 offers. So, where a claimant has won the case, but failed to 'beat' the offer, then the damages the claimant has won will be a fund out of which he can be asked to pay some or all of the costs due to the defendant after the initial period for accepting the offer expired (some of those costs can also be set off against those costs the defendant might have been ordered to pay the claimant). If costs still owing to the defendant exceed the damage award, then the order can only be enforced to the extent of reducing the damage award to zero (unless and until the court orders otherwise, which it might

---

49 As discussed above

50 The general rule or starting point of 'costs follow the event' is sometimes described as 'costs shifting' since the burden of paying the winner's legal costs 'shifts' from the winner to the loser. With QOCS the shifting can only go 'one way', and there are exceptions and so it is 'qualified' – hence the name.

51 CPR, r 44.16/17

do, for example, were the claimant to win the lottery).[52]

B. MULTIPLE DEFENDANTS

When a claimant sues two defendants and is successful against one but not the other, a strict application of the general rule that costs follow the event would mean that while the claimant would get costs from the unsuccessful defendant, he would have to pay the costs of the successful defendant. But where it was *reasonable* to proceed (and continue to the end) against both defendants (for example, because the defendants were blaming each other and it was impossible to anticipate who was liable), an adaptation of the general rule may be possible. The court has a discretion to order, in effect, that the losing defendant pay the winning defendant's costs. This sort of order comes in two forms:

(i) Bullock Order[53]

Here the claimant is ordered to pay the costs of the winning defendant, but once paid these can be recovered from the losing defendant in addition to the claimant's own costs. The order would sound something like this:

- Judgment for C against (unsuccessful) D1 with costs
- The case against (successful) D2 dismissed; C to pay D2's costs,
- D1 to pay to C the costs so paid by C to D2.

(ii) Sanderson Order[54]

Here the payment of the successful defendant's costs comes straight from the losing defendant, instead of being routed through the claimant. This sort of order is appropriate if the claimant is insolvent or publicly funded, as there may be greater certainty that the money will actually reach the winning defendant. Thus the order

---

52 QOCS is in its infancy, so watch out for refinements. See generally Sime, Ch. 47.

53 This gets its name from *Bullock v London Transport Omnibus Co* [1907] 1 KB 264, CA.

54 This gets its name from *Sanderson v Blyth Theatre Co* [1903] 2 KB 533, CA.

might sound like this:

- Judgment for C against D1 with costs.
- The case against D2 dismissed.
- D1 to pay D2's costs.

Finally, the various types (and permutations) of costs orders discussed earlier can also come in particularly handy when dealing with multiple parties. They provide flexibility. In the case of *McGlinn v Waltham Contractors* (No 5)[55] the claimants sued three defendants (D1, D2, D3) for £3.65 million. The claimant lost against D1 (who had offered to settle for £300,000!). The claimant did better against the other defendants, but only just. He was awarded just under £440,000 from D2, and just under £135,000 from D3, for a grand total of about £535,000 - less than 1/7th of his claim. The costs incurred by the claimant amounted to some £2.2 million. D1's costs were £880,000 and D2's were £1.2 million (D3's costs were put over to another hearing - case No. 6, probably!). The total costs so far were about £4 million. Issue-based costs were ordered on a percentage basis between the claimant and D2 in relation to liability and quantum. The claimant was ordered to pay D1's costs, the judge declining to make a Sanderson or Bullock order. On this aspect alone, the claimant was already out of pocket, even before taking into account the fact that he would have to pay his own costs of pursuing D1. Ouch!

C.   CLAIM AND COUNTERCLAIM

Where a counterclaim amounts to a total set-off (one that completely extinguishes the claimant's claim), then the defendant will have been successful and costs will (all other things being equal) follow the event. Where, however, a defendant's set-off is less than the claimant's claim (and there is no other answer to that claim), the defendant should make a Part 36 offer

---

55 [2007] EWHC 1419 (TCC). Any case with a (No 5) after it's name is going to be messy!

56 *Medway Oil and Storage Co Ltd v Continental Contractors Ltd* [1929] AC 88

on the 'balance' to protect himself on costs because, unless the set-off fails, the claimant can never 'beat' the offer.

Otherwise, where *both* claim and counterclaim succeed or fail, the traditional rule has been that there should be two judgments and two separate orders as to costs.[56] This is known as the rule in *Medway Oil*, which also said that in such a situation, a defendant is only entitled to costs 'exclusively referable' to the counterclaim. But this can cause hardship where much of what is referable to the counterclaim is also referable to the main claim (and so is not 'exclusive' to the counterclaim). This will happen where there is a high degree of interconnection between the actions, including a set-off claim which does not entirely extinguish that of the claimant. For a long time now, where the rule in *Medway Oil* would cause hardship, the court has been able to make a 'special order' on costs, either a single order or no order as to costs.[57] The court's options in this regard are now reinforced by the breadth of discretion in the CPR, and in particular by the use of percentage and other orders, as described above.

D. PRO BONO COSTS

Pro bono representation is (obviously) undertaken for free. A court can, however, order a losing party to make a payment to a prescribed charity (currently the Access to Justice Foundation) in respect of pro bono representation. *From April 2013, such orders are possible in all courts.* The discretion to make such an order will be exercised by reference to whether an adverse costs order would have been made in the ordinary course of events (that is, had the successful party not had pro bono representation). In essence the loser would be ordered to pay the costs he would otherwise have had to pay - but to the charity (not obviously to the person conducting the pro bono representation). Fixed costs would be awarded if applicable, otherwise the court would assess the costs by a summary or detailed assessment. A summary assessment would always be preferable, to save money and get the funds to the charity.[58]

---

57 *Chell Engineering Ltd v Unit Tool and Engineering Co Ltd* [1950] 1 All ER 378

58 Legal Services Act 2007, s 194(3) and LASPO Act 2012, s 61. See generally Access to Justice Foundation website

revision tips

- Be clear about the difference between matters of funding (how a party finances his own litigation) and costs orders (court orders that one party should pay some or all of the other party's legal costs).

- Make your own table of the possible orders which the court might make on an *interim* application and their meaning. Rank these interim costs orders from best for an applicant through to best for a respondent.

- Be able to recognise the common situations or circumstances where costs may not 'follow the event'. But bear in mind that every case is different.

- Be aware of the effect of public funding on costs outcomes, especially in so far as costs protection is concerned. QOCS works in the similar way

- Note the new triple effect of DBAs, QOCS and the *Simmon's* 10% uplift in personal injuries actions.

- Know the range of costs orders available to the court at the end of a trial, including percentage or time-specific orders, as alternatives (or adjuncts) to straight issue-based orders.

- Note the importance of 'proportionality' to the standard basis of assessing costs (CPR, r 44.3(2)-(5)) added by the Jackson reforms.

It is worth reading ...

The judgment of Dyson LJ (as he then was) in *Halsey v Milton Keynes General NHS* [2004] EWCA Civ 576; [2004] 1 WLR 3002 (don't worry about the *Steel v Joy* component). I think you are ready for this case now, having come something of a full circle from the one I suggested you read at the end of Chapter 2 (which gets a mention here, you will notice). This is a straightforward case, and the judgment reads a bit like a mystery thriller – you will be asking yourself: "What will the claimant suggest next?!"

CHAPTER 19

Judgment and beyond

Most litigants assume that once judgment is given in a case, it is all over. They would particularly like to think so if they have just been successful. But they would be wrong. In particular, the loser may want to appeal, or the winner may have to enforce the judgment. These are two particularly important aspects of the litigation process, which are discussed briefly below.

1. FINAL JUDGMENTS AND ORDERS

We have seen over these pages the various *orders* which the court might make on interim applications; at the end of a trial, what is handed down is a final *judgment* on the issues in dispute.[1]

After final judgment is pronounced, it must then be *drawn up*. The general rule is that the court takes responsibility for drawing up, but the court may order or give permission that a party do this. More particularly, however, in the QBD (including the TCC and Commercial courts, but not the Admiralty courts), the general rule is reversed so that unless the court orders otherwise, the judgment in those courts must be drawn up by the parties. A party who is required to draw up a judgment is

---

1   This is the typical nomenclature. The distinction is more rooted in the old rules than the new, and can be a bit fluid. In terms of enforcement, there is little practical difference between an 'order' and a 'judgment': CPR, r 40.1 and WB commentary

allowed *seven* days to file the relevant documents, failing which any other party may draw up and file them.[2]

Most judgments (and orders) must state the name and judicial title of the person who made it.[3] Unless the court specifies otherwise, they take effect from the date they are *given or made, not* the date they are drawn up, sealed and served.[4] Final (like interim) injunctions must contain a penal notice (to warn of the consequences of breach), and will not be enforceable until the respondent is made aware of the order (usually by being personally served, or being in court to hear it). This is just common sense - until a party knows it has been ordered to do or not do something, how can he (or it) comply?

A judgment for the payment of money (including costs) must be complied with within 14 days of the order, unless the court (or the judgment or the rules) say otherwise.[5] Interest will run (at the judgment rate, currently 8%) from the date judgment is given (again unless the rules or the court specify otherwise).[6]

When an order imposes a time limit for doing any act, the date of compliance must be clearly expressed - including the time of day and calendar date by which the act must be done.[7]

Many judgments or orders are made 'by consent'. A 'true' consent order is a record of a contractual agreement between the parties, and (once perfected) can only be varied or set aside on grounds rendering the contract void or voidable (for example, fraud or misrepresentation). 'Tomlin orders'[8] are a special kind of consent order, used when complex terms are agreed (or where the terms go beyond the original issues in dispute), which in any case are secreted away into a 'schedule'. Thus such orders are typically worded:

> And, the [claimant and defendant] having agreed to the terms set forth in the schedule hereto, it is ordered that all further proceedings in this claim be

---

2 CPR, r 40.3
3 Exceptions include default judgments and consent judgments: CPR, r 40.2
4 Unless the court specifies otherwise: CPR, r 40.7

5 CPR, r 40.11. The court can, for example, order payment by instalments. In personal injuries cases, the judgment will set out the amounts awarded under each head of loss, and the amounts which are to be 'diverted' to the state to repay relevant

benefits pursuant to the Social Security (Recovery of Benefits) Act 1997.
6 CPR, r 40.8
7 CPR, PD 40B, para 8.1
8 Named after Tomlin J. See Practice Note [1927] WN 290

stayed, except for the purpose of carrying such terms into effect. Liberty to apply[9] as to carrying such terms into effect.

Thus, with a Tomlin order, all proceedings are stayed, except as necessary for the purposes of implementing the obligations set out in the schedule.

Sometimes the court hands down a judgment on terms to which both parties are agreeable (indeed they may have suggested the terms to the court). This is not a true consent order in the contractual sense,[10] and will be enforced like any other court order or judgment.

2.   APPEALS

Litigants will want to know whether they can appeal a case they have lost - sometimes even before it has started! So it is important to have a working knowledge of the appeals structure. For examination purposes, the best way to learn the basics is by creating your own diagram (a pyramid, perhaps) incorporating the following: (a) where the appeal lies, (b) whether permission is or is not required and (c) whether grounds must be shown or the appeal is dealt with by way of re-hearing. PD 52 has a table you can work from, as does BCP, figure 74.1.[11]

The general rule is that an appeal lies to the next court tier up (for example, District Judge to Circuit Judge, Circuit Judge to High Court judge and so forth); but there are exceptions. In particular, if the appeal is a first appeal from a decision in the County Court (or from a master in the High Court), you will need to *distinguish between interim and final decisions* and (if the latter) note what *track* the case is actually on - this affects *where* the appeal lies, and in particular whether the appeal is 'fast-tracked' to the Court of Appeal. This is because a first appeal from a final decision of a District or Circuit Judge (or HC master) in

---

9   This part of the order allows parties to return to court if there are problems implementing the order and/or to enforce compliance. It does not signify an ability to come back to change the order.

10   See, e.g., *Siebe Gorman and Co Ltd v Pneupac Ltd* [1982] 1 All ER 377.

11   BCP's checklists 32 and 33 are useful too.

a Part 7 multi-track/specialist claim will go directly to the Court of Appeal.[12]

A decision is final if it is determinative of the entire proceedings. Clearly this includes a judgment on the merits of a claim. But it can also include a decision following a hearing of a preliminary matter, if it would have the same effect. An obvious example might be a decision on the question of whether an action is time-barred. Orders to strike out or grant summary judgment, on the other hand, are not final (although they might feel a bit that way to the parties). They are classic interim remedies.[13] *Most case management decisions are, in the nature of things, interim decisions.*

Similarly, but not often, appeals are allowed to 'leapfrog' an intermediate tier en route from the High Court, so that a decision of a master could go straight to the Court of Appeal (skipping the High Court Judge) or from the High Court Judge to the Supreme Court (skipping the Court of Appeal). This happens only very rarely, when the appeal raises significant points of principle or practice. A recent example came in the form of the appeal from Master McCloud to the Court of Appeal in *Mitchell v News Group Newspapers Ltd*, the first main decision on sanctions following the Jackson reforms in 2013.[14]

As regards leave to appeal, generally speaking, *permission* to appeal is *always* required *unless the liberty* of the individual appealing is at stake (not common in civil cases).[15] Permission can be sought 'from both ends', as it were, asking the court below first.

The appellant must, *within 21 days* of the lower court's decision,[16] file an appeal notice to initiate an appeal.[17] This must set out the *grounds* on which it is alleged the judge went wrong. If permission to appeal is required, the request (even if made orally to the court below) must be re-iterated in the appeal notice,[18] which must be served on the other side within seven days of being filed.[19] The appeal court can give permission to appeal on the paperwork alone, although (if permission is refused) the

---

12 Destination of Appeals Order, Art 5 and CPR, PD 52A, para 3.8

13 This aspect of the rules can get complicated, as even the WB admits at para 52.0.12. Do not get bogged down here- an exam should test you by using obvious examples of interim versus final orders.

14 [2013] EWCA Civ 1537 and see Ch. 13

15 CPR, r 52.3(1)

16 Or as the court orders: CPR, r 52.4(2)

17 This can be done electronically: PD 52, para 15.1B

18 CPR, r 52.4(1)

applicant can ask that the matter be reconsidered at an oral hearing (although if the case is hopeless, the court can refuse to do so).[20]

It is also necessary to *distinguish between first and second appeals.*[21] *Second* appeals *always* go to the *Court of Appeal.* Furthermore, it is easier to get permission to appeal if it is your first time: the test is 'real prospect of success' or some 'other compelling reason' why the appeal should be heard.[22] This should sound familiar - it is the same test that is applied in summary judgment hearings when deciding whether the defendant ought to be allowed to go to trial with his defence.[23] Not surprisingly, the test for permission to appeal is more stringent for second appeals, which after all will have been considered on appeal once already. Permission to bring a *second* appeal *must* be sought from the Court of Appeal and will *only* be granted where it raises an *important point of law or principle*, or there is *some other compelling reason* for that court to hear it.[24]

In any appeal a *respondent may* file and serve a 'respondent's notice'. He *must* do so *if* it is the respondent seeking permission to appeal (and so grounds must be set out); or the respondent wishes to ask the appeal court to uphold the lower court for reasons *different* to those given by the lower court (in which case the different or additional reasons must be set out, since appeal judges are not mindreaders!).[25]

Skeleton arguments are obligatory in appeals going to the Court of Appeal (and above). Otherwise, they should be used where the complexity of the case justifies their use.[26]

Finally, most appeals involve a *review* of the decision of the court below, *not* a re-hearing.[27] Judges have a great deal of discretion and so appeals are won or lost on the question of whether the lower court's decision was plainly '*wrong*' or otherwise *unjust* because of some procedural or other *irregularity*. For this reason, the appellate court (unless it orders otherwise) will not receive new evidence which was not before

19 CPR, r 52.4(3)
20 See generally PD 52, section IV and *Shlaimoun v Mining Technologies International plc* [2012] EWCA Civ 722. See also CPR, r 52.3(4A), newly added to avoid wasting court time

on unmeritorious applications.
21 'Second appeals', perhaps rather obviously, are those where the issue has been dealt with once already on a first 'rung' of the appeal ladder.

22 CPR, r 52.3(6)
23 See Ch. 5
24 CPR, r 52.13(2). And see BCP, para 71.15
25 CPR, R 52.5(1),(2)
26 See CPR, PD 52B, para 8.3
27 CPR, r 52.11(1)

the lower court. It would be illogical to criticise the lower court's decision on the basis of evidence it had not even heard.[28] Thus fresh evidence will only *rarely* be permitted on appeal - for example where *credible* evidence was simply *not available* at trial, but its impact would have been very *important* to the outcome. If the courts are not pretty strict about this, all appeals would be very susceptible to becoming re-hearings. This is sometimes known as the rule in *Ladd v Marshall*, which these days is applied in keeping with the overriding objective. [29]

JUDICIAL REVIEW

Judicial review is a vast subject and beyond the scope of this book. It is important, however, to distinguish it from the appeals system. Judicial review describes the process by which the courts exercise a supervisory jurisdiction over the acts and omissions of *public* bodies (including, but not limited to the courts), to ensure that they are lawful. The applicant must have sufficient standing ('locus') to invoke the Administrative Court's powers; and the grounds will have a very identifiable ring to them. Decisions of public bodies are usually attacked on one or more of three bases: illegality, irrationality, or procedural impropriety.

Permission to apply for judicial review is *always* required - this in itself is an involved procedure. The time periods are tight too (compared to normal limitation periods); the application must be made 'promptly' and in any event within three months of the decision complained against. There is a *pre-action protocol for judicial review cases*.

The typical orders sought by way of judicial review are:

(i) A *mandatory* order (an order that the public body in question carry out its public duty);

---

28 CPR, r 52.11(2). This is why it is important to get all relevant evidence in front of the court hearing the case.

29 [1954] 1 WLR 1489. See, e.g., *Terluk v Berezousky* [2011] EWCA Civ 1534, at 1751 and discussion at WB para 52.11.2

and/or

    (ii) A *prohibitory* order (an order restraining the public body in question from acting outside its jurisdiction or otherwise unlawfully);

and/or

    (iii) A *quashing* order (an order in effect setting aside the order of the inferior court or public body in question);

and/or

    (iv) A *declaration or injunction* (which can be ordered alongside one of the others above, if appropriate).

For detail, as necessary, consult CPR, Part 54. Practitioner commentary is extensive, both in the WB and BCP. The latter also has a useful Checklist 34 which is worth consulting. Check your exam syllabus to see whether and to what extent, judicial review is assessed.

3. ENFORCEMENT OF JUDGMENTS AND ORDERS

Parties who get judgment in their favour do not automatically obtain their remedy. The other side must do as the judgment or order says; in the case of money, this would be payment within a certain time (usually 14 days). Most people abide by court orders, but not all. Many a winning claimant has been distressed to find that the defendant cannot or will not obey the court's order.

'Cannot' is more of a problem than 'will not'. If, say, a money judgment has been made against someone with no money or assets, then it is probably not worth the paper it is written on. Legal advisors should be alert to such possibilities from the outset.

'Will not' leads to consideration of the powers of the court to enforce compliance with its orders, which are extensive. Enforcement of judgments is a solicitor's area of expertise, and so will figure most prominently on their professional examination syllabus. The BPTC requires an 'outline' or 'overview' (but confident) knowledge of the subject.[30] Whatever the level of detailed knowledge required, start with a basic understanding of the different kinds of enforcement order and marry them up with the type of asset or circumstance to which they relate. If, for example, a judgment debtor[31] is unemployed, it would be silly to seek to extract money from him by applying for an attachment of earnings order.

Let us first consider a money judgment. If too little is known about the judgment debtor's financial circumstances, then it will be necessary to obtain this information, either informally or by means of a court order.[32] Armed with such knowledge, it is then possible to consider the most appropriate method of enforcement. In particular, have a look at the following:

A.   SEIZURE AND SALE GOODS

This is a longstanding and common method of enforcement, but the language used to describe the means by which it is achieved (and some aspects of administration) have recently been modernised.[33] In the County Court, what were known as warrants of execution are now known as *warrants of control*. In the High Court, the old-fashioned writs of fieri facias ('fi fa') are now to be known as *writs of control*. The County Court cannot issue a warrant for judgments exceeding £5,000, so if a *greater* sum is involved the case (if not there already) will have to be *transferred* to the High Court.[34] Issuing a writ or warrant of control is normally purely administrative, although where more than six years has elapsed since the date of judgment, permission to enforce is required.

---

30 See note in BPTC syllabus, which can change year to year.

31 A 'judgment creditor' is a person who has obtained judgment for the payment of money. The person against whom such an order is obtained is called the 'judgment debtor'.

32 CPR, r 71.2

33 By the Tribunals, Court and Enforcement Act 2007 (Part 3, Schedules 12 and 13), effective from April 2014 by the Civil Procedure (Amendment) Rules 2014 (SI 2014/407).

34 The High Court can handle small amounts, however. So long as the judgment is not less than £600, the High Court can deal with this form of enforcement. This current County Court threshold could change over time.

Armed with such orders, the relevant enforcement officer of the court will call on the judgment debtor's premises. No forced entry is allowed (unless 'reasonable force' is sanctioned by court order). Once inside control can be asserted over named goods,[35] and (failing payment of the judgment debt within a minimum period of notice) sold to satisfy the debt. Be aware that certain goods are *exempt* for these purposes, for example, basic domestic necessities, tools of the debtor's trade and so forth. Watch out too for goods belonging to someone else (especially hire-purchase goods), which may not be earmarked in this way. You might be surprised how many things a judgment debtor has which do not belong to him!

B. CHARGING ORDERS (EXECUTION AGAINST AN INTEREST IN PROPERTY)

It may be possible to get a charge against property owned by the judgment debtor-this might be a good idea if he has a house.[36] But take care that there is some equity or beneficial interest in the property - it is no good if it is mortgaged to the hilt! The procedure involves *two-stages*; only the second stage involves a hearing and gives interested parties the opportunity to make submissions as to why the earlier interim order should not now be made final.[37] Getting the charging order (certainly the interim order) may be easy enough - and can act as an effective incentive to the judgment debtor to settle up. It also gives the judgment debtor security. But converting the charge to actual cash can be difficult because in order for that to happen the property must be sold, which is yet another step in the process.

C. THIRD PARTY DEBT ORDERS

This is useful if someone owes money to the judgment debtor. A typical example is a bank account in the name of the judgment debtor which is *in credit*. In effect,

---

35 The idea of these orders is to motivate the debtor to pay the judgment debt and so goods are not sold until notice is given and a minimum period of time is given (or agreed) for the debt to be paid. This is sometimes referred to as taking 'walking possession' of the goods.

36 It needn't be real property - shares or other securities qualify. Charging Orders Act 1979, s 2

37 See generally CPR, Part 73

this form of order requires the person owing money to the debtor, to pay an amount directly to the judgment creditor. It is no good, however, if the bank account is overdrawn - in such a case the debtor owes the bank money, not the other way around! Like the charging order, the third party debt order follows a similar *two-stage* procedure.[38]

D.   ATTACHMENT OF EARNINGS

This may be the only option if the judgment debtor has no assets other than a salary. It is in effect an order directed to the debtor's employer requiring the latter to deduct, and pay to the court, a named amount from the employee's salary. These orders can *only* be made in the *County Court* following an order for payment by installments which has fallen into arrears. The amount deducted is limited by a formula which is intended to ensure that a judgment debtor is left with enough to live on.[39]

Non-money judgments (for example, injunctions) are, as you might expect, enforced by different means. When a party does not do what a court says he must (or does what he must not), this can amount to 'contempt', which requires the direct intervention of the court in the form of a committal order.[40] Committal proceedings are very different to the kinds of enforcement procedures described above - they are up close and very personal!

E.   COMMITTAL PROCEEDINGS

Proceedings for contempt are essentially punitive, but with the added aspiration that any sanction given will result in future compliance with the court's orders. The two main punishments are imprisonment (for up to two years[41]), which can be suspended, and/or a fine (limited to £2,500 in the County Court) or sequestration of assets (the

---

38 See generally CPR, Part 72
39 See generally Attachment of Earnings Act 1971, s 24
40 CPR, r 81.4(1). The new Part 81 is now conveniently divided up into different types of contempt. Section II deals with breach of orders and judgments.
41 Contempt of Court Act 1981, s 14(1)
42 CPR, r 81.9
43 CPr, r 81.5/6/7
44 The WB's Practice Guide 9 (in Part D Vol 1) is useful

court can also give a stern warning). That all sounds very criminal, doesn't it? It is precisely for this reason that to establish the contempt, the breach must be shown to be *intentional* (a form of mens rea, in effect) and the standard of proof is the *criminal* standard: beyond reasonable doubt. Similarly, it must be shown that the relevant judgment or order contained a *penal notice*[42] (warning of the consequences of breach) and was served *personally* on the party (unless the court orders otherwise).[43]

Procedurally, committal orders are applied for using the Part 23 procedure (or Part 8 if no proceedings are underway). The application notice must set out full grounds, and this is one of the exceptional situations where the written evidence in support must be on *affidavit* (again, because of the criminal nature of the proceedings). The hearing will be in front of a Circuit or High Court judge.

It is useful to note too that committal proceedings can also be used to punish/ enforce a breach of an undertaking (that is, a promise) given to the court by a party, which are sometimes given in lieu of an order being made.

This is just a taster of the enforcement possibilities; if you need more detail, consult a practitioner text, which can point you to the myriad of sources for the various enforcement options.[44]

revision tips

- Do not run out of steam and be tempted to leave out enforcement altogether. It is usually worth a question or two. Be able to apply your knowledge to the facts of an SAQ. In terms of enforcing money claims, check which method is best and whether you are in the right court (you may need to transfer up or down). Does the procedure involve one or two stages?

- Make your own table on the appeals structure, from whatever source you choose. Do not just mindlessly copy the information - create your own representation. The idea is to get the knowledge into your head, not merely transfer it from one piece of paper to another!

revision tips *continued ...*

- Remember that generally first appeals go to the next court rung up, but some are 'fast-tracked' to the Court of Appeal (CA). Assuming the appeal is a first appeal from the County Court (or from a HC master), ask yourself (1) is the decision final? If the decision is interim (as most case management decisions are), the appeal just goes up to the next court rung as usual. If the decision is final, then (2) look to see what track the case is on. If the case is on the multi-track, then the appeal will go to the CA. If not, it will go to the next court rung up as usual. Second appeals always go to the CA.

- Note key words and concepts, but do not get bogged down in too much complexity. For example, an exam should use obvious examples of interim versus final decisions when testing your knowledge of whether an appeal is fast tracked to the Court of Appeal. Do not confuse the tests for granting *permission* to appeal (which itself varies depending on whether it is a first or second appeal) with the basis for a court's actually granting the *substantive* appeal.

- There can sometimes be an overlap, but remember to distinguish conceptually between *appeals* (which attack the judge's decision itself), *applications to set aside* a judgment or order (which itself cannot necessarily be faulted), and *judicial review* (which basically asks to Administrative Court to review the process by which a decision has been made).

It is worth re-visiting ...

Two cases:

The judgment in *R (Lawer) v Restormel Borough Council* [2007] EWHC 2299 (admin), which I mentioned at the end of Chapter 4, for its discussion on the function and limitations of judicial review, and a warning against the over-enthusiastic making of such applications.

The judgment in *Charlesworth v Relay Roads Ltd (2)* [2000] 1 WLR 230, which I mentioned at the end of Chapter 11, where judgment had been prounced, but not drawn up- an interesting reminder that the opera is never over until the big lady sings.

CHAPTER 20

Approaching the exams

As the time for your assessments approaches, you will need to think about a revision plan. You want to go into the examination hall alert and in a good frame of mind, knowing what sorts of questions you are likely to find on the paper. It is important to remember that examinations are (or should be) designed to allow you to show off what you know and the extent to which you know it - not calculated to make you fail. If you are well prepared, there should be a part of you (possibly a very small part) which is looking forward to the test.

Since 2011/12, the procedure and evidence exams for the BPTC have been centrally set by the Bar Standards Board (BSB). The result is that, although the various teaching institutions have provided information, professional guidance and raw materials for these examinations, they no longer have much (if any) say in how questions are formulated or judged. Assessors are bound by very strict, often very narrow, mark schemes. This sometimes requires exam candidates to give a bit more in written answers than the question, on the face of it, may seem to be asking. You don't have to be psychic, but you must not be too literal-minded either.

1.   REVISION

Revision is a very personal thing - some people make lists, some people use index cards, some people like mind maps - vive la différence. Having said that, there is some general guidance which is worth imparting. The first thing is to ensure that you are very clear about what is on your year's syllabus and how it will be tested. Take any and all mock exams which your course provides, both for the experience and to highlight any weaknesses in your understanding of the subject. It is important to know what you know (and what you have yet to learn) - and what to expect on the day of the examination.

Secondly, I believe it is important to revise 'little and often' and in sensible chunks, giving yourself breaks in between and rewards for what you have accomplished. For example, you might spend a couple of hours in the morning revising limitation and then (after a break for lunch or a run or whatever) come back and tackle amendment. Take a break, in other words, if only a short one. My own view is that the brain (well, certainly mine) can only take in so much in one sitting and it helps to let what you have covered sink in for a while before going on to the next item on the list. Studying just before falling asleep is supposed to be good - maybe because what you have just been working on 'marinates' all night! In any event, whenever you do it, *always* make sure that you really *understand* what you are revising. It is almost impossible to learn and recall information you do not fully comprehend. It also makes for more 'intelligent' guesses on exams when the need arises.

When reading judgments as part of your study or revision (or indeed anything from which you are extracting knowledge or information), note the gist (in your own words) and highlight the one or two sentences or paragraphs which encapsulate the reasoning and principle. If you find that all you are doing when you read something is colouring the entire text with highlighting pen, then you are not being discriminating enough - you may have just changed it from white to yellow! You must extract, and understand, the *essence*.

Similarly, in terms of legislation, rules and so forth (of which there are a lot), always make a note of the *key* concepts, words and requirements. Sometimes the differences seem rather subtle. Take default and summary judgment, for example. If default judgment has been entered (under **CPR**, Part 12), to get that judgment set aside a defendant has to show that he has a 'real prospect' of successfully defending the claim *or* that there is some other '*good*' reason for having a trial. This test has obvious (and necessary) similarities to that for summary judgment, but is articulated a little differently, so that in order to get summary judgment a claimant must show that the defendant has no 'real prospect' of successfully defending the claim and that there is no other '*compelling*' reason for a trial. The test is essentially the same, but the procedural prospective is slightly different, and for that reason, so too is the wording.[1]

As your learning and revision progresses, aim towards reducing down to a page of A4 (or a few index cards) the fundamentals of each area you are revising, noting key principles, rationales and vocabulary. These in a sense represent a 'snapshot' of the subject matter. Not only will this help you distil the subject, but as you approach the exam date you will have a handful, rather than a file (or worse, a room) full of revision notes for a last minute run through.

Do not enter the exam room sleep deprived. My own view is that a good night's sleep before the exam is a good thing - what you do not know by 11 pm that night is either not worth knowing, or it is too late. Having said that, I appreciate that many people get exam fever and are too excited to sleep. If you are one of these people, it is especially important that you get plenty of sleep as you approach the exam dates. Do not stay up two or three nights in a row. Besides a pen and pencil (and a calculator), all you are taking into the exam is your brain, and you want that working to full capacity.

For similar reasons, make sure you enter that exam room appropriately fed - you don't want to be faint from hunger or so full that you feel sleepy. Have a reasonably hearty and healthy breakfast (or lunch as the case may be). This would not be a good time for a bag of crisps and a coke. But by all means bring water and some polos into the exam (if allowed) to get you through the next three hours.

2. EXAM QUESTIONS

Litigation and evidence[2] on the BPTC are now tested by a combination of multiple choice questions ('MCQs') and short answer questions ('SAQs'). If you have not taken a multiple choice test recently, or if you are used to exams where you can get marks for telling the assessor something you know, even if you were not asked, then you will want to familiarise yourself with both of these formats for testing knowledge. There is no room for waffle on these sorts of exams.

1   See generally Ch. 5   2   And remedies, in the case of
                                      the civil paper

No doubt you have been given a lot of information about the assessments from your tutors and course directors. Make sure you take it on board. Remember that you need to be as good at SAQs as at MCQs because (for the BPTC at least) you must get a minimum mark in both halves of the paper. If you only pass one half, the whole test is failed and the whole paper needs to be taken again. You do not have many re-sit opportunities anymore, so make the most of this one.

SAQs and MCQS are designed to test a general level of knowledge, understanding, and application to be expected of a newly qualified lawyer about to embark on a pupillage (or other form of internship or early practice). The exams are challenging because the syllabus is very wide and centrally set exams are always something of an unknown quantity, but the questions are not directed at abstruse, historical or academic points of law which a practitioner might need to research. Nor do they test minutiae such as form numbers (although notice periods are considered fair game). Similarly the principles and rules are more important than the rule numbers in themselves. These may be referred to in a question, but as part of the description, not something to be tested as such. Having said that, there are several cases you should know by name (for example, *American Cyanamid*), as well as the most important sections of the most important legislation (for example, s 33 Limitation Act 1980). But it is what such cases and statutes tell us which really matters. You will need to 'drill down' into the rules sufficiently to learn the key requirements. Sometimes synonyms will do for more general principles, but at times the actual wording is crucial. For example, the overriding objective requires the courts (amongst other things) to deal with cases justly and at 'proportionate' cost - not reasonable, or sensible or some other kind of cost!

Mock exams will help you become familiar with the nature of the questions and level of knowledge which is required. It is important to take them, so far as is possible, in *exam conditions*. In particular, do the mock test to time and with no access to materials - these are closed book assessments!

Finally, the MCQ and SAQ formats are very different. Half of the exam will be taken up answering some 40 MCQs (the emphasis on the civil paper is on procedure, only about 25% of the question will be purely on evidence); and the other half, some five SAQs (again, most of these will focus on civil procedure). In other words you will spend (on average) some two minutes on each MCQ, but nearly ten times that (about 18 minutes) on each SAQ. So they demand different exam technique.

A.   THE MCQs

The MCQs themselves come in two slightly different formats. The standard version will have a paragraph or two setting out a particular factual scenario. There will then be a sentence posing a question (such as *Which one of the following is CORRECT?*), followed by four possible answers: [A] to [D]. You are required to select one answer, which you record on a separate sheet of paper. All four possible answers will be credible (to a greater or lesser degree, obviously), but only one will be the appropriate answer to the question. If you choose that answer you get one mark. You get no marks for choosing any other answers, and no marks are deducted for wrong answers.

My advice when tackling this sort of MCQs is:

(i)   Read any factual scenario carefully...

... noting things like whom you are advising, the cause of action, the type of loss and damage (personal injuries or non-personal injuries), what court you are in (County Court or High Court), whether the claimant is an adult or child, whether the limitation period has expired or not - and so forth. Underline or highlight this detail. As you do this you should be able to identify what aspect of procedure or evidence the question is testing. You may even anticipate the answer!

(ii)   Read the sentence which poses the question carefully too.

Sometimes this asks for the WRONG answer, or asks you to identify which proposition is INCORRECT. Note this carefully (it is always set out in capital letters). If you do not, it can be surprisingly easy to make a mistake by identifying a correct procedural or legal proposition, when you were supposed to pick out the incorrect one! To get the right answer you sometimes have to find the wrong one.

(iii) Read *all* four possible answers.

This is so even if the first one seems like the right one. It might well be, but you *must* double check that there is not a better one below it. Sometimes one choice is only *partly* correct, or another choice is more accurately worded. Watch out for words like 'never' or 'always' (or 'must' instead of 'may') in a choice you are given (which leaves no room for exceptions or the exercise of judicial discretion, of which there is a lot in civil cases) - this can sometimes be the one thing which makes it an incorrect answer.

(iv) Be methodical

For example, because you are asked to distinguish between correct and incorrect statements, it can help to put a mark (for example, T or F) by each one as you go along (if unsure, put a '?'). This can make it easier to answer the ultimate question accurately. Assuming you can mark all four choices either T or F, the odd one out should be the answer.

(v) The process of elimination can help...

... to get you to the correct answer. This is often an effective way of answering this kind of MCQ question. You can be a bit doubtful about which answer is correct, but more confident about those which are not. What often happens is that you can fairly easily narrow down the field to a choice between two of the answers, but the difference between those two can be quite subtle sometimes. Eliminating the wrong one should leave you with the correct one.

There is also a somewhat more complex variation of MCQ which you should be prepared for. In these you are given a series of three or four propositions (numbered (i) to (iv)) about a particular subject (sometimes, but not necessarily with a factual scenario) and asked to consider how many (if any) are correct. Below that, in a separate list, you are given a choice of various permutations (for example, 'all of them', '(i) and (ii) only', 'none of them', and so on), as possible answers [A] to [D]. Again, only one of these will be the appropriate one and you only get a mark for choosing that answer. In respect of this sort of question it is important to:

(vi) Be doubly systematic.

It is particularly useful with this type of question to *first decide* and then mark each of the *initial* propositions as True or False. You will then be able to see, by reference to your own notation system, which (if any) of those statements are true and which (if any) are false. *Only then*, should you move down to the second list of four possible answers and look for the correct one. With this approach, you are actively finding your answer amongst the available choices (if it is not on the list, you may have to go back and start again), rather than considering each choice individually. Again, a process of elimination can help. If you are not systematic about these more convoluted MCQ questions, you risk getting confused darting back and forth between the initial set of statements and the ultimate choice of four possible answers. Just because statement (ii) is correct does not mean option [B] is correct, and you do not want to confuse the two different sets of alternatives.

And in respect of *all* of the MCQs:

(vii) Record your answers carefully...
... on the separate answer sheet. Take a second to make sure you are doing this accurately and recording the right answer to the right question. This is especially important if you are wanting to skip a question you are unsure of, so that you can go back to it later. One idea about skipping questions is not to leave such answers blank, but to record the best answer you can first time round and note on your question sheet that you want to come back to it. Then, if you do go back and change your mind about the answer, just make sure you erase well and make your revised choice clear. And if you do not go back, at least you have taken a stab at the answer. The important thing is to ensure that you do not get out of sequence!

(viii)   Circle the correct answer
... on your examination paper *before* making the appropriate mark on the separate answer sheet - just in case you need to go back and remember what your answer was for recording purposes.

(ix) Treat the examiner as infallible
If your initial reaction when you read a particular question is that there is no correct answer or there are two correct answers or it is impossible to give a correct answer, read it again. If you still feel that way, swallow your pride and choose the *best* answer you can in the circumstances. You can complain later. Mistakes can (and do) happen, but they are still more apt to be committed by students than examiners, so have a go at the question whatever you think. If there is an error in the question, it can be taken into account when the questions and answers are all analysed after the examination.

(x) Keep the momentum going

Do not slow yourself down with unnecessarily time-consuming methods of highlighting detail as you read, or let a question stop you in your tracks. Even if the question is a 'stinker' (and there is bound to be one!), don't let it bug you, just keep going. Obviously some questions will take you a bit longer than others - the two minutes or so for each question is an average. But do not linger too long over any one question or let a question derail you so that you cannot do your best on the rest of the test. Having said that...

(xi) Do not rush

Remember that two minutes is quite a long time. Just because the factual scenario you are given seems a long one, read it carefully. If you have taken the detail on board (and know the subject matter), it only takes a few seconds to find, circle and record the correct answer. If you are well prepared you will not need the full two minutes for each question, but do not worry when you do.

(xii) If necessary make an intelligent guess

You do not lose marks for a wrong answer, so this is always worth doing. Narrow down the field as much as you can, make a sensible choice and move on. Remember to think laterally and apply basic principles when guessing - it should be as informed a choice as possible.

B.   THE SAQs

These are a very different sort of question. It may be worth just giving yourself a few deep breaths and a bit of a stretch before going on. Change your pencil (used for MCQs) for a pen.

A typical SAQ will set out a case study in several paragraphs, followed by two to five sub-questions (a), (b), and so on, based on that case study. There are ten marks allotted to the whole of the question, although not necessarily distributed evenly between the sub-questions, each of which will indicate in brackets how many points it is worth. A variation might be a single SAQ may have two five-mark case studies (one might follow on from the other), each with a number of sub-questions. Again the total is ten marks available for the entire SAQ.

Marks are *not* transferable from one sub-question to another and you *cannot get any more* credit for the answer to a sub-question than it is worth. Remember the tests you did in school, where you could see how many marks each question was worth. It's the same idea here. The BPTC exam may be harder than '*Ahmed has planted some bean seeds. What do they need to grow?* (2 marks)', but you should still make your distribution of writing time and energy commensurate with the marks each sub-question attracts.

SAQs are rather more nuanced and so can be more challenging than MCQs. They require more active participation and a greater degree of concentrated analysis. Not only do you have to know the relevant principles, but you have to answer specific questions about a particular aspect of that area of procedure, remedies and/or evidence. There is nothing (except the case study) to 'suggest' or 'trigger' the answer, and one question will often range *over more than one procedural topic*. In short, you have to apply a broader range of knowledge and do more of the work. It may be worth have a quick look at all five SAQs and answering them in order of 'preference' - that is, start with the questions you are most confident about (and so most apt to get full marks efficiently). It would be a pity to get to the last question without time to give answers you were well capable of giving!

Again, it is important to take any and all mock SAQs on offer during your course. In addition, here are a few suggestions about tackling these sorts of questions:

(i)   Do not write too much

It is called a short answer question, not a long answer question and it means what it says. Assessors appreciate *simple sentences or bullet points*, as opposed to verbose paragraphs with an answer buried somewhere inside it (although they will find it if it is there). Remember that you must *answer the question asked* - it does no good answering some other question or writing down a lot of irrelevant information. Typically a handful of focused and accurate statements is all that will be required for *each* sub-question, although obviously the *more marks* allotted to each of these, the *more points* you will need to make. If the sub-question is worth *two marks*, you may well want to make four valid points to cover yourself, if indeed there are four to make, but remember that the marks allotted to a sub-question are a maximum - no matter how brilliant any additional points you make are, you cannot get more than the maximum (and the points cannot be credited to any other sub-question). Once assessors have found that maximum, they move on to the next section, and they won't look back! Be careful, too, not to make contradictory points which undermine a sensible one which you have already made! There is no negative marking, but if the second half of an answer effectively cancels out the first half, then you will get no points. Know when to stop.

(ii) Do not write too little

You must not only answer the question asked, but do so with sufficient particularity and accuracy to get the maximum marks. You might write a few words which identify a correct general principle, but fail to provide salient detail or link your answer to the case study. A fuller and more focused response might have attracted more marks. Remember too that if you are asked to give reasons always do so, but it is a good idea to do this even if reasons are not explicitly sought. A correct answer *plus* a correct reason can often get you (*two marks*) if they are on offer (and you will invariably *need* both if only (*one mark*) is allotted). If you think the question could speak to two alternative scenario, then briefly set out the implications of each - thus if the examiner is thinking one way, and you are thinking another, you have both situations covered.

Indeed, sometimes you need to think outside the box just a little bit and extend your answer to include what might seem like peripheral (but still relevant) detail. So if, say, there are (*three marks*) allotted to a sub-question, you know that you must make at least three valid and relevant points. However, *for insurance purposes*, if you feel that six valid points could be made, put them *all down*. There are two reasons for this: sometimes the examiners award half marks (without telling you this!) if there are quite a few points which could be made and/or they may want slightly different information or more procedural detail than you feel the question is, on the face of it, seeking. This is just a safety precaution, however, so do not go overboard. And every question must be judged on its own merits - sometimes it is pretty obvious that one fully correct answer gets one mark, and that is that.

(iii) Do not write too soon

This is very important. You have about 18 minutes per SAQ and you want to use the time wisely. Remember two things: (a) you cannot formulate sensible responses until you think about the case-study and questions posed *and* (b) you want each answer to each sub-question to be pertinent and pack a punch (and not meander all over the shop). So, my advice is this:

(a) Always read the entire SAQ first...

... *and give it some thought before writing down your final answers to the individual sub-questions.* Do not be tempted to read the factual scenario and then immediately start answering each sub-question as it comes. By reading the whole question first, you will be able to see how the content of your answers should be *distributed* in order to get the maximum marks. If you give answers relevant to (b) in answer to (a), you will not get any credit. This may seem harsh, but that is just the way it is (although if you find yourself in this situation, you can circle the relevant bit of text and put an arrow to the place where this answer should be given, or reverse the numbering. Do not just write it all out again!).

(b) Jot down ideas on the exam paper as you read...

... through the entire SAQ (for example, noting relevant statutory provisions, key principles, procedure and so on). This reading time will give you an opportunity to think about *every aspect* of the question, so when it comes to writing out your answers, you will have a clearer idea of what is required. It is a bit like being in a firing range - you want to gather your thoughts, take steady aim and fire so as to hit the target each time. So, you might well spend *half* the 18 minutes thinking and formulating points for the entire SAQ, and the *other half* actually writing out the short pertinent answers to each sub-question, carefully and methodically, distributing your answers sensibly. Double check that you made the appropriate number of points (plus any insurance points) for each sub-question. Do not dawdle over one sub-question at the expense of another, although, as a matter of common sense (and assuming you can answer both) give a four mark question some priority over a one mark question.

(iv) Always double check...

... that you have clearly understood the detail and the demands of each sub-question. You might be surprised how often students lose points because they were not very careful to *answer the questions actually asked.*

Finally, as I tell my students before their exams, remember to -

P Prepare sensibly (little and often)
A Apply basic principles when in doubt (think analogously)
S Sleep beforehand
S Sustenance beforehand

This became known as the PASSword. Many of you, I am sure, can achieve much more than a mere pass. Now go and show them what you can do!